Etymology has been largely neglected since the beginning of this century. Professor Yakov Malkiel here sets out to rescue it from its fate. He inquires into the style, structure, presuppositions, and purposes of etymological inquiries over the last two centuries, and sets them against the practice of etymology in Antiquity and the Middle Ages. He also examines the complex and changing interrelationship between etymology and general linguistics in recent times, with the intention of revitalizing etymological research.

Professor Malkiel is undoubtedly one of the most distinguished practitioners of the discipline, and brings to this work a remarkable breadth and depth of scholarship. Wide-ranging and imaginative, *Etymology* will be welcomed by all historical linguists and Romance linguists.

ETYMOLOGY

ETYMOLOGY

YAKOV MALKIEL

Emeritus Professor, Department of Linguistics and
Romance Philology Program,
University of California, Berkeley

CAMBRIDGE
UNIVERSITY PRESS

Published by the Press Syndicate of the University of Cambridge
The Pitt Building, Trumpington Street, Cambridge CB2 1RP
40 West 20th Street, New York, NY 10011–4211, USA
10 Stamford Road, Oakleigh, Melbourne 3166, Australia

First published 1993

Printed in Great Britain at the University Press, Cambridge

A catalogue record for this book is available from the British Library

Library of Congress cataloguing in publication data

Malkiel, Yakov, 1914–
    Etymology / Yakov Malkiel
        p. cm.
    Includes bibliographical references and index.
    ISBN 0 521 32338 X (hardback). ISBN 0 521 31166 7 (paperback)
    1. Language and languages – Etymology – History. I. Title
P321.M34 1993   412 – dc2092–20773   92–20773   CIP

ISBN 0 521 32338 X hardback
ISBN 0 521 31166 7 paperback

TS

CONTENTS

PREFACE

The choice of an accurate and, at the same time, appealing title for this book has, I confess, cost me considerable headaches. The point is that etymology (unless one is willing to equate it with some such indifferent rendering as 'the discipline of word origins'), has tended to mean, in its actual applications and, above all, implications, entirely different things to successive generations of scholars and laymen alike, from Antiquity to the concluding years of the twentieth century.

In certain remote periods, the literal meaning of a given proper name and the messages encoded into it (especially but not exclusively in reference to proper names of persons) meant incomparably more to an average member of the speech community in question than the provenance of any common nouns. After all, parents in many places enjoy the privileges, within the framework of tradition, of selecting, for their newborn children, names not infrequently endowed with special messages or associations. Conversely, few individuals are invited, encouraged, or allowed to coin novel designations for, let us say, dishes or pieces of furniture. In the second half of the last century, which was marked by a new enthusiasm for science, accurate etymologizing mattered chiefly to those eager to reconstruct a plausible evolutionary chart of sounds and forms, viewed across the ages, since their development, as was then firmly believed, was governed by strict laws, best discoverable by those familiar at first hand with reliably established starting points for word trajectories. About sixty years ago, those fine French scholars Alfred Ernout and Antoine Meillet gave their unsurpassed etymological dictionary of Latin the revealing subtitle *histoire des mots*, i.e., 'word biographies'. They were lucky enough to find imitators. If one looked at the biographical vicissitudes of the lexical units in that perspective, then the 'cradle' of each word was not necessarily of more compelling significance than its subsequent transmutations, identified with heightened attention to its meaning and to the specific place it occupied within its family. For a while, the intoxicating success of 'dialect geography' compelled some of its devotees to reserve an equal share of attention to a word's temporal odyssey and to its sometimes astonishing travels through space, by way of land or sea. At that juncture one can invoke the spatio-temporal approach to etymological probing.

I myself initially toyed with the idea of smuggling into the title or subtitle of this book the phrase 'lexical archaeology'. In the first instance this indeed seemed defensible at that juncture, not least because it might discourage some potential readers lacking any flair for the past, any eagerness to engage in piecing together events and linking them in terms of cause and effect as closely as possible. What in the end prevented me from obeying that hunch was the disappointing discovery that archaeology is basically expected to concern itself with tangible objects as concrete witnesses to the zigzags of material civilization. (To be sure, no one denies that it can serve other, secondary, purposes as well, for example, by unravelling mythological knots or by helping one to reconstruct the zigzagging course followed by the various techniques of writing.) By blindly adopting the role of a verbal archaeologist, the student of historical (or 'diachronic') linguistics would almost unavoidably agree to lean towards concentration on pictorially representable nouns, a hazardous imbalance which, as has become clear in critical retrospect, was the chief fault of the various spokesmen for the Central European school of *Wörter und Sachen* (i.e., of tangible objects and of the labels for them) – an approach deservedly influential half a century ago, but also dangerously one-sided and ceaselessly running the risk of exhausting itself. After all, pronouns, verbs, prepositions, conjunctions, etc. are those ingredients of practically every language's lexis which are most likely to stimulate the imagination of any red-blooded linguist. Conversely, 'individual growth in lexis' (or, somewhat more loosely, 'individual growth in languages') underlines the legitimate and rhetorically effective contrast to 'pattern' or 'structure' or 'system', i.e., the key expressions for what represents the grammarian's delight and constitutes his principal tool of analysis, without (to revert to 'individual growth') adversely colouring this voluntary retrenchment or spontaneous limitation of the scope and style of his presentation.

Perhaps the moment has now at long last arrived for stating rather bluntly what this book has *not* been designed to accomplish. It does not aim to serve as a manual, as a pedagogically flavoured instrument of indoctrination, advancing from the relatively simple to the admittedly sophisticated. Nor will it lend service as an easily manageable 'How to . . . ' book, furnishing helpful bits of advice on how to learn to use certain reputable etymological dictionaries; how to ferret out relevant book reviews; how to conceive and formulate a truly original etymological idea ('guess', 'conjecture', 'hypothesis'); how to prove one's predecessors wrong or to disarm one's potential future critics; how to find a niche for a note or an article of one's own on an etymological issue in some highly esteemed learned journal; and the like.

To use, I trust justifiably, a fairly trite phrase: etymology is going through an unprecedented crisis of self-contradiction at present, on both sides of the Atlantic (but the drama is conceivably more visible in the New World). Let me cite a few paradoxes that seem to support my contention. With the rarest of exceptions, the best of our universities hesitate to offer at any level lecture courses or seminars on etymology, although they make a calculated effort to initiate the neophyte into the fundamentals, or even the intricacies, of phonology, morphosyntax, semantics, or else pragmatics; and the same, *grosso modo*, holds for special linguistic summer institutes. Several influential journals, including those which do not hesitate to include in their scope research in historical linguistics, nevertheless, either programmatically or, at least, in their day-to-day routine, hesitate or flatly refuse to publish perfectly legitimate inquiries into etymological issues, and so on. When a busy journal editor's attention is drawn to this disquieting state of affairs, he or she is apt to remark that some of the greatest linguistic scientists of the past, e.g., Jespersen, Sapir, Bloomfield, displayed scant excitement about etymological discoveries or controversies – a contention which, as a matter of fact, is not inaccurate but proves nothing. Should an inadequacy rank as a merit?

Disturbingly, while this policy of rejection goes on, tone-setting publishing houses in English-speaking countries and elsewhere, in revising and bringing up to date certain classics among the dictionary ventures they have sponsored, announce loose bits of etymological information or even introductory essays on etymological subjects as a newly added prestigious feature. Multi-volume etymological ventures, whether they concern languages living or dead, widely-known or obscure, acknowledge support received from government agencies or private foundations, and so on. Inevitably, amid such conflicting circumstances, the questions arise: who really needs etymology, and for what purpose? And, what positions are such linguists as practise etymology (or, far more advisably, include etymology in their many-pronged daily practice) expected to occupy in the world of organized scholarship, particularly as regards teaching and publishable research? For alphabetic dictionaries, however great the need for them, contrary to appearances happen not to be the logical outlet for advanced experimental research in etymology.

Affirmatively speaking, the purpose of the present book is, then, to ventilate these basic questions and, by so doing, to fill a gap in the information immediately available. It has been conceived as a series of three medium-sized essays, of chronologically determined scope, each of which a broadly educated 'lay' reader – whether previously exposed to the tricks of technical linguistics or not – should easily be in a position to assimilate in a few hours. The absence of footnotes, a deliberately planned feature, serves the same purpose. However, plentiful (and, one hopes, up-to-date) bibliographic information has been provided, both for those readers who are anxious to ascertain the writer's own sources of information, and for those who are eager to expose themselves to further intellectual stimulation.

It remains for me to record my sincere gratitude to those infinitely forebearing and understanding members of Cambridge University Press who have patiently borne with my inconsistencies and caprices, especially Judith Ayling and the indexer Fiona Barr, as well as to a string of part-time student assistants, all of them loyal and some of them talented, who have helped me to survive in the years 1985–93, notably Dawn Ellen Prince and Anne McCormick. Finally, I acknowledge with deep gratitude the help received from my colleagues and friends Anna Laura and Giulio Lepschy in handling the page proofs and in answering editorial queries.

Berkeley, California

1

The nineteenth century

In different times and at different places, etymology has meant slightly or entirely different things to the few or many people who, under varying sets of circumstances, have used that word, applying it to their own spheres of interests. Basically, etymology always meant something approximating to the paraphrase 'original meaning, or use, of a given lexical unit or proper name'. But the cultural implications of this lame descriptive statement can be entirely different. The core meaning of a word can be imagined as something wholly independent of the passage of time and endowed with magic messages or mystic overtones.

The appeal to etymology in a magic context may well have started with proper names and be so old as to have its roots in prehistory. Parents, by giving their newborn child a name whose 'real' meaning is wholly transparent to those familiar with the given language (like Spanish *Dolores*, *Consuelo*, or *Amparo*, or Hebrew *Rachel*), or transparent only in part, or else to experts alone, may to some extent be motivated in their choice by this chance to encode a wish for the child's future well-being or expected character (standard of behaviour), even though several alternative motivations may prevail. To the extent that the real meaning of a name titillates the speech community's, or certain outsiders', curiosity, the etymology comes close to resembling the riddle, and the etymologist, in being called upon to solve or clarify it, acts like a magus or a magician. Particularly relevant in this context are meliorative changes of names late in life, sometimes by order of a deity, inasmuch as they may involve a reward for past accomplishments, or a programme of character-building in the future.

The mystic approach to etymology was peculiar to medieval Europe; involved in it was the widespread belief in symbolism and the practice of parables, literally 'juxtapositions'. Just as a visual symbol stands for something else (e.g., the cross for 'salvation' or 'Christianity', the half-moon for 'Islam', 'Solomon's seal' – according to other authorities, 'David's shield' – for Judaism, the Hammer-and-Sickle sign for Socialism, etc.), so the outer shape and meaning of a word may conceal a distinctly deeper or more relevant ingrained message.

With the gradual move of linguistic curiosity in the direction of time-dominated disciplines, principally history, a word's etymology began to be tantamount to 'previous meaning', or 'earlier actually attested meaning', or else 'earliest reconstructable meaning', without the concomitant pretence that modern scholarship is invariably in a position to piece together primeval meanings, or, for that matter, pristine forms. Etymology thus changed its direction, aiming at the new status of a strictly identificational discipline; words and names were henceforth divested of any residual mystic or magic essence. Persons eager to satisfy their etymological curiosity consult an etymological dictionary, which tells them not what to do at present or what to expect from the future, but what shape the word at issue once possessed, with what principal meaning it was endowed, and, occasionally, through what intermediate stages of form and denotation it went after shedding its initial and before acquiring its present appearance. (Only under very special circumstances has etymology in the twentieth century been called upon to act not cognitively, but as an active force – as when certain poets fond of polysemy want the 'etymological meaning' to blend with other semantic shades of the word pressed into service.)

The discovery of the time factor and the adaptation to linguistic material of theories, methods, and techniques germane first to history and, later, to the evolutionary sciences represented only one of two relevant major advances of modern times. The other side of the progress achieved has been the discovery that certain words, perhaps the majority of lexemes, have the built-in capacity to migrate from one locus, or one speech community, to another – as parts or particles of the general cultural heritage. A few words seem to be continuously on the move (and have therefore been properly called migratory); so are the objects (usually merchandise), the concepts, the institutions, and kinds of people which they designate. Strictly speaking, the discovery represents nothing revolutionary. The ancient Romans, unless they were hopelessly stupid, easily recognized isolated Greek words (Graecisms, Hellenisms) absorbed into the flow of Latin speech that surrounded their lives. With the advent of travel and foreign-language teaching, and with the wide spread of bi- and multi-lingualism in many modern societies, there has been in the air a keen awareness of the fact that countless words in one's own language not only have a significant time-depth, but have also been adopted from a whole spectrum of foreign tongues – ancient or modern, neighbouring or distant, cognate in content and structure or exotic. As had been the case in Antiquity, the presence of lexical diffusion (perhaps a better label than 'borrowing') is being dimly felt even by the less sophisticated twentieth-century person, no less than the aforementioned power of time, together with the capacity for causing attrition or distortion inherently attached to both of them.

The systematic exploration, from the vantage point of modernity, of those earliest stirrings of etymological curiosity has not consistently been in the hands of the same groups or coteries of researchers. Originally, it was classicists, biblical scholars, and conventional comparative linguists (among them the especially versatile and erudite Heymann Steinthal) who busied themselves with such issues, and part of that heritage is unquestionably still alive. Over the last half-century, however, literary critics, from Ernst Robert Curtius in Bonn to R. Howard Bloch at Berkeley, have also manifested active curiosity about those aspects of etymology in its infancy which were doomed not to survive into later periods, marked by more sober approaches.

One step towards organized knowledge was the collection of loosely floating legends about the more exciting cases of word origins into a sort of corpus or inventory. As far as the West is concerned, this feat was accomplished by a brilliant figure, Isidorus, the Bishop of Seville, who, standing at the threshold of the Middle Ages yet having free access to numerous sources of Late Antiquity in part no longer available to us today, found the necessary leisure, among his feverish activities as a theologian, moralist, law student, and historiographer, to compile a priceless volume of antique etymologies concerned chiefly, as one would expect, with Latin, the so-called twenty books of *Etymologiae*, sometimes referred to as *Origines*. Few books throughout the following centuries were so avidly read and so studiously copied by trained scriveners in several European countries (including Germany) as was this Isidorian treatise. In addition to providing small capsules of knowledge – by no means devoid of value if measured by the standards of the time – the Isidorian *Etymologiae* also stimulated other influential figures to emulate the great initiator. When, in the third quarter of the thirteenth century, Alfonso X (called the Learned), King of Castile and León, assembled at his court a number of scholars, 'scientists', and translators to prepare historiographic, legal, astronomic, and other accounts capable of sating a truly encyclopaedic range of curiosity, part of the responsibility of this private academy attached to the royal court was to learn how to intersperse their writings with parenthetic remarks on the true meaning and extraction of certain key words and key names.

One can liken this gradual systematization of scattered etymological insights into treatises to the slow emergence of glossaries, both monolingual and bilingual, through consolidation of individual glosses – at the outset, marginal or interlinear annotations of difficult words found in literary texts entering into the prescribed curriculum – into initially modest and haphazardly compiled *glossaries*, out of which, little by little, our better-balanced *vocabularies* and *dictionaries* were allowed to develop. As a matter of fact, by eventually merging these two genres, the collections of etymological hypotheses and the bare glossaries, the West finally hit on a new genre of erudite writings, which has survived unimpaired to this day: the *etymological dictionary*.

The transmutation of strings of guesses and anecdotes – which frequently suffered from the further disadvantage of mutual overlapping – into a tightened and increasingly respectable body of knowledge has had to overcome a battery of obstacles. Not everywhere, to begin with, was etymology equated with the systematic search for word origins. In Eastern Europe, for example, where scholarship was presided over by inveterate Byzantine traditions, etymology came to mean what we call morphology and, in particular, inflection, with heavy stress laid on declension and conjugation. In pre-Revolutionary Russia, paradoxically enough, *etimologija* was so interpreted on the secondary-school level. Accordingly, the teaching of grammar to teenagers fell traditionally into two halves (with separate textbooks produced for appropriate exercises), etymology and syntax, apparently to the exclusion of orthoepy. At university level, however, etymology, entering into a programme of philological training, meant much the same thing as in the West, and etymological dictionaries, starting with those devoted to the Russian language (e.g., the one compiled by A. G. Preobraženskij, originally published in 1910–16), pursued much the same goal as in the rest of the civilized world. Through a further twist of irony, present-day Russia happens to be one of the very few countries that has a learned periodical devoted to etymology exclusively (*Ètimologija*, founded in 1963, in addition to a slightly older venture *Ètimologičeskie issledovanija* . . . , devoted to the Russian language alone).

To revert to the West: until fairly recently there was little understanding of the kind of etymological scholarship that was cultivated between roughly 1500 and 1800 in several advanced European countries. That scholarship, with all its faults and limitations, was merely one thread in a whole strand of tentative linguistic explorations, which were not always forcefully defined or skilfully co-ordinated. There were language students, during those three centuries of preliminary gropings, who were mainly concerned with the ultimate provenance of individual words of their own tongue – the etymologists *par excellence*. There were others who were passionately involved in discovering the roots of their language as a whole, and who drew the illustrations for whatever turned out to be their favourite thesis from individual identifications of ancestral prototype and contemporary product, to the exclusion, as a rule, of all and any intermediate stages. Also, there were those, perhaps least conspicuous as a group and, as a result, sometimes overlooked by later historians of linguistic science, who prepared miniature historical phonologies, striving to equate certain sounds (which they would call 'letters') of their tongue, e.g., of French, Italian, and Spanish, with those of the reputed parent language – in the given cases, of Latin. Other groups of trail-blazers were active in those years – e.g. missionaries compiling word-lists for exotic languages or carrying out urgently needed translations of catechisms, etc. – but they are, in retrospect, of less concern to us. Among 'pure' etymologists one may mention, in early seventeenth-century Spain, Sebastián de Covarrubias (H)orozco and, in mid-seventeenth-century France, Gilles Ménage. Among authors of treatises on the origins of particular languages (as distinct from those philosophical minds that were ruminating on the genesis of human speech, in the most general terms possible at that time), we note the early-seventeenth-century Spaniard stationed in Italy, Bernardo Aldrete, and, towards the middle of the following century, that erudite Spaniard of transparently Catalan stock, Gregorio Mayáns y Siscar (their respective treatises were titled: *Del origen y principio de la lengua castellana o romance*, 1606, and *Orígenes de la lengua española*, 1737). Finally, the clumsy miniature 'phonologies' were not sufficiently extended to qualify as separate book ventures, but were, typically, hidden away as introductory chapters to normative grammars and dictionaries, or as parts of other sections, starting with a few relevant pages in Antonio de Nebrija's tone-setting *Gramática castellana* (1492). The important thing to remember is that pioneering etymologists did not yet deem it advisable or mandatory to test their proposals, or any earlier conjectures of which they were cognizant, against any sets of phonetically phrased correspondences, or laws, or rules, precisely because those equations, apart from being very poorly phrased, were not recognized as binding, i.e., endowed with sufficient probatory force to militate for or against acceptance of an etymological conjecture still left pending. What did etymological operations, as conducted between c.1500 and 1800, actually look like?

It is important to realize that most of the Renaissance and post-Renaissance etymologists were (measured by the standard of their time) men of considerable learning, eager to absorb a good many facts about as many languages as possible and equally anxious to consult the erudite writings of their contemporaries and predecessors, several of them available only as manuscripts (not a few of which have, in the meantime, been irretrievably lost). In addition to Latin, Greek, and some Hebrew they strove to acquire adequate insight into languages cognate to their own (thus, the Frenchman Ménage had a respectable command of Italian and a commendable knowledge of Spanish). Moreover, be it only for the sake of a certain intellectual piquancy, Covarrubias, as a participant in the Spanish Golden Age *maurofilia* ('enthusiasm for things Moorish'), made a point of familiarizing himself with Arabic lexis, perhaps under the tutelage of Pedro de Alcalá's record of Granadino speech (1504?), whereas Ménage, with equal justification, being aware of the Celtic character of Brittany and also of what Caesar as well as the historians and geographers of Antiquity had reported about most of pre-Roman Gaul, became one of the first victims of *celtomania*. We can thus credit the 1500–1800 period with (a) some widening of horizons, as regards possible source languages outside the Graeco-Roman world, and (b) a willingness to cull rival hypotheses from a variety of eagerly collected earlier treatises (which, unfortunately, its representatives were in the habit of leaving unidentified in each single instance). The trouble, once we look at things and judge values from our vantage point, was that these pioneers seldom, if ever, sized up those rival conjectures in a truly critical vein, stating which looked more persuasive or, at least, more promising than the rest and, if this was the case, why. Their ineptness about applying phonological criteria – the chief cause of certain absurdities of which they made themselves guilty and which later exposed them to ridicule – should, however, be balanced against their impressive flair in ferreting out borrowings. Covarrubias, for example, was particularly deft at catching Italianisms in Spanish, Ménage not infrequently captured Castilianisms and Italianisms in Classical French and even assembled whole lists of them in supplements to his dictionary. Towards the end of the eighteenth century, Tomás Antonio Sánchez, in glossaries appended to his pioneering editions of medieval Spanish texts, even believed he had recognized the Old Provençal provenance of certain Old Spanish lexical items.

As the crowning flaw of those early ventures one may finally single out a certain absence of any sense of proportion. If awareness of some colourful myth or entertaining fable was deemed useful to explain a word-origin at issue, a scholar of Covarrubias' calibre would not hesitate to narrate the whole story, including its less relevant details, over a total of two or three pages, barely reserving a few lines for the genetic identification of less amusing words.

The late nineteenth century, known for the rigidity of its prominent theorists ('Neo-grammarians'), was particularly pitiless in exposing and condemning the amateurishness of pre-1800 pioneers. Tracing French *fermer* 'to close, lock' to *fer* (or its Latin prototype *ferrum*) 'iron', rather than to *firmāre* 'to make firm, fast, lasting', was deemed irresponsible and unforgivable nonsense. Today's attitude tends to be a shade less condescending. To be sure, *fermer* basically echoes *firmāre*, but the fact that the meaning 'to lock' emerged from further development makes the association of the activity with an iron lock, or bar, or latch in the minds of that group of speakers highly probable. One could even invoke *ferrum* as a secondary etymon or, at least, as a collateral evolutionary factor. Moreover, there are several other word histories in Romance confirming the role of *ferrum* as an intruder, as when Latin *veruculum*, literally 'small javelin', was allowed to develop into *ferrolho*, rather than 'ideally correct' *verolho*, in Portuguese. The fact that *firmāre*, without some support from *ferrum*, was apt to evolve in a radically different direction is revealed by the state of affairs in Italian, where *fermare*, in transitive and reflexive uses, actually means 'to stop'. So the old etymological treatises, irritatingly bad as they are, need not be rashly discarded. Here and there they do contain tiny grains of useful information or molecules of ideas that lend themselves to cautious salvaging.

With the advent of the nineteenth century, historico-comparative linguistics came into its own. Its birth, during the Napoleonic Era, coincided with the rise to unprecedented prominence in linguistics (or in linguistic science, *Sprachwissenschaft*, as it was admiringly called henceforth) of Germany and the Scandinavian countries. The new chain of events was apt to influence the further course taken by etymological explorations, but the impact was not immediately felt. One conceivable reason for the delay was that two among the most prominent advocates of the new approach, namely Rasmus Rask in Denmark and, shortly thereafter, Jakob Grimm in Germany, tried out their forces and tested the validity of the new subdiscipline by attacking morphology (*Formenlehre*) first, and in so doing placed heavier emphasis on inflection than on affixation or composition, not to mention morphosyntax.

Only in revising his *Deutsche Grammatik* (which means 'Comparative Germanic', rather than 'German', Grammar) for a second edition did Grimm invert the sequence of morphology and phonology, thus creating a widely imitated model for posterity. The upshot of the new schema was that the bonds between etymology and historical grammar, as reinterpreted in the second quarter of the nineteenth century, were measurably tightened.

Diachronic phonology, especially as it was conceived in the last century, fundamentally involved the pairing off of words assumed to have been essentially the same lexical units seen at different evolutionary stages, as when present-day English *desk* and, through a strange coincidence, *dish* are both traced, albeit through different channels, to Latin *discus*, itself an adaptation of Greek *dískos* (δισκος), from *dikeîn* 'to throw'. The third reflex of the Graeco-Latin word in English, and a far more technical one, is *disk*, or *disc*, and the fourth is *discus*. In Antiquity, *dísk-os* / *disc-us* principally designated a 'quoit', i.e., an implement for exercise in gymnastics. Only secondarily did it refer to a 'dish', or to a 'sundial', on account of the similarity of their roundish shapes. A quick look at English *disk* (= *disc*), *discus*, *desk*, and *dish* suffices to show that the first two forms, details apart, involve the unaltered adaptations of the core of the Graeco-Latin prototype; and that the fourth form deviates more radically from the first two than does the third, mainly because *dish* has only three sound units (/dɪš/) instead of the four in /dɪsk/, /desk/. While *disk*, I repeat, is merely a learned adaptation of *disc-us* (and *discus* is hyperlearnèd), *desk* and *dish* differ from one another as a result of radically different conduits of transmission, which exposed the word at issue to different conditions, or constraints, or pressures customarily associated with changes. Scholars now believe that *desk* is merely a post-medieval adaptation of Italian *desco*, which indeed had descended in a straight line from *discus*. *Dish*, conversely, though in the last analysis also credited to infiltration of *disc-us* into English, boasts a far more complicated biography. As scholars have gradually pieced together its biography, *dish* goes back, via Middle English (Chaucerian) *dish*, to Old English (Beowulfian) *disc* 'plate', which – in the company of Old Saxon *tisk* 'table' and of Old High German *tisc* 'dish, table' (cf. modern *Tisch*) – goes back to a reconstructed, i.e., unrecorded, archaic parent language, conventionally known as West Germanic which, two thousand or so years ago, indeed appears to have borrowed the very same Graeco-Latin word, against a background of favourable conditions of contemporary material civilization.

To understand this complicated process one should, consequently, have familiarized oneself with archaeology and with conventional history as well (namely with the record and character of protracted contacts between Roman and Germanic civilizations). One should next have acquired some knowledge of the history of writing and spelling, e.g., of the widespread interchangeability of the letters *c* and *k*, as carriers of the sound /k/. But, above all, one needs a firm grasp of the – temporally and spatially limited – transmutations of relevant speech sounds: the relation of word-initial /d/ and /t/, or word-final /sk/ and /š/, or else word-medial /e/ and /i/ or /ɪ/, as among individual languages, and as among successive stages of, basically the same languages. These fluctuating relations are, in the aggregate, precisely the province of diachronic phonology.

Given this exceptionally close connection between the history of words and the history of sounds, it becomes clear that the newly refined and expanded diachronic phonology was bound to revolutionize etymology, by occasionally suggesting new solutions to old riddles, but, even more frequently, by weeding out as untenable certain pedigrees that had been for millennia accepted as unadulterated truth.

There were, at bottom, two possibilities left to a new generation of etymologists to adjust their favourite discipline to a new climate of opinion and to an arsenal of new tools. Either these scholars would aim at being all-round language historians, capable of alternating the writing of historical (especially historico-comparative) grammars, with self-immersion in etymological investigations, often conducive to the preparation of a fully organized etymological dictionary; or, though imbued with the new knowledge expounded in historical grammars, they would prefer to concentrate on etymology (or, as some soon preferred to term it, word history) cultivated for its own sake, not infrequently in the closest attainable connection with broad-based cultural history. These two groups of investigators, not necessarily antagonistic to each other or irremediably divided, simply corresponded to two diverse temperamental categories of explorers.

The former approach, which deserves to be known as *integrative*, because it tends to combine etymology with historico-comparative grammar, can be illustrated with a brief survey of the writings of two near-contemporaries and compatriots, Franz Bopp and Friedrich Diez.

Bopp (1791–1867), the father of Indo-European comparatism, manifests in the ensemble of his publications a much heavier commitment to grammar than to lexis and, accordingly, etymology. It can be shown, step by step, that his primary interest was strictly grammatical and that his secondary concern with etymology gradually branched off from grammatical preoccupations, without ever succeeding in overshadowing them. In a nutshell, his career started with an 1816 monograph (later revised in an English version of 1820) that dealt with the conjugational system of Sanskrit viewed in comparison with Greek, Latin, Persian, and Teutonic or Germanic, aiming to 'show the original identity of their grammatical structures'. Despite Bopp's self-immersion in Sanskrit over the next two decades, he managed, between 1826 and 1832, to present five short memoirs to the Berlin Academy, which were jointly devoted to the comparative 'dissection' (*Zergliederung*), i.e., analysis, of Sanskrit and cognate languages. The specific topics on Bopp's agenda were, at that stage, functional words lying at the intersection of purely grammatical and lexico-etymological lines of curiosity: (a) personal pronouns of the first and second person; (b) reflexives; (c) demonstratives in their relation to case endings; (d) certain radicals of demonstratives and their connection with miscellaneous prepositions and conjunctions; and (e) the influence of pronouns on word-formation. Highly characteristic of this period of transition was another monograph, *Vokalismus* (1836), critical in tone and scope, whose peculiarity consisted in its discussion of two earlier books of great prominence, one of them grammatical, the other lexical in content: J. Grimm's *Deutsche Grammatik* and E. G. Graff's *Althochdeutscher Sprachschatz*. This picture is completed by a shorter piece of the same period (1835), which deals with Indo-European numerals and thus likewise straddles the realms of grammarians and etymologists. Bopp was now ready for his vast syntheses. The years 1833–42 witnessed the appearance of the original four-volume edition of Bopp's trail-blazing *Vergleichende Grammatik*, which embraced Sanskrit, Zend (i.e., Avestan), Greek, Latin, Lithuanian, Palaeo-Slavic (or Old Slavonic), Gothic, and older stages of German. The publication of the comparable etymological venture took place in 1828. It was written in Latin, and its title was distinctly less pretentious, advising the reader that this was essentially a *Glossarium Sanscritum*, in which all widely used Sanskrit roots and vocables were explained, with some attention reserved for comparative references to Greek, Latin, Germanic, Lithuanian, Slavic, and Celtic counterparts. Interestingly, the pioneering edition of Bopp's grammar was promptly translated into English, by Edward B. Eastwick (1845–53), while the revised second German edition (1857–61), which – by way of innovation – paid some attention to Armenian, was translated into French by a major fellow-scholar, Michel Bréal (1866–74). Both adaptations were later re-issued. In contrast, Bopp's dictionary until the end remained available in Latin alone.

Diez's *œuvre* reflects a comparable, but somewhat more advanced and, above all, better balanced state of affairs in regard to the relationship between the two disciplines here focused upon. A minor poet, a translator, and an historian of literature at the start of his career, Diez (1794–1876), after specializing in Old Spanish and Old Provençal poetic texts, began to toy with problems in straight diachronic linguistics in his exegetic annotations to selected medieval poems. By the mid-1830s, his plans for an all-embracing historico-comparative grammar of the Romance languages thus far identified were ready. It appeared before long (1836–44), trailing Bopp's initial Indo-European venture by the narrowest of margins. From the outset, phonology occupied a pride of place, making Diez more modern in his architectural design than Bopp and Grimm had been at the outset. Indirectly this arrangement also countenanced the cause of etymology. However, the opening volume also had its share of flaws and limitations. The matter of level of transmission (vernacular vs. learnèd) was still disregarded throughout, and the perspective chosen, invariably leading from the parent tongue to the corona of daughter languages, was one-sided. A sharp reversal of the tide occurred in 1853, when Diez's complementary project, the *Etymologisches Wörterbuch der romanischen Sprachen*, ran off the press. On that occasion, the author's debt to his predecessor Bopp became inconspicuous; it showed, at most, in the choice of a 'privileged' daughter language, except that, where Bopp had elevated Sanskrit to that rank, Diez, for reasons no longer held valid today, enthroned Italian, assigning a slightly more modest position to French and Provençal as well as to Spanish and Portuguese, while relegating Romanian to the rear of the gradually emerging landscape. This bizarre detail apart, Diez offered a real string of miniature analyses of each etymological problem selected for inclusion, paying full and understanding attention to earlier pronouncements by pre-1800 trail-blazers. More significantly, in revising his grammar for a second edition, he enriched it with new insights gained on his etymological safari, adding, for example, a whole section on ancestral (Graeco-Latin, Germanic, Arabic) sources of innovative Romance sounds, such as certain sibilants and affricates. The next edition of the dictionary (1861) and its sequel (3rd edn, 1869–70), in turn profited from the grammar having been properly brought up to date (3rd edn, 1870–72). This brilliantly executed zigzag movement lasted until the end of Diez's life, and placed grammatical and etymological analyses on comparably high pedestals, unlike Bopp's scale of values. Incidentally, one not unimportant side-effect of the newly awakened curiosity about language history repeated itself in the case under study: Diez's comparative grammar was translated, albeit late, into French (by A. Brachet, G. Paris, and A. Morel-Fatio, 1874–6),

11

and the long introductory section was translated into English by C. B. Cayley (1863). No such token of attention can be reported concerning the etymologicum.

There exists an opposite side in the community of professional students of language, namely those disinclined to subordinate etymology almost routinely to the exploration of historico-comparative grammar, or to place the two disciplines on the same level. Even though such linguists may have gone through a period of intensive, rigorous training in formal diachronic phonology, they might appositely be called *separatists*. Less felicitous by far would be the label *isolationists* for this splinter group, because it would fail to do justice to one crucial circumstance. Although somewhat luke-warm – chiefly for temperamental reasons? – to the structuring of grammatical edifices, scholars of that ilk often excel at bracketing their private conception of linguistics with ethnography, mythology, and other disciplines towards which grammarians and semi-grammarians, in turn, display less open-mindedness, not to say total antipathy.

One paradigmatic example of that converse attitude was August Friedrich Pott (1802–87), a student of Bopp's in Berlin, but one ever more strongly attracted to, and influenced by, that *Originalgenie*, Wilhelm von Humboldt. Already in his early thirties Pott began swerving from the prescribed course of academic respectability by plunging into an ambitious two-volume project, *Etymologische Forschungen auf dem Gebiete der indogermanischen Sprachen* (1833–6), which a critic as perspicacious as Georg von der Gabelentz, in his many-splendoured necrological essay on Pott (1888), called the actual lexico-etymological counterpart to the near-contemporary original version of Bopp's comparative grammar. Be that as it may, Pott, just appointed to a professorship in Halle, was cautious at the outset, adding, by way of subtitle, the lengthy qualification 'with special reference to the sound shift[s] (*Lautumwandlung*) in Sanskrit, Greek, Latin, Lithuanian, and Gothic'. The second and last edition, sweepingly expanded into a six-volume venture (1859–76), exhibited greater daring on the author's part. The strong allusion to the primacy of sound shifts was altogether omitted (at the very juncture at which younger scholars began toying with the rigidifying concept of 'sound laws'). As if in compensation, the corpus of raw data tapped was energetically expanded, so as to include Avestan, Persian, Slavic, Germanic (rather than Gothic exclusively), and also Celtic. The indexes to this monumental enterprise, compiled by H. E. Bindseil, dealt, characteristically enough, with roots, words, proper names, and units of lexical meaning. Even this did not exhaust Pott's commitment to the rehabilitation of a neglected perspective, a special favourite of his. In 1863 there appeared a 100-page monograph from his pen, on etymological legends that had circulated in Antiquity, written with all the more authority as the author already had a book of studies on Greek mythology to his credit.

The way von der Gabelentz painted the intellectual portrait of Pott, the Halle professor must further rank as the forerunner, or founding father, of: (a) onomastic studies; (b) onomasiology interpreted as the reverse side of semasiology (or lexical semantics); and, conceivably most memorably, (c) sound symbolism (or phonosymbolism). All three approaches were intimately interwoven with traditional etymology, yet were by no means irrevocably divorced from newly acquired, i.e., historico-comparative, grammatical knowledge. A brief comment on each of these breakthroughs may be in order. Pott's research in proper names culminated in a 900-page, cross-linguistic inquiry into anthroponyms or personal names (2 vols., 1853–9), which paid special attention to family names and gave full consideration to toponyms or place names. As if this stiff quota were insufficient, Pott also wrote shorter monographs on Basque and Old Persian names, thus firmly bringing the study of proper names into the fold of etymology and, on balance, of diachronic linguistics as well. Although the concept of onomasiology was alien to Pott and his generation (the term was minted by Adolf Zauner as late as 1902), he began early to experiment with that approach, which lets its practitioners start out not from a given form, or cluster of forms, but from a given meaning, then collects across the board the words serving to convey that meaning (i.e., cross-language synonyms and near-synonyms), while seeking to draw conclusions from identity of message as against diversity of forms. Pott thus studied numerals (and, in the process, paid attention to discrepant systems of numbering, e.g., quinary vs. vigesimal) on two occasions (1847, 1868), but also became fascinated by the implications of the names of fingers (1847) and crossed over into the realm of zoonymy (including the names of the elephant) before any one else thought of the advantages of such investigations. Pott's ability to pre-empt phonosymbolism has been inferred from the title and slant he gave to a whole series of articles – a sort of common denominator vaguely reminiscent of Roman Jakobson's thinking in our own time 'about the diversity of linguistic expression along the axes of sound and concept'.

In addition to all these accomplishments, slanted almost without exception in the direction of etymology and of disciplines germane to it, Pott included in his purview numerous modern non-Indo-European languages (especially South and Central African), Old Egyptian, Javanese, and Japanese. As a theorist, he bridged the gap between Humboldt (whose philosophy, cast in the so-called Sapir–Whorfian key, he espoused) and Steinthal, operated with both genetic and areal groupings of languages, setting off, *inter alia*, the whole of Europe as one such territory (*Sprachverschiedenheit in Europa*, 1868; *Zur Litteratur der Sprachkunde Europas*, 1887), and launched successful inquiries into the long-elusive language of Gypsies (1844–5), thus paving the way for Graziadio Isaia Ascoli (1865), Francisco Adolfo Coelho (1892), and many others – inquiries which, with astonishing foresight, he called 'geographico-linguistic'. To be sure, there were also darker sides to Pott's performances – one is reminded of his insufficiently polished and compressed style of writing, of certain monographs of his being programmatically polemic, of his disquieting burst of enthusiasm (1856) for Count Gobineau's controversial (to say the least) writings on human races. But, all told, it is Pott who deserves the credit for having laid the cornerstone for modern-day 'pure etymology'.

In yet another respect Pott's *Etymologische Forschungen* represents a landmark. Until the middle of the nineteenth century, issues in etymology were ordinarily laid out in special dictionaries alphabetically arranged, so that they could be consulted with relative ease by sophisticated laymen and by fellow-scholars alike. To be sure, certain variations on this pattern were possible. Such dictionaries could be programmatically selective, such as Ramón Cabrera's posthumous *Diccionario de etimologías . . .* (1837), or they could be inadvertently lacunary. Some were ushered in by methodological treatises, as with the long section on the rudiments of etymology preceding Pedro Felipe Monlau's *Diccionario etimológico . . .* (1856), or by miniaturized language histories, as with the aforementioned treatise by Aldrete prefixed to the second, posthumous edition of Sebastián de Covarrubias' *Tesoro*. A few were eventually revised by other scholars, a hazardous undertaking in the case of a discipline as highly subjective as etymology has been traditionally (here Benito Remigio Noydens' 1674 Supplement to Covarrubias' thesaurus comes to mind). In Cabrera's experiment, a selective sketch of diachronic phonology was designed to balance a dishful of etymological titbits. Whatever the varying circumstances, the underlying shape of a reference work remained clearly recognizable. With Pott's *Etymologische Forschungen*, that frame of reference was abandoned. We have before us a string of case histories of assured concern to the specialist alone, and this adds a new dimension of dignity and a quota of autonomy to etymological anatomy. Before long, imitators would join Pott, one's thoughts wander off, for example, to the Berliner Karl August Friedrich Mahn's *Etymologische Untersuchungen auf dem Gebiete der romanischen Sprachen*, which made its appearance in twenty-four freely assorted specimens or instalments (1854–64).

Yet this is only part of the profound changes that set in around 1850, in the heartlands of the Old World and, ten to twenty years later, at its periphery and in the New World – changes as regards channels through which the fruits of one's own etymological thinking, as well as one's critical reactions to other qualified persons' thinking, could be appropriately offered. To the pre-existing category of academy memoirs and bulletins there was added, starting in the 1840s, a host of new periodicals (typically, quarterlies sponsored by learnèd societies), an innovation which made it possible to publish smaller chunks, and even crumbs of newly acquired etymological knowledge in the form of articles, notes, mere page-fillers, and, above all, formal reviews of all sizes concerned with etymological dictionaries and monographs. There were also, under exceptional circumstances, meek replies to unfavourable assessments or angry, sarcastic rebuttals (provoking counter-rebuttals). In a matter of two or three decades, the tone of etymological probing was radically revised.

It might be tedious to offer here a catalogue of all the newly launched humanistic periodicals that encompassed in their offerings significant articles and bits of serious criticism concerned with historical linguistics, including its etymological ingredient. Any complete inventory of this kind would also suffer from being overburdened with items that were destined to perish after a few experimental fascicles or volumes, whatever the specific reasons for the decline and eventual demise in each individual case. Ferreting out today scraps of valuable material from those early and, more often than not, ephemeral ventures is something of an art even if the sources themselves are within fairly easy reach. For one thing, many pioneers – especially those toiling in the German-speaking countries – had the strange habit of identifying, in references, the budding journals not by their full titles, but, misleadingly, by the names of their editors. Thus, the venerable *Zeitschrift für vergleichende Sprachforschung*, which exists to this day, was long advantageously known as *Kuhn's Zeitschrift*, in tribute to Adalbert Kuhn, a second-rate scholar who had started it in 1852. (There also existed a mysterious *Techmer's Zeitschrift*, etc.) Furthermore, the scope of certain journals blessed with longevity has changed radically over the years. Thus, the *American Journal of Philology* has served, of late, so consistently as a mouthpiece for classical learning that few dedicated students of, for instance, Romance etymology would reckon with the possibility of detecting articles and book reviews pertinent to their own interests in its early volumes (from which such items were actually by no means absent). A student of Italian linguistics, a discipline known or notorious for its deep-seated etymological flavour, even bias, is fully expected not only to have ascertained what periodical is masked by hermetic references to *Bezzenbergers Beiträge* (the answer is: *Beiträge zur Kunde der indogermanischen Sprachen*, 1877–1906), but also to stand prepared to pick morsels of information directly or indirectly valuable for the study of Italian from the opening volumes of the *Zeitschrift der deutschen morgenländischen Gesellschaft* (1847–), which later became more careful about toeing the line of strictly oriental themes.

But, all such amenities and eccentricities apart, etymological research almost overnight became a scholarly endeavour which required the constant use of academy bulletins, the files of miscellaneous, sometimes unpredictably uneven journals, on occasion even daily newspapers, and the like. This sort of increasingly heavy-handed research clamoured for an appropriate locale – preferably a generously stocked university or seminar library. Only at its preliminary or initial stages could it be undertaken and, for a while, conducted at the practitioner's home, provided that this home happened to be equipped with a superb library, its shelves bursting with reprints received from fellow-scholars. And the successful practitioner of the new-style etymology, on average, was no longer some assiduous and imaginative *aficionado* or, basically, a *littérateur* who, like Gilles Ménage, had chosen the elucidation of word origins as a genteel pastime, a side interest, or hobby, or plain intellectual *divertissement*. In most instances, he was henceforth either a celebrated university professor, or at least a professional librarian attached to an academy or a major research library; on increasingly rare occasions, he was a university-trained teacher active at a respected *lycée*, or *Gymnasium*, or *college*. The transmutation of etymology into an esteemed and even admired academic discipline was thus, to be sure, not exclusively, but to a large extent, due to this rapid expansion of its academic underpinning, which made progress time-consuming and subject to controls, and thus sharply curtailed the margin of free-wheeling, spontaneous guesswork.

The existence of sharp divergences in assessing the role of etymology in linguistic practice, coinciding as it did with a dramatic increase in the number of media available to all language historians (etymologists included), led to an utterly confusing situation by the middle of the nineteenth century. To illustrate this imbroglio, I shall report on three radically discrepant attitudes towards the quest for word origins, struck by that same group of influential European students of language, and try to add an extra touch to the picture by briefly reporting on the American scene a decade or two later.

The comparatist August Schleicher (1821–68) was a man of many talents and of diversified interests, and there is a certain irony in the fact that lexicology remained for him evenly divided between diachronic phonology and morphology (basically, inflection), while etymology pursued for its own sake was almost wholly absent from the range of his active interests. He compiled a few glossaries, but these were doomed to remain ancillary to other pursuits. A glossary, for example, serves as a key to a chrestomathy which, in turn, accompanies a grammar of Lithuanian of slightly earlier vintage (1856–7). Then again, almost exactly one half of Schleicher's edition (1865) of the poems of Christian Donalithius (1714–80) – again a Lithuanian – was reserved for a glossary. Furthermore, the sample texts ('Schriftproben'), in an impressive variety of Indo-European languages, assembled in Schleicher's posthumous *Indogermanische Chrestomathie* (1869), were accompanied by a battery of exegetic glossaries; but these had been contributed, in large part, by Schleicher's collaborators and intellectual heirs – H. Ebel, A. Leskien, and J. Schmidt. Schleicher was by no means a one-sided or 'dry' person – his active curiosity encompassed, for example, folk poetry, down to the musical ingredient of both Lithuanian and Thuringian folk songs (1857, 1858). But, as the very title of his *magnum opus*, a two-volume comparative grammar of Indo-European, immediately reveals (*Compendium der vergleichenden Grammatik der indogermanischen Sprachen*, 1861–2, 2nd edn, 1866), his purpose was to compress diachronic phonology and morphology into highly concentrated treatises ('kurze Abrisse'), conducive to the reconstruction of the proto-language, which was all-important to him; and this aim, he doubtless felt, could be reached with a modicum of secure lexical illustrations. Contributing to succinctness was also the use, first experimented with by Schleicher, of an asterisk in lieu of all sorts of lame paraphrases to signal neatly the conjectural (or hypothetical) character of a form adduced in a grammatical context. The fact that Schleicher impressed his contemporaries, primarily (and perhaps to the point of one-sidedness) as, preeminently, a grammarian follows from the circumstance that D. Pezzi, in preparing for a Turin publisher a translation of his principal treatise, made a point of pairing it off with a parallel translation of Leo Meyer's lexicon of Indo-Italo-Greek roots, as if to restore the balance between grammar and lexis. Only in the least familiar of Schleicher's far-flung publications, for example, his periodic contributions, phrased in Russian, to the Memoirs (*Zapiski*) of the St Petersburg Academy of Sciences, may the author's repressed lexico-etymological concerns have come to the fore.

Schleicher's almost studied aloofness from any personal commitment to monographic research in etymology did not prevent at least one of his followers from using the master's classificatory schema for the Indo-European language family in coming to grips with a large-scale etymological venture. The case alluded to is August Fick's – for a while, remarkably successful – *Vergleichendes Wörterbuch der indogermanischen Sprachen* (1870–1; 3rd edn, greatly expanded, 1874–6), which operated with such a system of cleavages within the asssumed family tree as allowed the analyst at once to assign the lexical unit at issue either to the parent language ('the trunk'), or to one of the branches, or sub-branches. So there was no dearth of potentialities for advanced, innovative etymologizing within Schleicher's system. But the system itself was arrived at through the author's dialogue with Darwin, Haeckel, and other leading naturalists of his time, with a modicum or minimum of independent etymologizing.

Almost the opposite side of the mid-century spectrum of opinions on etymology was occupied by the *Grundzüge der griechischen Etymologie* by Georg Curtius (1820–85), the climactic point in the career of an unusually prolific classicist and comparatist. The original publication dates of the two volumes were 1856 and 1862, even though the editions preferably consulted today are the fourth (1873) and the fifth (1879), which had the benefit of an unusually thorough revision by the noted Celticist Ernst Windisch, a close friend of the author, and are further available in a translation into – slightly quaint – English. Upon opening the heavy tomes, an unforewarned reader will be confused at first, for, after skipping the lengthy introductory section (Book I), devoted to Indo-European as a whole, he is bound to discover that Book II, running to c. 350 pages, is devoted to a well-organized succession of processes normally dealt with in historical phonology, with a much larger dosage of attention here reserved for consonants than for vowels. Only then will he recognize that the same section is, additionally, subdivided into 619 etymological miniatures, each item mandatorily revolving around some Greek word, but also taking into account as many congeners as had by then been ascertained. The individual etymological discussions are arranged, then, in such a manner as to illustrate the highest possible number of points whose aggregate constitutes the edifice of Indo-European historical grammar, with emphasis on Greek. Book III shows an even higher degree of atomization. Here an ensemble of as many as 400 pages, reserved for a long chain of irregular, or sporadic, changes, also dissolves into an analysis of unnumbered, but doubtless even more numerous, etymological case histories. There is, then, a strident discrepancy between the arrangement and the content of the book. While topically it is indeed concerned with neatly individuated word histories, in each of which Greek is allowed to sound the dominant note in a chorus of voices, the collocation of these etymological anecdotes has been so planned as to illustrate not the various patterns of lexical transmission, as visible through the prism of the divergent vicissitudes of the core vocabulary, but the scheme of sound shifts. Only the inclusion of very generous indexes, running to c.100 pages, brings one back entirely to the lexico-etymological domain announced by the title of the book.

The third mid-century event worth reporting here as a contributing factor to the growing confusion about the exact status of etymology was the appearance, in 1852, of a slim article by a Germanist who was just beginning to make a name for himself, namely Ernst Förstemann (1822–1906), on 'German Folk Etymology'. The paper lacked any potentially unsavoury overtones which a piece so titled might have acquired had it been published, perhaps ninety years later, in a politicized academic milieu. Nevertheless, despite its unquestionable analytical brilliance, the paper managed to cause confusion, introducing as it did into the terminological toolkit of a linguist the previously unheard-of label *Volksetymologie*. In addition, making its appearance as the opening piece in Vol. I of the trail-blazing *Zeitschrift für vergleichende Sprachforschung*, it produced a real 'splash'.

To put it briefly, the author proposed to reserve for cognitive or scientific inquiries into word origins the ponderous composite label *gelehrte Etymologie*, while applying the alternative tag *Volksetymologie* to, fundamentally, two unequal situations: (a) the transfer, within the bounds of a given language, of some isolated word, occasionally opaque, from its residual (moribund) lexical family to some other, more vigorously thriving family; and (b) the assignment of borrowed words or names (or else of bare fragments of such items) to appropriately similar native word families enjoying unimpaired health – at the cost, not infrequently, of some semantic stretching, or even of a comic effect, deliberate or unintentional. Thus, the elements *-dam(m)* and *-burg* of the Central European toponyms *Potsdam*, *Brandenburg*, and *Merseburg*, involve reinterpretations, through *rapprochement* with familiar German common nouns, of originally Slavic words or word segments. Similarly, the hydronym *Bodensee* 'Lac Léman' (situated at the Swiss–German-Austrian frontier) contains a Celtic unit gone astray and later embroidered upon in much the same way, through playful association with German *Boden* 'bottom'.

19

Had a more experienced and cautious Förstemann used for his purpose some such neutral words as, if I may repeat myself, 'transfer' or 'reinterpretation', or else 'adjustment', he would have wrought no harm. But his romantically inspired idea of picturing the entire speech community as a sort of collective brain performing analytical operations seems, in retrospect, severely misleading. The resulting damage increased when the celebrated book carved out posthumously from Ferdinand de Saussure's lectures (*Cours de linguistique générale*, 1916) turned out to contain some sparkling pages on folk etymology, contrasting with its dogmatic refusal to include genuine etymology within its purview. The situation scarcely improved when Anglophone linguists, in an effort to assimilate *Volksetymologie* to the arsenal of their own tools, began to toy with such ambiguous terms as 'popular etymology' or, worse, 'false etymology'.

Finally, there arose, approximately at that juncture, the self-contradictory situation of a many-sided linguist putting, *qua* theorist, a premium on etymological inquiry while practising that scholarly art on an astonishingly modest scale. This slightly paradoxical description fits rather neatly the performance of the pioneering Yale scholar William Dwight Whitney (1827–94). Thus, that classic – popular and, at the same time, sophisticated – from Whitney's prolific pen, namely *The life and growth of language* (1875), contains the following memorable passage, entirely unequivocal in its endorsement of etymology:

> The whole process of linguistic research begins in and depends upon etymology, the tracing-out of the history of individual words and elements. From words the investigation rises higher, to classes, to parts of speech, to whole languages. On accuracy in etymological processes, then, depends the success of the whole; and the perfecting of the methods of etymologizing is what especially distinguishes the new linguistic science from the old. The old worked upon the same basis on which the new now works: namely on the tracing of resemblances of analogies between words, in regard to form and meaning. But the former was hopelessly superficial. It was guided by surface likenesses . . . it was heedless of the sources whence its material came; it did not, in short, command its subject sufficiently to have a method. A wider knowledge of facts, and a consequent better comprehension of their relation, changes all this. (pp. 312ff.)

Yet, as one scans Whitney's many-faceted *œuvre* (disregarding, for the purpose of this inquiry, the elementary grammars and readers of English, French, and especially German, often prepared in collaboration with others, as well as annotated collegiate editions of plays), one discovers at its core a magnificent Sanskrit grammar (1879), which pays sustained attention to the classical stage of that language and to older Vedic, with a bulky supplement volume (1885) inventorying 'roots, verb forms, and primary derivatives'. There are also a few exegetic editions of Sanskrit texts, and a collection of companion articles; two – slightly overlapping – wide-ranging introductions to linguistics; and one polemical tract against a – briefly influential – Oxford scholar, Max Müller (1892). But, all told, there is amazingly little that qualifies as etymological spade-work, except where it is inextricably interwoven with grammar. One might mention the incidental fact that the *Compendious German—English dictionary* (1879, 1887) which Whitney compiled with the assistance of A. H. Edgren was equipped, according to the title page, 'with notations of correspondence and brief etymologies'. Also, among his *scripta minora*, we detect one rather uncharacteristic item, on 'A botanico-philological problem' (1877), which qualifies for classification as a contribution to creative etymology. It discusses the Indo-European dendronyms for 'beech', 'oak', and 'fir', yet is, unfortunately, marred by an excess of polemic against Max Müller, Whitney's arch-opponent. Even by throwing into the balance Whitney's thirty-page review (1873–4a) of the revised edition of John Peile's *Introduction to Greek and Latin etymology*, one falls short of restoring the balance.

Theodor Benfey must have had a sort of premonition when, in 1869, he published his bulky history of linguistics and Oriental philology in Germany because, precisely in that country, the relevant course of events began to change radically just a couple of years later. A loosely organized contingent of younger scholars known under the nickname of 'Neogrammarians' (*Junggrammatiker*) began to assert itself dynamically, aspiring to place historical linguistics on a firmer, more scientific foundation. The group, at the start, comprised mostly Germans; the few foreigners included lived under the aegis of German culture (thus Karl Verner, a Dane, was attached as a researcher to the Dresden Library). The vigour of this movement cannot be separated from the general upswing of Bismarckian Germany in the early 1870s, while the scientific pretensions of Neogrammarianism echoed the esteem in which exact sciences, notably chemistry, were held by German society at that juncture.

How did etymology (and the etymologists) fare under this new regime? The emphasis that Neogrammarians placed on phonology is widely known. If Förstemann, by 1852, had invoked 'severe, strict sound laws' (*strenge Lautgesetze*), these laws, real or alleged, two decades later, became 'exceptionless' (*ausnahmslos*). Morphology, in particular the study of declension and conjugation, also continued to enjoy prestige, witness the slant of Hermann Osthoff's investigations. Etymology was tolerated to the extent that it allowed researchers to sift out the core vocabulary of a given speech community from later admixtures, through borrowings from neighbours or, alternatively, through culturally conditioned deliberate adoptions from an earlier ('classical') stage of the language under investigation. Within the core vocabulary, a neat distinction was to be drawn between such lexical units as had developed through the sheer interplay of sound laws, regular to the point of predictability, and those in whose growth extraneous forces ('analogy') had intervened. The latter part of the total material invited constant re-examination, since one could hope to identify, through careful scrutiny, certain recurrences of minor sound changes in such a slightly amorphous mass. In that eventuality, the researcher could expect to transfer such lexical items as displayed a certain evolutionary resemblance that had previously remained hidden to the more attractive pile of pieces that had passed muster, in terms of scientific analysis. Thus a new scale of values gradually developed – one decidedly less than favourable to the cause of etymology.

The influential members of this – informally constituted – school of thought never signed any manifesto, making it unfair for anyone to lump together their individual philosophies and sets of preferences. But certain informal agreements do stand out, in free variation with more personal tastes. Thus, Hermann Paul (1846–1921), a distinguished Munich professor of Germanics, in the end did consent to busy himself with applied lexicography; but particularly the early editions (1896–7, 1908) of his superb *Deutsches Wörterbuch* pay a minimum of attention to the provenance of entries, contrasting in this respect with Friedrich Kluge's earlier, but more frequently revised, *Etymologisches Wörterbuch der deutschen Sprache*.

How did Neogrammarian doctrine, specifically, affect etymological analysis, apart from stimulating its converts to segregate relative newcomers to the lexicon (the aforementioned layers of borrowings) from the ingredients transmitted by word of mouth from time immemorial? The common denominator of etymological decisions among Romance scholars attracted to the Neogrammarian stance was, for example, a distinctly higher reliance on a given word's form than on its meaning. Antoine Thomas was willing to disregard the semantic factor altogether, on account of its elusiveness, if essential identity or resemblance of shape sent a strong message; see the three collections of his articles and notes: *Essais de philologie française* (1897); *Mélanges d'étymologie française* (1902, 1927); *Nouveaux essais de philologie française* (1904). According to that philosophy, Italian *cansare* 'to avoid, eschew' (at present a mere by-form of *scansare*) and Spanish/

Portuguese *cansar* 'to fatigue, wear out', must be cognates and, as such, go back to the same prototype. Then again, Wilhelm Meyer-Lübke, in the two editions of his comparative Romance etymological dictionary (1911–20, 1930–35), bracketed certain forms so as to mark their learnèd or semi-learnèd transmission – indiscriminately so, even when of the, let us say, five criteria to be used in judging such an issue, four militated in favour of normal development and only the fifth pointed to the learnèd (or retarded) channelling.

The Neogrammatical approach was beneficial in a negative way, by forewarning the analyst that something must, or may well, be 'special' about a word history where some deviation from a widely accepted norm was involved. In this way, hundreds of previously accepted cross-temporal equations were discarded upon careful re-examination of the evidence. Conversely, the Neogrammarians, from today's vantage point, appear to have been disappointingly weak in dealing with general phonological shifts (dissimilation, haplology, and the like) and with the effects of phonosymbolism, to the extent that etymologizing was concerned. They failed to do full justice to individual word histories and, in particular, paid woefully insufficient attention to the imagerial side of semantic history, to the localization of words on the geographic map, and to social dialects, as well as to the extended co-existence of variants, not to mention matters of 'style in language' and levels of formality.

On balance, the aforementioned Hermann Paul represented, within Neogrammarianism, the more liberal, humanistically coloured current, so that etymologists to this day can draw on his *Prinzipien der Sprachgeschichte* (1880). The second edition (1886) contains, for example, two chapters of crucial relevance for advanced etymology, going far beyond the narrow corridor 'sound laws' vs. 'analogy'. One deals with the shifts in the configuration of etymologically bracketed word families, the other with spontaneous creation ('Urschöpfung'), which exceeds the realm of ono-matopoeia. This is not all. In the Preface the author confesses that, after some wavering, he decided against including a separate chapter on the dichotomy of regular sound shift (independent of the word's meaning or function) vs. the reshaping of a given word in response to its function ('Scheidung des Lautwandels von den durch Rücksicht auf die Funktion bedingten Umgestaltungen der Form'), referring the reader instead to an earlier journal article from his pen on the subject. As the reason for having extricated himself from his previous plan he cited, without giving away the names of the culprits, the studied indifference or hostility of certain critics; 'in which camp?', one might ask.

Other members of the group displayed a certain ruthlessness in pushing through their ideology and programme, and succeeded in creating the image of an 'establishmentarian' type of diachronic linguistics, in which etymology and disciplines inherently akin to it were relegated to the very periphery. This prevalent scale of values had a discouraging effect on not a few potential linguists, whose imagination the new regime of withering austerity failed to kindle. Gustav Gröber, for exampler, a first-rate Romance philologist, cultivated in the 1880s a perfectly legitimate and judicious kind of lexical reconstruction, piecing together, by the hundreds, Vulgar Latin bases from Romance reflexes ('Vulgärlateinische Substrate romanischer Wörter', 1884–9), but before long gave up any active involvement in linguistics for the sake of medieval Latin literature. Other scholars over-reacted by writing titillating articles, pamphlets, and books on the very topics that were apt to irritate those policing the newly marked-off domain. Thus, Karl Abel (1837–1906), for a while popular on both sides of the Atlantic, philosophized on the origin of language; the semantic polarization of pristine words; the kinship between Old Egyptian and Indo-European; the discrimination of synonyms; expressing the concept of 'love' in languages old and modern; and language as the expression of national modes of thought.

To the minds of staunch establishmentarians, Hugo Schuchardt (1842–1927) was the implacable opponent, the scourge *par excellence*, of Neogrammarianism. It might be more reasonable to view him not only as one of the most brilliant, but also as one of the most eccentric, linguistic scholars of all time. Certainly his slim, whimsical pamphlet of the year 1885, which earned him the above-cited reputation, namely *Über die Lautgesetze. Gegen die Junggrammatiker*, lacked any pivotal importance. What actually makes the protean Schuchardt's many-pronged *œuvre* appear as a seductive (according to others, dangerous) alternative to the Neogrammarians' theory and practices is the fact that, starting with a certain cut-off point in the mid-1870s, when he was still in his early thirties (and just embarking upon his long academic career at Graz University in southern Austria), he, privately, tended to find boring what almost every one else in the profession was proclaiming, pledging, and practising, while the others, conversely, were taken aback by his daring eccentricities. Not for nothing did one of his concluding academy memoirs (1925a) discuss 'Individualism in Linguistics'. This attitude of an outsider can easily be demonstrated with special reference to etymology.

The start, though hardly conventional, was relatively smooth, inasmuch as Schuchardt, bowing to the *Zeitgeist*, was willing to subordinate individual

word history to the delineation of sound developments, as he did successfully (a) in his three-volume *Der Vokalismus des Vulgärlateins* (based on
newly published epigraphic evidence, 1866–8); (b) in his professional thesis
(*Habilitationsschrift*), accepted by a university as demanding in those years
as Leipzig, *Über einige Fälle bedingten Lautwandels im Churwälschen*
(1870); and (c) in an invitational journal article (bizarrely titled 'Phonétique
comparée'), in which he riveted attention to the unstable word-initial
consonants in certain Sardic and South-Central Italian dialects (1874).
Soon thereafter his prime interest veered in the direction of word biographies pursued for their own sake – not merely conceived as a tool
serving to fill residual gaps in historical grammars. One can comfortably
follow this new development by examining, one by one, the volumes of the
newly founded, prestigious journal *Zeitschrift für romanische Philologie*,
which absorbed many of his shorter, yet increasingly extensive contributions
on this theme.

Even though Schuchardt knew at all times how to resort to such
conventional weapons as regular sound correspondences, he excelled at
trying different approaches, which were not at all times mutually compatible. For one thing, he succumbed to the fascination of migratory words,
paying special attention to sources infrequently tapped by the average
'modern-language man', as when he explored Romance words that had
percolated into Berber (1918) or examined the reciprocal influences exerted
between Basque (one of his favourite hunting grounds) and, again,
Romance (1906). For another, he began to concentrate on 'spontaneous
creation' (*Urschöpfung*), a category which, we recall, even the more
conservative Hermann Paul had unhesitatingly endorsed. In addition, he
became aware of the degree to which the shape of material objects (their
sharpness, obtuseness, angularity, roundness) and their impact on our
sensory faculties (through display of softness, harshness of surface, etc.)
could co-determine the names we are apt to attach to them. Little by little,
the study of *realia* behind the world of words began to loom as not one whit
less exciting than the austere formal analysis of labels alone. Etymological
studies from his pen started making their appearance equipped with graphic
illustrations – either drawings or photographs – of characteristically con-
toured tools, containers, dwellings observable in rural life, past or present.
They also, I repeat, grew in length from statements running to a few lines to
standard-sized articles or beyond. This development reached its peak in
Schuchardt's consecutive Vienna Academy memoirs, *Romanische Etymologien*, of the years 1898–9. In preparing the second of these monographs,
which discussed the provenance of French *trouver* 'to find', a celebrated

etymological crux, Schuchardt, who leaned towards *turbāre* as the source of the elusive word (muddying the water being one of the widespread techniques used by fishermen as a preparation for catching, i.e., 'finding', the fish), is rumoured to have temporarily transformed one of the rooms of his home into a small-scale museum of fishing gear. Two years later, he wrote a shorter piece on 'Sickle and Saw, Sickle and Dagger', whose slant is self-explanatory.

Not surprisingly, when Schuchardt encountered Rudolf Meringer (seventeen years his junior), the two dissenters before long joined forces. Meringer, an Indo-Europeanist and Germanist by earlier specialized training, was representative enough of that group of scholars to have been entrusted by a highly respectable publishing house with preparing a turn-of-the-century introductory account of ongoing Indo-European research for the tone-setting Göschen Series, an assignment he conscientiously fulfilled. Yet, his heart was beating for all sorts of innovative and unorthodox approaches. Thus, with Karl Mayer he published, as early as 1895, a 'psycho-linguistic inquiry' into saying the wrong thing and misreading. Thirteen years later, he chose an excellent title for a book apt to circumscribe the range of his maverick curiosity: *Aus dem Leben der Sprache: Versprechen, Kindersprache, Nachahmungstrieb*, i.e., freely translated, '*Speech observed in its dynamics: making a twist of the tongue, children's talk, drive for imitation*'. An independent line of anthropological curiosity prompted him to examine rural material civilization, especially the regional layout of German peasant homes. By 1909, Schuchardt and Meringer had pooled their intellectual resources and launched their own journal, *Wörter und Sachen*, i.e., 'Words and Objects [designated by them]', which was to revolutionize one dimension of etymology, by linking it henceforth to archaeology and ethnography, rather than to historical grammar.

The reverberations of Schuchardt's (and, to a smaller extent, Meringer's) thinking continue to hold our attention. Meanwhile, the preponderance of Central European scholarship, as shown not least in the sheer massiveness and assertiveness of the productions rolling off German printing presses, need not seduce us into overlooking relevant work done elsewhere, on a more modest scale.

France and Belgium plunged into historical linguistics generally, and into etymology and related disciplines in particular, shortly after 1860, i.e., after a delay of over forty years, through the initial efforts of a small group of devoted workers, most of them with strong ties to Germany. As the senior member of this group one may single out Émile Littré (1801–81), not a career university teacher, but a highly respected intellectual, with strong attachments to tone-setting philosophers (e.g. Comte) and physicists (e.g., Ampère). Littré's *Dictionnaire de la langue française*, in four volumes (1863–72), immediately became a classic; it was not meant to be genuinely historical, but, for most entries, had a built-in historical dimension ('la partie historique . . . l'étymologie'). Thus it dramatized the importance of etymology for broadly educated readers. This dimension gained in prominence in the revised edition (1875–89), which included a separate Supplement Volume featuring Marcel Devic's etymological vocabulary of exotica, *Dictionnaire étymologique de tous les mots d'origine orientale*, a model for future ventures tried out in Spain by Eguílaz y Yanguas and in Germany by Lokotsch. Littré's prestige made him a frequent contributor to élitist journals with a strong appeal to professionals and non-professionals alike (*Journal des savants, Revue des deux mondes, Journal des débats*). Some of his articles concerned toponymy and lexicology, and included a trail-blazing essay on the health, as against ailments, of certain words ('Pathologie verbale, ou lésions de certains mots dans le cours de l'usage'), which paved the way for the later approach of dialect geographers. The influence of these shorter writings increased after they were assembled into a sturdy volume (*Études et glanures* . . . , 1880), designed to flank another major work from Littré's pen, namely his *Histoire de la langue française*.

A new generation of academics before long showed appreciation of Littré's pioneering role, Michel Bréal, easily the most influential among their ranks, published, in 1888, an annotated posthumous edition, in book form, of his predecessor's essay, *Comment les mots changent de sens*. Thus etymology, launched as a quest for ultimate word origins, began to change, at the hands of a small coterie of talented Parisian scholars, into a piecing-together of mosaics of word histories.

Auguste Brachet (1844–98), in retrospect, appears as a dynamic reformer of the teaching of grammar at secondary-school level, through his injection of historical perspectives. As a precocious younger man, he was, until c. 1875, also esteemed as a scholar. His easily assimilable *Dictionnaire étymologique de la langue française*, prefaced by the classicist Émile Egger and launched in competition with a similarly superficial piece by the Belgian Auguste Scheler (1862), was even translated into English (1873), as had been previously his *Grammaire historique de la langue française* (c. 1868). While these gropings have become mere 'curios' today, Brachet's slim monograph of doublets, i.e., on words transmitted through two or more socio-educational channels (*Dictionnaire des doublets, ou doubles formes de la langue française*, 1868; *Supplément*, 1871), contained potentialities for progress in etymology which were later exploited by scholars of distinctly higher stature, e.g., Carolina Michaëlis de Vasconcelos in Germany and U. A. Canello in Italy. Michel Bréal immediately applied Brachet's idea to Latin, in a transactions volume (*Mémoires* . . .) of the newly founded Société de Linguistique de Paris.

Gaston Paris, the founder of a major school of Romance Philology in Paris, practised etymology only at intervals; but when he engaged in it, he did so with gusto and consummate skill, demonstrating a mastery of methods and techniques developed in German-speaking countries – witness his skill in dissecting the innovative Romance designations of the 'liver' (in lieu of Latin *iecur*), minted in a culinary context, in a piece written for the Ascoli Testimonial (1901).

As an out-and-out Indo-Europeanist and a devotee of anthroponymy, Michel Bréal, appropriately enough, started his careei with a slim dissertation on Old Persian proper names in Greek disguise (1863). Later, he pooled resources with Anatole Bailly in issuing collegiate dictionaries of Classical Greek and Latin in which formal (genetic, etymological) classification of entries was balanced by a semantic counter-system. Only at the ripe age of sixty-five did he produce a work that deserves to rank as a classic, the first foundation of what one is tempted to call, at present, 'lexical semantics': *Essai de sémantique* (*science des significations*), which was promptly translated into English under the title *Semantics: Studies in the science of meanings* (1900). The book had its roots in Bréal's earlier collaboration with Bailly, but its preparation also tied in with Littré's aforementioned essay, *Comment les mots changent de sens* (1888), in whose posthumous publication Bréal, we recall, had a prominent share.

Of all late nineteenth-century scholars who clustered around the 'grandes écoles' of Paris, Arsène Darmesteter (1846–88), an indefatigable worker, probably more than any fellow-researcher, had a knack for deftly striking a balance between grammar and lexicology. Small wonder that the rules presiding over word-formation, both in descriptive and in historical projection, before long became his favourite hunting-ground. Regarding synchrony, he specialized in contemporary patterns of word coinage (1877). With respect to diachrony, he authored the first major treatise on word-compounding in French (1874) and, that same year, salvaged the manuscript of a closely related monograph by L.-F. Meunier (left unfinished by that short-lived colleague). These and similar involvements took Darmesteter to the threshold of etymology proper. He made the decisive leap in 1887 through a book, *La vie des mots étudiée dans leurs significations*, that was not only recognized almost at once as a masterpiece, but also was to enter, with Littré's slightly earlier essay and with Bréal's somewhat later book venture – each already mentioned – into a sort of triptych of Paris-sponsored studies tending to change etymology into a genuinely historical discipline rather than an exercise in reconstruction. This goal all three could expect to reach by transmuting a collection of conjectures, however sophisticated, into a series of fleshed-out word biographies. In connection with the suddenly fashionable biological metaphors, observe the contrast between A. Schleicher who, fascinated by the vogue of Darwinism, toyed with likening the 'lifespan' of an entire language to that of an organism, and the group of Parisians who merely invoked the vicissitudes or fortunes of individual lexical units.

Independently, Darmesteter, by the time he died, left either completed or in a state of advanced draft his quota of work on a new-style dictionary of French which he had undertaken for a private publisher in collaboration with A. Hatzfeld, the celebrated *Dictionnaire général*, which was to offer a challenge to Littré's bulkier model. The circumstantial sketch of a historical grammar to be prefixed to the dictionary proper had already been finished by 1885, while for the revision of etymologies (earmarked for accompanying the individual entries, with formulaic brevity), Antoine Thomas had to be called in by way of an emergency solution. (Meanwhile, Hatzfeld was, and remained, responsible for sketching in the relevant ramifications of meaning.) The manufacture of a first-rate dictionary with this peculiar distribution of responsibilities among its editors was something of a novelty and subsequently served as a model for certain twentieth-century experiments in etymological dictionaries (e.g., *mutatis mutandis*, those by Bloch and von Wartburg, and by Ernout and Meillet).

Having watched Antoine Thomas (1857–1935) casually cross our path on two occasions, we owe him a formal introduction. Not unlike Gaston Paris, he was by training primarily a medievalist who concentrated early on conventional history as well as on the history of literature, to the extent that they applied to France (and also, on a small scale, to Italy). In addition, his early teaching career at Toulouse University acquainted him thoroughly with Occitan, old and modern. Between the late 1880s and the opening lustrum of the twentieth century he rose to prominence in Paris and, at the same time, experienced a change of heart, becoming immersed in lexico-etymological studies. His speciality became sharply pointed etymological vignettes, each running typically to a printed page or two, which he astutely alternated with somewhat longer inquiries into derivational affixes. These miniatures, originally published in journals, were, we recall, eventually assembled in three volumes. As a rule, the items chosen for identification were selected haphazardly, rather than serving to test a questionable sound correspondence or in the context of some group tied together by semantic bonds. Thus, Thomas practised etymology for etymology's sake, rather than for some ulterior purpose. His strength lay in his enviable command of mediaeval sources, in his palaeographic skill, which enabled him to propose emendations, and in his virtuoso ability to extract maximum information from scores of dialect glossaries, a genre of semi-scholarly literature favoured by well-intentioned and sometimes knowledgeable amateurs. His weaknesses lay in his incapacity to handle languages and dialects other than Gallo-Romance, in his refusal to come to terms with fieldwork-style inquiries and with the projection of their results onto maps, and in his apparent hesitation to attack broader problems or to draw bolder conclusions from the small-scale discoveries he was ceaselessly making as a talented miniaturist. Despite these shortcomings, Thomas' precise methods produced a long string of model etymologies, based on studies of dialect, which placed far heavier reliance on form than on meaning.

Before long, Antoine Thomas' slightly precious *l'art pour l'art* approach to etymology, including its presuppositions, encountered severe criticism. It ran foul of the attitude of devoted dialectologists, who, apart from siding with Schuchardt in matters of theoretical orientation, seemed to prefer solid data-gathering through fieldwork to aloof armchair etymologizing; and it irritated generalists and comparativists of the calibre of Maurice Grammont. Thomas, after 1904, continued publishing valuable articles in the quarterly *Romania*, but these were no longer assembled in handy volumes, with or without revision.

To conclude: Darmesteter's lectures on historical grammar were issued posthumously and even translated into English, but easily the most original ingredient of his lexico-etymological commitment, namely his work on Old Judaeo-French rabbinical glosses, was carried on, with *élan*, by the Baltimore scholar David S. Blondheim, rather than by anyone in his own environment.

Gaston Paris was getting old. Clearly, the generalities established in writings such as *La vie des mots* or *Essai de sémantique* made for stimulating reading, but offered no concrete problems, or riddles, into which younger scholars responsive to etymology could confidently sink their teeth. Thus, around 1900, the first French school of etymology was facing a lull.

A certain latent lay curiosity about word origins (particularly those of the 'colourful' order) has been extant in the British Isles for a long period of time. Suffice it to thumb through the parenthetic etymological remarks with which the early Hispanophile Captain John Stevens interspersed, or spiced, his *New dictionary, Spanish and English, and English and Spanish* (published in 1726, the year of his death). But it took a distressingly long period of time for this sort of titillation to harden into a truly professional performance. The finest pioneering example of mature, unhurried work taking into account whatever had in the meantime been accomplished on the European continent is, indisputably, the first edition (1882) of Walter W. Skeat's *An etymological dictionary of the English language*, a genuine classic. The seriousness of the author's preparation, which transcended by a wide margin his sheer expertise in English (or even in German, note the author's 1876 pamphlet on 'English words, the etymology of which is illustrated by comparison with Icelandic'), shines forth in the many auxiliary sections either preceding the dictionary proper or appended to it. These include such items as: notes about the languages cited (xiii–xx); canons for etymologies (xxi–xxii); books referred to in the dictionary – a bibliography remarkably complete for its time (xxiii–xxviii); lists of prefixes and suffixes (727–8); a list of Aryan (i.e., Proto-Indo-European) roots (729–47); distribution of words, i.e., a grouping of lexical items by their common descent (English proper, Old Low German, Dutch, Scandinavian, etc.), all the way to hybrids and to words of unknown extraction (747–61); examples of sound shifts, i.e., samples of diachronic phonology (761); a list of homonyms (762–71); a list of doublets (772–4) – apart from a more conventional section of errata and addenda. Clearly, this book marked a bold and respectable attempt to integrate etymology with a whole range of language sciences. Moreover, being aware of the randomness of the dispersal of lexical material in an alphabetically arranged reference work, Skeat recast the sum total of his knowledge in a more systematically arranged counter-view, namely his two-volume *Principles of English etymology*, with one half of the venture being reserved for 'the native element' and the other for 'the foreign element', i.e., borrowings. If we add to this inventory of accomplishments a string of toponymic monographs concerned with geographic sections of England, in addition to extended philological inquiries into selected older English literary texts (an activity which, by way of fringe benefit, doubtless gave him a much firmer grasp of the denotations and connotations of countless lexical units), we will begin to recognize the magnitude of Skeat's breakthrough.

Of course, not all the extra features of Skeat's dictionary were equally innovative, or turned out to be equally fruitful. The laying-down of 'canons for etymology' strikes one, in our Age of Theory, as a major step in the right direction. However, as early as 1856 Pedro Felipe Monlau had included a far more extended section titled 'Rudimentos de etimología' in his Spanish-language *Diccionario etimológico*, while the idea of balancing a selective list of cameo-sized word biographies against a still very primitive outline of sound shifts can be traced, once more in Spain, to Ramón Cabrera's posthumous *Diccionario de etimologías* (1837). Skeat's decision to compile a list of 'Aryan' roots turns out, upon closer inspection, to be more an archaism than a bold innovation, reflecting as it does a common mid-nineteenth-century attitude, which failed to distinguish between the needs of, for example, a classicist and those of a student of medieval and modern languages; as a random example, one may cite Giovanni Bolza's quaint *Vocabolario genetico-etimologico della lingua italiana* (1852). Still, Skeat's stamp of approval and the quality of his information and workmanship served to prolong traditions which rapidly perished in neighbouring domains. Thus, the *American heritage dictionary*, in general tailored to late twentieth-century tastes and needs, has nevertheless resumed the (conceivably pointless) tradition of a separate major section titled 'Indo-European Roots' (written by an expert of the rank of Calvert Watkins, pp. 1505–50), in addition to briefer sections on 'Indo-European and the Indo-Europeans' (pp. 1496–1504) and, entering into the preliminary matter, 'The Indo-European Origin of English' (xix–xx), from the pen of the same Harvard scholar.

Skeat's dictionary made its appearance (1st edn, 1882) when the author (1835–1912) stood at the zenith of his life. He lived long enough thereafter to witness and no doubt savour its success (2nd edn, 1884, 4th edn, 1909–10). He had to his credit a number of shorter companion studies, e.g., *A glossary of Tudor and Stuart words, especially from the dramatists* (1914), posthumously published (repr. 1968), in addition to miscellaneous items channelled principally through the *Transactions of the Philological Society* (e.g., 'Notes on English etymology', 'Words of Brazilian/Peruvian/West Indian origin', 'A rough list of English words found in Anglo-French') and eventually assembled in a sturdy volume (1901), all of which adds to his stature, but hardly explains the failure of a British school of etymologists to arise. Henry Sweet (1845–1912), to be sure, was a major figure, but he impressed his contemporaries and posterity chiefly as a leading practitioner of phonetic sciences, even though (especially in the years 1879 to 1885) he had diligently practised Old English etymology. While his experiments along that line ultimately became accessible through absorption into the *Collected papers* (1913), it is not irrelevant to remind oneself that they were originally published in two German periodicals, *Englische Studien* and *Anglia*.

There are many other symptoms of thwarted growth, despite tokens of goodwill displayed by undaunted individuals. As regards etymological desk dictionaries of English composed by Englishmen, the appearance, in 1921, of *An etymological dictionary of Modern English* by Ernest Weekley (1865–1954) marked something of an anticlimax. Weekley's venture gave the impression of being a pruned version of Skeat, divested of its forerunner's antiquarianism, but otherwise failed to offer anything significantly innovative. True, it would be unfair here to omit mention of the fact that Weekley's dictionary lacked the centrality to his entire *œuvre* that Skeat's earlier and weightier experiment had had to his own. After 1921, he remained as active as ever, publishing in rapid succession collections of notes tastefully phrased and easily assimilable, including *Words, ancient and modern* (1926), *More words, ancient and modern* (1927), *Adjectives – and other words* (1930), *Words and names* (1932), *Something about words* (1935). Perhaps it is proper to call him the major popularizer of the discipline in the United Kingdom.

The tale of woe continued with Alan H. Gardiner's *Theory of speech and language* (1932). During World War I, the noted Egyptologist became intensely concerned with the gradually emerging new discipline of 'general linguistics' (initially also known under the name of 'general philology' in Great Britain), and after reading Steinthal, Paul, von der Gabelentz, Wundt, Saussure, Meillet, Kalepky, and Bühler, he embarked on a two-volume venture of his own on the subject. The projected second volume might have been – at least indirectly – relevant to etymology, because it was to 'deal mainly with the word and its kinds, as well as with various extensions of the word', so the author announced in the Foreword to Vol. I (p. 13). Unfortunately, the second volume was never written (or, at least, never appeared), unlike the revised second edition of the first (1951). This is a pity, because Gardiner, as the author of the 'controversial essay' *The theory of proper names* (1940, 1954; see also his *Ancient Egyptian onomastica*, 1947), might have had something worthwhile to contribute. The few British scholars who, before 1950, felt attracted to etymological puzzles usually followed in the wake of foreign models. Just as Henry Sweet, a century or so ago, for a while, we recall, leaned on German patterns, so Harold Orton (Leeds), a word geographer and a spokesman for the *Wörter und Sachen* approach, operated with a basically German–Swiss scheme, while John Orr (Edinburgh), fascinated by clashes of homonyms, sailed comfortably in the wake of Jules Gilliéron's methodology.

The turn of the century seems to be the right cut-off point for terminating this introductory chapter. Many relevant things were then in a state of flux, thus arousing heightened expectations. The continued hegemony of Central Europe in everything that related to historical linguistics – including its etymological dimension – continued unchallenged, with Austria (Graz, Vienna) competing for attention more and more with Germany, and with German Switzerland (especially Zurich) just beginning to strike out in original directions. Paris, if not the whole of France, showed how intelligent management even of limited human resources can yield high dividends in a discipline that is not yet fully established, such as etymology.

The comparative method, of such crucial importance for progress in etymology, had of course been devised long before. But the period around 1900 witnessed, in rapid succession, the rise of various novel, or newly organized, subdisciplines whose growth turned out to be beneficial for the crystallization of a new style of etymological inquiry: (a) (lexical) semantics, as represented by Bréal; (b) biologically flavoured lexicology, spearheaded by Darmesteter; (c) synonymics or onomasiology, especially when concerned with certain tightly ordered real-life domains (kinship terms, chromonyms, numerals, names for the parts of the body); (d) dialect geography, especially to the extent that it was word-oriented rather than remaining sound-oriented; (e) approaches and techniques (including iconography) devised to bring together facts of language and the near-parallel evidence of material civilization (*Wörter und Sachen*).

Conceivably even more significant than the alliances between etymology and these relatively new approaches, enthusiastically pursued in those years, was the discovery being made in the concluding quarter of the last century that the compilation of etymological dictionaries was necessarily the highest goal, or, worse, exhausted the possibilities, of imaginative etymological research. Hugo Schuchardt's experimental mood and insouciant attitude toward stale academic traditions – coming, true enough, in the wake of Pott's distinctly earlier pioneering work – was exactly what was needed (in addition, of course, to the newly gained availability of numerous learned journals) to develop, among a younger set of linguists, a taste for cultivating individual word histories as a separate and highly rewarding genre. The transition was marked by the appearance of articles concerned with whole clusters of pending etymological issues, sometimes wholly unrelated, each running perhaps to a half-page on the average. Romanists will remember such composite studies, traceable to the 1880s and 1890s, from the pens of G. Baist and C. Michaëlis de Vasconcelos. These became, before long, the prototypes for incomparably more extended and sophisticated monographs, each devoted preferably to the vicissitudes of a single word which had proved refractory to previous genetic analysis. Preparing such a monograph, by the same token, presupposed more and more an insightful combination of art and science (in the humanistic vein).

While we have, repeatedly and on good grounds, stressed the potential complementarity of etymology and historical grammar, no account of the gropings of nineteenth-century etymologists would be complete without, at least, some passing mention of three other recurrent instances of disciplinary solidarity. There was a prolonged close alliance between etymology, on the one hand, and, on the other, (a) folklore, (b) mythology, and (c) the systematic study of proper names (a scholarly endeavour for which there seems to exist no cumulative technical label): anthroponymy, toponymy, hydronymy, etc. Apart from being separately related to different phases and facets of etymological inquiry, these three humanistic endeavours also display strong mutual affinities among themselves. In the past century, it was by no means uncommon for representative practitioners of etymology (or of historical linguistics as a whole, including grammar) to cultivate with identical and comparably generous apportionment of time and resources any imaginable combination of these disciplines, which were equally prestigious at that juncture; while shortly after 1900, and especially in the concluding half of the present century, the likelihood of such ranges of active involvement has gradually receded.

One can almost randomly cite names, titles of books, monographs, or articles, and dates to hammer home this interlocking pattern. Among pioneers of historico-comparative linguistics whose paths we have already crossed, Fick was more concerned with names than with myths or legends. As an accomplished Hellenist, he became immersed early on in anthroponymy (1874) and, towards the end of his lifetime, in toponymy (1905, 1909), operating with the noteworthy concept of 'system of names' in the former monograph, while stressing the importance of place names for substratum research in the latter. Also, he believed he had discovered the category of 'namelike formations' in Ancient Greek (1876). Mahn supplemented his experimentally oriented *Etymologische Untersuchungen* . . . (1854–64) in the Romance domain with the more narrowly based *Etymologische Untersuchungen über geographische Namen*, of almost identical vintage (1856–64). The monumental edifice of Pott's far-flung, many-tiered *œuvre* contains at least three mythologically slanted items which quickly succeeded one another (one harking back to 1859, two to 1863), in addition to a slightly earlier 'großer Wurf' on all sorts of proper names, with heavy emphasis placed on surnames (1853). Also, in his old age he tossed off one shorter piece on Basque family names (1875). Examples can be multiplied almost indefinitely. In contemporary Paris, a many-sided prolific scholar of the calibre of Michel Bréal (who was also an able spokesman for the cause of dynamic scholarship) not only started his career, we recall, with an inquiry into Old Persian names in Greek garb but also that same year (1863), submitted as a companion thesis a monograph geared to 'comparative mythology', on Hercules and Cacus. Bréal's later publications include a successful miscellany, characteristically titled *Mélanges de mythologie et de linguistique* (1877; 2nd edn, 1882) and also, in collaboration with Anatole Bailly, an innovative *Dictionnaire étymologique latin* (1885; 10th edn, 1992), with the programmatic subtitle, 'Les mots latins groupés d'après le sens et l'étymologie'.

It is easy to guess what initially tied together these, in certain respects disparate, lines of investigation. Close familiarity with folklore was helpful for diachronists grappling with languages till then little known and hardly boasting a major corpus of literature, such as Lithuanian. Thus Schleicher (in whose programme of research etymology, we remember, was represented, at best, peripherally) fell back on Lithuanian proverbs, riddles, songs, and even fairytales (thus walking in the footsteps of Jakob Grimm) in an effort to supplement the meagre information supplied by normal literary sources (1857). As a Germanist, he did not spurn the resources of Thuringian folk culture either (1958). Mythology, on the other hand, in addition to providing a treasure-trove of names awaiting etymological analyses, was replete with fabulous accounts of the descent of tribes and of their diversified tongues, with the ever-present possibility that the fables might contain grains of historical truth and thus stimulate long-delayed legitimate research.

By way of anticipation, let me state that, contrary to what we have so far been observing by watching the strategy of the trail-blazers, it gradually became more and more exceptional for a truly distinguished twentieth-century linguist to extend his or her active curiosity to folklore and mythology, two fields which simply drifted away from the area cultivated by linguists, without losing in the process any of their original academic respectability. Conversely, the study of proper names, which can of course be conducted on a very high level of scholarly seriousness, in several influential quarters (including the New World) has lost much of its erstwhile professional standing, tending to function, at best, as an auxiliary discipline, whose resources diachronically minded linguists and students of the history of settlement can, to be sure, advantageously tap at intervals, but which lacks a methodological and theoretical foundation of its own, despite Alan Gardiner's attempt to prove the contrary. Its major appeal at present is to well-intentioned, educated laymen, and its societies tend to thrive on a sub-academic level. The contrast with the times of Förstemann, Skeat, and especially Weekley could scarcely have been stronger. Offerings from the last-mentioned Anglicist's pen such as *The romance of names* (1914) and *Surnames* (1916), along with certain writings by Albert Dauzat on the other side of the Channel, for better or worse represent a sort of rearguard action.

Guide to readings

A classic in the early history of linguistics, which inevitably pays some attention to etymological speculation, is Heymann Steinthal (1823–99), *Geschichte der Sprachwissenschaft bei den Griechen und Römern, mit besonderer Rücksicht auf die Logik* (Berlin: Dümmler, 1863; rev. 2nd edn, 2 vols., 1890–1; photostatic reproduction, 1961).

There is no dearth of briefer histories of linguistics at present. As a rule, they are fairly slim one-volume ventures. In the English-speaking countries R. H. Robins ranks as the foremost expert in that line of curiosity. For the older periods, his booklet *Ancient and medieval grammatical theory* . . . (London, 1951) is relevant, despite its main emphasis on concerns other than etymological. For a bird's-eye view of other introductory manuals (including those by Milka Ivić, Giulio C. Lepschy, Maurice Leroy – with a side-glance at Glanville Price's translation into English of his relevant book – and Bertil Malmberg, in addition to Thomas A. Sebeok's parallel *Portraits of linguists: a bibliographic source book*), see Yakov Malkiel and Margaret Langdon's review article, 'History and histories of linguistics', in *Romance Philology*, 22:4 (May 1969), 530–74.

Some information on etymological analysis as part of an ensemble of operations is shed by general introductions to historical (diachronic) linguistics. This sort of information is apt to be more parsimonious in items of fairly recent vintage than in some of the 'classics'. For a bird's-eye view of newly launched textbooks and introductory volumes, see the review article by Carol F. Justus, 'The textbook of historical linguistics: summary of the past or guide to the future?', in *Romance Philology*, 33:2 (Nov. 1979), 299–309, covering experiments conducted by James M. Anderson, Raimo Anttila, Anthony Arlotto, Theodora Bynon, D. L. Goyvaerts, and W. P. Lehmann. Edgar H. Sturtevant's *Linguistic change: an introduction to the historical study of language* stands apart, inasmuch as, despite the new Introduction contributed by Eric P. Hamp – an eager etymologist in his own right – to the edition undertaken by Chicago University Press ('Phoenix edn', 1961; 5th printing, 1973), the book goes back to a distant past (1917) and thus reflects the author's thinking before he reached the zenith of his long life (1875–1952). It thus antecedes by a sizeable margin his *Introduction to linguistic science* (New Haven: Yale University Press, 1947). Among the classics alluded to above, the one easily most generous with information about techniques for identifying word origins was Hermann Paul's *Prinzipien der Sprachgeschichte* (Halle: Niemeyer, 1880; rev. 5th edn, 1920; 2nd edn translated into English, 1891).

On the negative side of the picture, the failure of several highly respected linguists to arrange for separate chapters on etymological methods in their influential summations has contributed to the discipline's temporary loss of appeal, especially to the *avant-garde*. This has been especially true, in Europe, of Ferdinand de Saussure's posthumous (1916) *Cours de linguistique générale*, extracted from lecture notes taken at the start of the century, and of Joseph Vendryes' *Le langage: introduction linguistique à l'histoire* (Paris, La Renaissance du livre, 1921, but finished by 1914; available in English in Paul Radin's translation, 1925). It is also true, in North America, of the well-known syntheses by Edward Sapir (1921), by Leonard Bloomfield (*An introduction to the study of language*, New York: Holt, 1914; *Language*, New York; Holt, 1933, and, as a result, *Language history*, extracted by Harry Hoijer from the latter book, 1965); and by Charles F. Hockett (*A course in modern linguistics*, New York, Macmillan, 1958). One minor exception was the brief Chapter 10 ('Etymology and linguistic method: the historical aspect of words') in Louis H. Gray's reputedly conservative *Foundations of language* (New York: Macmillan, 1939). Given the chilly reception of that book by younger critics and readers, this authorial stamp of approval actually sealed the flat rejection of etymology by, and the blunting of etymological curiosity in, an entire generation of potential enthusiasts.

The countertrend, so far only infrequently observable, began with Émile Benveniste (1902–76), who, even though exposed to the most tempting formulations of all manner of 'modernisms', nevertheless, in his definitive book (*Le vocabulaire des institutions indo-européennes: économie, parenté, société; pouvoir, droit, religion*, ed. Jean Lallot, Paris: Les Éditions de Minuit, 1969; translated into several languages, including English by Elizabeth Palmer, London: Faber & Faber, 1973), managed to reserve for etymology an important niche as part of lexicology – a point I have tried to make in my necrological essay 'Lexis and grammar', in *Romance Philology*, 34:2 (Nov. 1980), 160–94.

One notes a regrettable scarcity of book-length initiations into the theory, methodology, and techniques of etymology; also, the arrival on the scene of this peculiar genre of scholarly-didactic literature was much delayed. As regards the present century, one of the earliest among the guides to the subject was Vittore Pisani's *L'etimologia: storia, questioni, metodo* (Milan: Renon, 1947; rev. 2nd edn, Brescia: Paideia, 1967) – a relatively slim book when placed alongside certain monumental ventures by the same comparatist. Lecture courses dedicated specifically to etymology (as against incidental allusions to etymological issues) have likewise been few and far between – Vittorio Bertoldi used to offer a few during the years of his professorship at Naples, and occasionally the relevant lecture notes ('dispense') would ripen into a quotable book. It would thus appear that Italy offered the best environment for introductory texts of this kind; the tradition has been continued of late (witness the venture by a much younger scholar, Alberto Zamboni). Interestingly, doctoral dissertations on narrowly circumscribed etymological subjects have also been shunned in many quarters, possibly on account of the risks involved for the candidate. As a result, the places where methodological problems set in an etymological key have been typically thrashed out have included: prefaces and introductory chapters to etymological dictionaries; leisurely critical reviews of fascicles of etymological dictionaries and rebuttals occasionally provoked by sharply worded criticism; lists of addenda to strings of dictionary entries; and also initiations into related approaches, for example, into lexically coloured dialect geography, starting with the volume of Jules Gilliéron's essays written in collaboration with M. Roques (1912) and encompassing the deservedly well-known introductory volumes of Ernst Gamillscheg (1928) and Karl Jaberg (1936).

Several reasons can be offered for this remarkable restraint on the book market: the notorious inherent subjectivity of the discipline, the presupposition of considerable maturity on the part of the would-be practitioner, and so on. Because Romance material, at the stage of mere apprenticeship, may only confuse the budding Germanist, and vice versa, stray attempts have, of late, been made to prepare introductory manuals with more narrowly selected documentation. Examples of this latest, not unwholesome, trend would be: Max Pfister, *Einführung in die romanische Etymologie* (Darmstadt: Wissenschaftliche Buchgesellschaft, 1980) and Elmar Seebold, *Etymologie: eine Einführung am Beispiel der deutschen Sprache* (Munich: Beck, 1981).

2

The first half of the twentieth century

So far, we have managed to describe the shifting positions of etymology, at first outside the edifice of historical grammar and later on in close connection with it, in splendid isolation from political events and social changes as it were, with practically no reference to such real-life situations as the Napoleonic Era, the Crimean War, or America's Civil War, to cite three examples at random. In this undertaking we have received support from the oft-cited fact that, between 1871 and 1904, Europe went through a protracted period of relative peace – of respite from involvements in serious wars and from all sorts of revolutionary concussions.

But as one approaches the next half-century, things begin to undergo a radical change, not necessarily for the better. The period 1900–1950, at present visible in clear retrospect, was marked by two world wars which were not only exceptionally devastating, but were also characterized by all sorts of ideological implications and by energetic reshuffling of centres of intellectual prestige. Allusions to the impact of changes of such magnitude can no longer be swept under the carpet. The fortunes of historical linguistics and of etymology alike were very strongly and, I repeat, by no means always favourably affected by the resulting redistribution of intellectual ammunition.

It should suffice, in this context, to mention two influential circumstances. First, by 1900, the reputation of German scholarship, both pure and applied, stood at its zenith the world over. German-born or German-educated scholars, including those with heavy commitments to a brand of 'linguistic science' deeply rooted in Central European traditions of historicism, were in high demand on both sides of the Atlantic. One need only refer to Max Müller's regime at Oxford, to Franz Boas' at Columbia, to Maurice Bloomfield's at Johns Hopkins, and also to Rudolf Lenz's and

Friedrich Hanssen's at Santiago de Chile. The peculiar pattern of 'Geisteswissenschaften', into which linguistics was supposed to enter smoothly, was adopted almost everywhere, along with an idiosyncratic division of academies of sciences into two branches and of universities into, typically, four 'faculties', except that France, standing somewhat aloof, tried desperately to assign to advanced linguistics, a relative latecomer to Paris, the appearance of a social science rather than that of a purely humanistic discipline.

With the weakening of German academic influence as a direct consequence of World War I and its aftermath, linguistics either tended to decline altogether in the given country or, to regain its severely weakened momentum, had to fall back on those approaches to analysis and those styles of research, starting with data-gathering, that showed a bare minimum of dependence on no longer fashionable German models. As a result, etymology, reputedly a quintessentially German subdiscipline, rapidly receded into the background of supply and demand. Thus, in the United States, the vigorous resurgence of linguistic scholarship after the early 1920s is ordinarily associated with three almost charismatic names, those of Edgar H. Sturtevant, Edward Sapir, and Leonard Bloomfield. Yet one practically never hears even the staunchest admirers and supporters of these pioneers assert that their idols were deft etymologists – a detail, they usually hasten to add, of minor relevance, given the currently marginal status of etymology in the alliance of linguistic disciplines.

The effects of World War II, its preludes and its unsavoury accompaniments, were different, yet even more disastrous for the well-being of etymology. The misleading indoctrination associated with atrocities committed in connection with forced resettlement, segregation, extermination, and the like began to throw singularly unattractive light on such dimensions of research – previously held to be innocuous – as the study of toponyms and anthroponyms, of certain layers of loan words, and so on. Before long, such intellectual pursuits became distasteful to a whole generation of potential Central European *Wortforscher*, not to mention their foreign counterparts. An entire school of West German Romanists, based in Bonn, under the leadership of Harri Meier, has after 1960 specialized in attempting – with varying success, it is true – to reassign characteristic ingredients of Romance lexis to non-Germanic, preferably Latin, stocks. Such an atmosphere, permeated by politically flavoured pro and contra sentiments, seems unhealthy for the growth of impartial etymological research.

Economic considerations also gradually became a matter of unprecedented concern. In the nineteenth century, a typical one-volume dictionary slanted in the direction of word origins could easily be sponsored by a private publishing house catering for academics. Conversely, monumental collections of words viewed in their phrasal contexts (thesauri, concordances) – aiming at exhaustiveness by definition – were prepared by teams of trained investigators and launched by generously endowed academies, the prime examples being Jakob and Wilhelm Grimm's *Deutsches Wörterbuch* and the Munich Academy's *Thesaurus Linguae Latinae*. Such ventures were compatible with, at most, parenthetic etymological remarks. After 1920, however, experiments began to be made with producing mergers between, on the one hand, an etymologicum and, on the other, some blend of a time-honoured historical dictionary and a new-style dialectological treasure trove. These stirrings led to the creation of Walther von Wartburg's sophisticated but overextended and, consequently, unwieldy *Französisches etymologisches Wörterbuch*, which the Swiss scholar, despite much help received from co-workers, left unfinished after half a century of unremitting toil. As he has since found imitators, including Max Pfister, there arises the problem of the optimum relation of a thesaurus and an etymological guide; of the wisdom of engaging in an etymological balance-sheet outlasting a half-century of concentrated labour and involving numerous decision-makers; of drawing financial support under intellectually defensible conditions; and of recognizing the best possible dividing-line between a reference work and a series of individual monographs, each geared in its structure and slant to the particular problem at hand.

The final non-scholarly issue enmeshed with our central problem is the well-established fact that, in several influential and economically powerful societies, the public at large, in a simplistic way, is titillated by colourful, exotic, or amusing anecdotal word histories and by tantalizing clues to certain haunting proper names, a state of affairs apt to create a less than healthy demand for appropriately spiced etymological dictionaries. In extreme cases, such pressure may produce hazardous imbalances by challenging budgetarily hard-pressed publishers to issue etymological dictionaries unworthy of the reputation of their firms. Few laymen would dream of buying copies of historical grammars or phonological treatises, with or without embellishments. As often happens, the wrong sort of success threatens to spoil the best-meant undertaking.

There has tended to emerge one more link of etymology's shifting fortunes to real-life conditions and caprices. Because, in the joint estimate of experts and outsiders alike, scholarly inquiry into word origins enters into the ensemble of lexicographic and lexicological concerns, and because cultivation of these word-centred disciplines, which place a premium on slow, patient long-range data-gathering, is all too frequently entrusted to mature, even ageing scholars, it began to be widely assumed, after a certain cut-off point, that the responsibility for etymological decisions should and can be safely entrusted to the older generation. This view, understandable even to those who happen not to share it, before long led to the untenable belief that there cannot, plausibly, come into existence anything worthy of being called etymological *avant-garde*, rebellion, or revolution capable of attracting young and restless minds, since no intellectual upheaval can be staged by an ill-assorted group of senescent men and women. One important lesson that a close look at the segment of time here selected for inspection, namely 1900–1950, teaches the unbiased observer is that passionate commitments to etymology, cultivated almost for its own sake, can demonstrably develop under favourable sets of circumstances. A Jakob Jud, if I may here evoke the memory of that great Zurich teacher (who, I dare say characteristically, died in 1950, at the age of seventy) was nothing if not a wholeheartedly dedicated etymologist, from the earliest awakening of his curiosity about language and languages.

Let us return to the concluding decades of the nineteenth century, which can be interpreted as having formed a prelude to the watershed date of 1900. The etymological article and, *a fortiori*, the etymological monograph, as we know them, were not yet in existence, even at the most advanced centres of learning. The book-length etymological dictionary – traceable, we recall, to the pre-1800 years – continued to prosper, and was generally held in high esteem. Journals, bulletins, and annual transaction volumes contained either isolated etymological notes (in addition to whole clusters or loose scatterings of such notes, geared sometimes to some ulterior purpose), or, at best, full-sized articles dealing with features of recognized disciplines (including historical grammar) in which dubious points of etymology were incidentally touched upon or even thrashed out. But, outside its faint visibility in such subordinate roles, etymology cultivated, with zest, chiefly for its own sake was seldom, if ever, seen in action.

Illustrations can be cited by the hundreds. Let us examine from this standpoint, for the sake of concrete documentation, the randomly chosen volume for the years 1880–1 of a British venture, the *Transactions of the Philological Society*, with less heavy emphasis on actual accomplishments, as they emerge in critical retrospect, than on the various competing bends of a nascent intellectual curiosity.

With this goal in mind, we can set off, as conducive almost directly to fresh etymological insights, J. P. Postgate's pithy note '*Dare* "to give", and **-dere* "to put"' (pp. 99–105). Since Russell Martineau, when at work on his lengthy piece, 'On the Romontsch or Rhaetian language in the Grisons and Tirol' (pp. 402–60), included in his survey sections on 'Non-Latin and obscure words' as well as on 'Peculiarities of vocabulary', this piece, which was doomed to being consistently overlooked on the Continent, may contain a handful of etymologically relevant remarks. Beyond this point, however, the chances of the material being genuinely useful to dedicated etymologists begin to decline. Viewed as a mass of potentially helpful raw data, and in deference to the writer's general prominence, Walter W. Skeat's 'Rough lists of English words found in 13th–14th centuries Anglo-French' (pp. *91–*168) invites rapid scanning. There is an off-chance that Walter R. Browne's twin papers on the distribution of place-names in (a) England and (b) the Scottish Lowlands contain tiny bits of etymological enlightenment. Any sustained concern with diachronic phonology, such as is embodied in Charles Rieu's 'Remarks on some phonetic laws in Persian' (pp. 1–22), is apt to offer fringe benefits for research in pure etymology, whether the author did or did not intend to reach that secondary goal. But the prime performer in that context, namely Henry Sweet, busied himself with the issue of 'Sound Notation' (pp. 177–235). The Society's 1880–1 President, J. A. H. Murray, on two occasions entertained the membership mainly with reports on spelling reform and on the progress made by the Society-sponsored monumental dictionary, barely allowing Henry Sweet to squeeze in a few fleeting remarks on the 'Investigation of the Aryan *Ursprache*: the Indo-Germanic vowel system' (pp. 155–62). Prince Louis-Lucien Bonaparte's experiments with what we are tempted to call contrastive synchronic phonology (Portuguese vs. an alliance of Spanish, Italian, French, and English, and the ensemble of Slavic tongues vs. Scando-Germanic) eclipse his atypical self-immersion in 'Neuter Neo-Latin substantives' (pp. 45*–64*). The other studies, judging from a hasty inspection of the topics they cover, are poles apart from any exercise of, or reasonably close association with, etymological curiosity.

On the European continent, the drift, or calculated movement, towards the gradual emancipation of individual etymological inquiries gathered greater and quicker momentum. There were several convergent avenues of approach to the goal of individuating more and more the separate word biographies (a term, it is true, not yet appealed to a century ago). The more deliberately selective the etymologist was from the start, the better were the chances he stood of achieving a high degree of circumstantiality. Increased concentration on the ingredient of peculiarity (and even of uniqueness) could be aimed at, if not necessarily reached, if the etymologist was prepared to confine his verdicts to a single ethnoglottal strain of the lexicon under study (e.g., to words of Germanic extraction in a given Romance language); or to limit them to a single form-class, be it nouns or verbs or prepositions; or else to circumscribe his objective in social terms (e.g., vocabulary known to have been favoured by peasantry or by college students, and the like). With fewer items designedly under study, each one could be focused upon in a more leisurely fashion and with far closer attention either to formal variation and semantic nuances, to specific conditions of spatio-temporal extension, or else to the inexhaustible supply of real-life correlates. Moreover, the words selected for leisurely inspection could very well have shared, as a sort of common denominator, the fact that they occurred, predominantly or even exclusively, in the same literary text (ideally, one of known authorship, or at least datable and localizable when viewed through the prism of its manuscripts), or that their use invited association with a particular literary genre.

Adducing a few examples should suffice, and the dates cited are not devoid of importance in their own right. For a while there threatened to develop a real rash of modern-language glossaries reserved for words of oriental (principally Arabic) extraction. Nothing short of a classic in that field was W. H. Engelmann's pioneering venture (1861) devoted to Spanish and Portuguese, later expanded in collaboration with R. P. A. Dozy (1869), who had independently studied Arabic, Hebrew, Aramaic, Persian, and Turkish words in his native Dutch (1867). But L. de Eguílaz y Yanguas' counterpart (1886), not restricted to Arabisms, and L. Marcel Devic's application of the pattern to French (1876), through ingenious collaboration with Émile Littré, are also worthy of mention. (Experiments conducted in the reverse direction, i.e., through confinement of the survey to the majority's source, are likewise on record, especially with regard to Romanian – witness Sextil Puşcariu's (1905) and J. Aureliu Candrea-Hecht/O. Densuşianu's (1907) ventures, apparently undertaken after the last-mentioned scholar's preliminary testing (1902) – but belong to a slightly later period and failed to produce the effect here hinted at. They clash with Alexandru de Cihac's spade-work (1870–9), which aimed at doing justice to Romanian lexis as a whole.) So much for ethnoglottal strains. Confinement to grammatically defined and controlled minorities of words is best illustrated with Rufino José Cuervo's idiosyncratic, if forceful and brilliant, *Diccionario de construcción y régimen de la lengua castellana* (1886–93, with reverberations as late as the mid-twentieth century), a mere torso of a work rich – counter to expectation – in etymology yield, but programmatically limited to lexical entries abounding in syntactic implications, i.e., well-nigh exclusively to verbs and prepositions. In Germanic studies, Friedrich

Kluge's monograph on German university-student slang (1895), wedged in between the fifth (1894) and the sixth (1899) revised editions of his influential etymological dictionary, exemplifies the planned isolation of a sample along the socio-educational scale, while a later work from his pen (1911), dealing with the lexis of German sailors over a protracted period of time, concerned itself with a neatly detachable social dialect. An inventory of German names of diseases (1899) by Max Höfler, a seasoned expert in folk medicine, offers a different sort of specialization, equally welcome to etymologists, namely, familiarity not with a privileged group of speakers, but with a sharply delimited range of topics (cf. Dozy's 1845 monograph on the Arabic names of garments). The late nineteenth-century flowering of philology, which was moored to the critical interpretation of challenging ancient texts, brought with it the preparation of etymological glossaries as supplements to, or companion volumes of, elaborate editions, with the aim of stimulating fellow scholars and goading students.

The range of possibilities was immense: the compiler of such a vocabulary could afford simply to list the recommended etymon, perhaps in parentheses, alongside the page- and line-references for the given lexical unit, as did Wendelin Foerster, leaning on Hermann Breuer for help, in the context of his once seminal edition of Chrétien de Troyes' romances; or he could expand certain favourite entries almost indefinitely, at the risk of converting them into miniature monographs, as was Ramón Menéndez Pidal's decided preference in the case of his edition of the venerable *Cid* epic (1908–11; but the plans were laid out as early as 1898). Not infrequently, amid such exegetic fervour, some investigator deemed it appropriate to publish, in the guise of inescapably uneven journal articles, mixed miscellanies of textual observations, half-grammatical, half-etymological (e.g., Jules Cornu in 1884), unaware of the damage to the causes they espoused that might accrue from such a policy a century later. Another oddity imitated in America somewhat later (Jeremiah D. M. Ford, 1911), was the spicing of glossaries appended to anthologies with etymological *bric-à-brac*. Such eccentricities have meanwhile receded – observe Lucien Foulet's praiseworthy restraint in his model glossary of 1955 and the tendency, even among hard-boiled Beowulfians (Friedrich F. Klaeber, C. L. Wrenn), to relegate discreetly camouflaged etymological hints to their notes rather than their glossaries. Nevertheless, the highwater mark of commitment to often otiose etymological information, coinciding with the protracted absence of well-rounded, engagingly worded etymological articles is certainly worth noting. The mere sight of a Boston-sponsored book title (1898) such as *English etymology: a select glossary serving as an introduction to the history of the English language*, by Friedrich Kluge and Fredrick Lutz, will serve to prepare us for the later recoil.

Any approach or pretext that tended to single out certain words for separate consideration in their historical dimension – for an analysis, that is, more leisurely than the quota of attention accorded to others – directly or indirectly paved the road for future etymological notes or sketches. Even though the sporadic study of doublets was already practised in the late seventeenth century, Auguste Brachet's more 'scientifically' grounded *Dictionnaire des doublets* (1868) and a succinct supplement to it, issued that same year, gave rise to a real vogue, not to say fad, which not very much later led to the publication of monographs (concerned, at first, with related languages) distinctly more sophisticated than their model, by Carolina Michaëlis de Vasconcelos (1876) and Ugo A. Canello (1878), spilling over eventually into adjoining domains, including German Philology ('Doppelwörter', 'Zwillingswörter'). The situation, surveyed by myself in 1973 and 1977, need not be reexamined here in tedious detail. The implicit need to etymologize with appropriate care, at least, the vernacular partner of each pair or team of doublets greatly stimulated etymological curiosity and thus spawned not a few notes on the subject. The accuracy of this projection of cause and effect is shown by the splendid record of Carolina Michaëlis de Vasconcelos who, precisely after the cut-off date of 1876, became a first-rate practitioner of etymology, writing series of almost invariably persuasive notes. However – again wisely – she stopped short of compiling any premature etymological dictionary of Spanish and/or Portuguese.

For three entirely different reasons, the etymological note (often running to less than a half-page in its printed version), was favoured, as a size-defined genre of linguistic research, over an etymological article, not to mention a full-grown monograph, at the threshold of the present century. For one thing, the extant etymological literature which had to be taken into account was still anything but extensive. The proponent of some new conjecture would, at most, mention two or three earlier guesses or opinions – let us say, one culled from a pre-1800 dictionary abounding in pronouncements on word-origins, one from a pioneering historical grammar, and one more from a nineteenth-century book-length etymological venture. To round out the expected modicum of documentation, a few bits of older textual documentation could be adduced: a passage or two extracted from a chronicle, an epic, or a ballad. After a brief hint at the inconclusiveness or, worse, vulnerability of the previous commitment(s), the new idea would be ventilated as crisply and, at the same time, as engagingly as possible. There were few, if any, previous notes and practically no book reviews to be checked before the completion of the dossier.

The second reason, being less anecdotal, can be credited with a more noteworthy set of implications. Since the recurrence (or regularity) of sound changes began to be taken for granted in most responsible quarters, leaving unconverted only a gradually thinning fringe of amateurs, and since the chief advantage of proposing some new etymological explanation was the strengthening it bade fair to provide for the weakly supported among such 'laws' (as sound correspondences were called in those days), the demonstration of the accuracy of the proposal was, in most instances, simple. Only the slightly erratic trajectories of loan words or word histories disturbed by analogical interferences invited somewhat more detailed discussions. Again, a tightly worded note was all that was needed.

There was one more justification for relative parsimoniousness of wording, namely the size and character of the readership aimed at. Any prospective reader, whether stationed at Oxford, in Petersburg, or in Boston, could be safely expected to boast almost the same level of preliminary wide-ranging education, to be familiar, for example, with the same three or four world languages, in addition to the classics. Thus it was deemed advisable to skip the glossing of any Latin or Greek lexical unit adduced. In addition, while readily allowing for certain glorious exceptions, practically all participants in the glotto-historical game reckoned, more or less explicitly, with the fact of academic life that any, let us say, Old English word-studies would be examined carefully only by professional Anglicists, while enigmas of Old Russian lexis might, at best, attract Slavicists, and so on. The crossing of the dividing lines between the gradually congealing specialities was made more and more difficult by increasingly desultory and cryptic references to obscure texts, manuscripts, writers, copyists, editors, and investigators, most details being withheld on the assumption that the potential reader was well prepared for his task on the side of 'philology'. The likelihood of a Romanist wanting to read, for example, some Scandinavian inquiry, or vice versa, for the sake of a typological analogy, simply did not occur to those generations of workers, given the protracted absence of any organized body able to represent the legitimate interests of general linguistics, which are so readily understood and appreciated at present.

Through the coincidence of these three circumstances, the many pungent notes produced during those years were indeed short, but, less gratifyingly, make disproportionately difficult reading for any but the narrowest and best-initiated specialists.

Yet, in many quarters the urge to write clusters or constellations of notes on disconnected issues in word origins seems, for a while, to have been uncontrollable. A few examples can be cited from the Romance field. As a rank beginner, Wilhelm Meyer-Lübke, in 1886, launched a twelve-pronged congeries of such hypotheses, under the title 'Romanische Etymologien', squeezing the whole into less than five printed pages of an influential journal. The following year, under the still vaguer title 'Etymologisches', he again tried to do justice to twelve problems (concerning French, Old and Modern, in addition to Italian, Spanish, Franco-Provençal, etc.), spreading out the discussion over less than eight printed pages.

At this juncture one is tempted to ask: what was the authors' aim in releasing such ill-assorted collections of pithy etymological comments? Or, to fall back on a more legitimate phrasing: how did they, at later stations in life, manage, if at all, to make good use of such piles of motley material?

The answer is that, in not a few instances, there simply was no visible intention on the writer's part, of transcending the stage of highly competent and scrupulously documented notes. This applies, for example, to Paul Barbier's concluding effort, 'Nouvelles études de lexicologie française' (1947–55), as well as to the aggregate of his earlier attempts, which were published in Leeds. (True, the material painstakingly collected was eventually used, with the authorization of Barbier's heirs, for certain fascicles of Walther von Wartburg's thesaurus.) Some scholars of the first magnitude were in the habit of writing scattered etymological notes, presumably to acquaint themselves at first hand with a method or a technique; they then allowed the material assembled to lie fallow for decades. Thus, one cannot persuasively argue that a young Antoine Meillet's ten-page venture 'Notes d'étymologie grecque' (1896) led directly to his *Aperçu d'une histoire de la langue grecque* (1913), still less that any bridge connects his discernibly more advanced *Études sur l'étymologie et le vocabulaire du vieux slave* (1902–5) with two masterpieces of his mature age, each dealing with a cognate language, namely the *Esquisse d'une histoire de la langue latine* (1928) and the *Dictionnaire étymologique de la langue latine* (1932), which he compiled in fruitful collaboration with Alfred Ernout. Conversely, where a lapse of just a few years separates a loose constellation of etymological vignettes from a full-sized etymological dictionary, one can justifiably speak of the notes being a harbinger of the future book. This condition holds, for example, for Ernst Gamillscheg's gropings (*A–F*), in the very early 1920s, *vis-à-vis* his subsequent etymological dictionary of French (1926–8) and, to an even higher degree, for Juan Corominas' experiments conducted throughout the 1940s (1941–2, 1942–4, 1947–8) in relation to the original version of his ambitious Spanish etymologicum (1954–7).

The prototypes, however, go back to the late nineteenth and the early twentieth century. The classic example was furnished by Antoine Thomas. Obviously, by the time that fine scholar (whose name has already figured in the preceding section) was publishing his pioneering contributions (many of them amounting to conglomerations of etymological notes) in the late nineteenth-century volumes of the prestigious Parisian journal *Romania*, neither he himself nor anyone else could have foreseen the subsequent appearance of several volumes into which many of them were ultimately absorbed: *Essais de philologie française* (1897); *Nouveaux essais* . . . (1904); *Mélanges d'étymologie française* (1902). Nor could one have foreseen the reappearance of the *Mélanges* in a generously expanded form (1927), still less the devolution of all etymological responsibility upon himself for the *Dictionnaire général*, after Arsène Darmesteter's unexpected death. Nor do we know for certain what adverse circumstances prevented the later series of such journal notes (e.g., 1909, 1911, 1913), of equal or even superior excellence, from being collected into easily manageable volumes. It is a safe guess that researchers who, at the start of their careers, a century or so ago, invested a good deal of their time and energy in such explorations, were simply eager to build up a sort of intellectual bank account against unforeseeable eventualities. Gottfried Baist, for one, who for years specialized in this genre (as David A. Pharies' helpful bibliography recently demonstrated), eventually skimmed from that 'account' the hoped-for interest when he was invited to prepare for Vol. I of Gustav Gröber's encyclopaedia (1888, 1904–6) two highly concentrated miniature sketches of Spanish historical grammar. Ramón Menéndez Pidal's first constellation of etymological conjectures (1900) could have served him as a stepping-stone to two bold projects that, in all likelihood, were already in his mind: an authoritative book-length manual of Spanish historical grammar and a wide-ranging glossary planned as a companion piece to his palaeographic and critical editions of the *Cid* epic. Carolina Michaëlis de Vasconcelos candidly labelled some of her meatiest assemblies of etymological notes (1908, 1910–1) as tentative contributions to a future etymological dictionary (she discreetly refrained from stating by whom she expected such a synthesis to be compiled).

While certain characteristics of etymological probing here at issue were perhaps most vigorously pronounced in Romance quarters, they were by no means confined to that corner of the edifice.

One more concatenation of circumstances gave the almost haphazard ensemble of stray etymological observations a privileged status and a strong impetus in the 1875–1920 period: the apparently unlimited availability of editorial space (especially in quarterlies, but also in monograph series and the like) for lavishly detailed assessments of etymological dictionaries. These verdicts, as a rule, reached their crowning achievement in innumerable counter-proposals which were almost impressionistically hazy in phrasing. The situation tended to get completely out of control when the (not infrequently) offended authors insisted on placing in the same media their (rarely exciting or convincing) rebuttals, which were similarly organized. As a result of this dispersal of information and of its critical appraisal, not to mention the ensuing chaos, the general esteem for etymology was not destined to gain momentum.

Even a scholar as balanced in general as Friedrich Diez deemed it necessary to issue a pamphlet (1858) against certain (he felt) prejudiced critics of his dictionary (1853; 2nd edn, 1861). Interestingly, he did not stoop to inveighing against any morose reviewers of his historico-comparative grammar. It could even happen that the critics far surpassed the author of the work reviewed in intellectual stature. Thus, in the Preface of his etymological dictionary of Romanian (1905) Sextil Puşcariu listed among the assessors of the first two editions (1891, 1901) of Gustav Körting's notoriously mediocre *Lateinisch–romanisches Wörterbuch* such luminaries as W. Behrens, O. Densuşianu, E. Herzog, Wilhem Meyer-Lübke, Carlo Salvioni (twice), and J. Subak. Conceivably, the cause of scholarship would have been better served had the publisher of Körting's ill-fated *Lateinisch-romanisches Wörterbuch* been persuaded to launch, in 1907, not a (lightly revised) third edition, but a carefully indexed collection of improvements suggested by those critics. The fashion reached its peak with the experts' often discordant reactions to the original version (1911–20) of Meyer-Lübke's *Romanisches etymologisches Wörterbuch*. From the staff of a single Madrid institute (the venerable Centro de estudios históricos) came, in close succession, a book-length critique (actually, a single series of mostly extra-short notes) by Vicente García de Diego, the useful commentary by Américo Castro (spread over several instalments), and the splendid elaborations from the pen of Ramón Menéndez Pidal (1920) which were incomparably superior to that same polymath's earlier attempts of 1900. In the concluding decades of our own century, this approach, though still practised, in a friendly vein, by Kurt Baldinger with respect to a fairly recent revision of the Bloch–von Wartburg venture and, above all, by Harri Meier in relation to the Corominas–Pascual mammoth undertaking, has gradually tended to acquire a slightly archaic tint.

The above remarks must not be misunderstood as a flat denial of the very existence, over an extended period of time, of the genre of the etymological full-length article, side by side with a liberal representation of pertinent reference works, on the one hand, and on the other, of loose clusters of (sometimes ill-assorted) notes. It suffices to demonstrate the temporary atypicality and marginal status of the etymological article (despite the availability of talent, of widespread curiosity, and even of the requisite editorial space, in highly esteemed journals and bulletins), then to inquire into the ascertainable causes of that protracted state of affairs. By way of acid test we may switch our attention, once more, to the domain of Palaeo-Indo-European studies (at that time at the zenith of their growth), as cultivated mainly on the European continent at the turn of the century. We can accomplish this, I submit, by subjecting to almost random scrutiny the fat Vol. XXXVI, of the year 1900, of what was then easily the world's most prestigious periodical on the subject: the *Zeitschrift für vergleichende Sprachforschung*, launched by Adalbert Kuhn almost half a century before.

Our initial impression is not unencouraging, as we discern, appended to the 500-page volume, a meticulously subdivided word index running to almost sixty pages, alongside a preceding topical index of merely thirteen pages. But that first impression of facing a sort of lexico-etymological paradise quickly turns out to be illusory. Of words purposefully cited in that context there was indeed an undeniable wealth, but – with relatively meagre exceptions – the search for them was palpably subordinated to goals other than major etymological schemes or breakthroughs.

As we look less hastily into the arrangement of the volume, we recognize before long, as the major chunks, articles (not infrequently of impressive size and often contributed by highly regarded investigators who are still vividly remembered today) which deal, above all, with comparative phonology and, on a more modest scale, with morphology. As spokesmen for the cause of Proto-Indo-European phonology, that inner sanctum of the discipline at the given juncture, we encounter, in quick succession, H. Pedersen, E. Zupitza and (writing from far-off Russia) F. Fortunatov; the last-mentioned also delves separately into Sanskrit phonology. That Swedish expert, K. J. Johanson, contributes a piece of crushing weight on Indo-European initial *b*-. Then his Danish counterpart Pedersen reverts to the jousts, this time with an even longer item on the gutturals in Albanian. Morphology barely holds its own thanks to the attention that Johannes

Schmidt, *qua* Hellenist, lends to a pair of numerals and to nominal plural formation.

Lexis is also represented, I hasten to add, but not quite on a par with phonology, as regards size and depth of the individual contributions. Relevant in this respect are not such trivial facts, all told, as the incomparably greater length of H. Zimmer's contribution here to Old Irish grammar than the same noted Celticist's light-winged ensemble of eight lexical notes on different members of the favoured subfamily, or as the involvement, *passim*, in lexico-etymological or onomastic probings of such relative second-raters as Oswald Richter, Richard Meister, Willy Foy, or Wilhelm Luft (their names are practically forgotten today). Far more symptomatic of the prevailing *Zeitgeist* seem to be certain matters of emphasis and interpretation. Thus, H. Hübschmann, certainly a major figure by any standards, presents as a single offering an attractive combination of a quintet of lexical studies (with raw data culled from Old and Modern Persian, and also from Old Armenian) and one overtly phonological inquiry, but apparently does not hesitate to title the whole 'Zur persischen Lautlehre', thus clearly and explicitly subordinating etymological to phonological analysis. In other instances, it is not the ancillary status accorded to word study as such that causes a shock to present-day readers, but the earlier tendency to group etymological observations with exegetic remarks (for example, the proposed emended reading of difficult lines of some privileged text) as a sort of *bric-à-brac*. Other writers consistently mix random grammatical and lexico-etymological comments, as can be said of that highly competent student of Irish, Whitley Stokes. A similar ingredient of haphazardness seems to pervade the, otherwise no doubt meritorious, but conspicuously patchy, contributions by Albert Thumb and Paul Kretschmer. The former combined into a single package, as it were, inquiries into three Greek, two Albanian, and five Gothic words, the latter concocted a miscellany from a much briefer examination of one Latin and two Greek lexical items. The total impression left by such strategies was that etymology was doomed to concern itself with residual problems that somehow refused to be smoothly fitted at once into the commanding grandiose structure of phonology and allied grammatical disciplines. To clear away that more or less embarrassing residue, a loose collection of, ideally, brief notes was all that was, strictly speaking, needed or welcome. As one could, not so long ago, hear certain veteran scholars remark, etymological conjectures are, in essence, footnotes to exercises in historical grammar, the implication being that footnotes, in most instances, can be safely skipped by readers who happen to be in a hurry.

The situation here described was singularly disadvantageous for any further growth of etymology as an autonomous discipline, chiefly because it was associated with the reckless atomization of knowledge and, independently, because its pursuit was haunted, so rumour had it, by an excessive dosage of subjectivity and haphazardness. This unpromising state of affairs clamoured for some speedy remedy.

One quick way out was simply to exclude etymology from the alliance of a serious linguist's legitimate concerns – undoubtedly, at a certain price. Ferdinand de Saussure decided to strike such an attitude towards the start of this century in the experimental lecture courses he delivered before small élitist audiences in Geneva on 'general linguistics' or, as one might be tempted to rephrase the topic at present, on linguistic theory. As if to drive home his point even more energetically, Saussure declared that a linguist's eagerness to extend his curiosity to 'folk etymology', was perfectly defensible while he brushed off the serious quest for word origins as a pursuit far too whimsical and, consequently, too idle to qualify for recognition among analytically minded practitioners of the arcane discipline. The heavy price he paid was the incipient subordination, at first by himself and later by a widening circle of closer disciples and other followers, of diachrony to synchrony. Fortunately, for the well-being of etymologists the world over, his trenchantly worded advice was not immediately heeded.

An alternative solution to abdication was for etymologists the gradual abandonment of certain objectionable practices – including the scattering of flimsy contributions – apparently dear to a whole generation of pre-1900 trail-blazers. Essentially, the task before their successors was to replace the inveterate habit of stirring up dust-clouds of loosely floating conjectures by publishing series of substantial, memorable, and well-organized articles of appropriate length.

The transmutation of trifling, disconnected, anecdotally flavoured notes into significant articles could be achieved in several ways. One approach to that goal was the preparation of a sort of retrospective dossier or record of earlier attacks on the given issue – outlining what French scholarship pointedly calls 'l'historique du problème'. This possibility fell, so to speak, into the lap of each practitioner (provided he had the necessary knack for dramatizing the zigzags of the reconstructed discussion) simply because a steadily increasing number of authoritative, if not infrequently conflicting, pronouncements was rapidly becoming available. A layman, at best casually interested in the provenance of certain proper names or words, will ordinarily be satisfied with consulting the latest available edition or printing of some standard dictionary recommended to him. Not so the expert. He realizes that the second edition (1924) of Erich Berneker's (unfortunately, incomplete) Slavic etymological dictionary (1908–14) involved bare reprinting, but he also knows that Alois Walde's revised Latin etymological dictionary (1910), even though issued scarcely four years after the completion of the original version, carried with it a heavy quota of revision, as did the successive editions of August Scheler's pioneering dictionary of French, of Diez's comparative dictionary of six Romance languages, and so on. Greater piquancy attaches to the fact of celebrated 'Schlimmbesserungen', i.e., unintentional changes for the worse. Of approximately every ten improvements upon Diezian conjectures proposed by his principal successor Meyer-Lübke, it is estimated that one, in the end, turned out to be a step back rather than forward. Even more embarrassingly, the same specialist, in polishing or updating an earlier piece from his own pen against the prospect of some new edition, occasionally slipped and offered an inferior interpretation. A few instances to that effect can be culled from Meyer-Lübke's otherwise deft revision (1904–6) of his chapter previously written for the original edition (1888) of Gröber's encyclopaedia. Then there are supplements, by younger fellow-scholars, to dictionaries – obsolescent or left incomplete – compiled by deceased predecessors (e.g., Scheler's to those by Diez and Grandgagnage), as well as thorough revisions proposed by aggressive publishers, witness J. B. Hofmann's recasting of Walde's aforementioned venture in the field of Latin. If one recalls that the eighteenth edition (1960) – long thought to be definitive – of Friedrich Kluge's fabulously successful *Etymologisches Wörterbuch der deutschen Sprache* not only included the dialect geographer Walter Mitzka's additions and qualifications, but also contained the fruits of earlier editions by Alfred Götze, Hans Krahe, and Alfred Schirmer ever since the eleventh edition (1934), then it will immediately dawn on today's practitioner that one cannot, in fairness to all parties involved, operate with the latest 'Kluge' alone, given its composite character and the partial identifiability of the many confluent sources of thinking. Add to these book-length treatises the myriads of verdicts reached in lengthy book reviews, page-filling notes, and the like, and you will grant that, with a measure of patience and good will, a richly orchestrated chorus of not infrequently dissenting opinions can be brought together. Whether these are tersely listed in the opening paragraph of an article gradually gaining momentum or, even worse, in a compressed footnote to it, or expanded into a highly readable digest of a protracted controversy will depend on the talent and intentions of the writer busy with drawing the balance sheet, of a protracted discussion or on the accompanying circumstances.

With all due allowance for the amenity of such an elegant recreation of a significant, long-lasting controversy (one thinks of the fluctuating discussion that has lasted decades on the background of the French verbs *aller* and *trouver*), the idea that the injection of such an ingredient could help scholars transform nonchalantly tossed-off etymological conjectures into weighty articles of strategic value is, in the long run, untenable. The unravelling of a plot, with etymologists portrayed either as its protagonists or as the detectives in charge, presupposes on the part of the narrator a literary talent rather than a gift for fresh linguistic insights. Moreover, any accumulation of such spicy reports could easily become counterproductive. What we have identified here is just an occasionally welcome infusion.

In addition to trying to increase the volume of competing analytical conjectures one could defensibly aim at operating with an expanded (not just inflated) inventory of linguistic facts under inquiry. The philosophy behind that tactical step is the realization that the genetic explanation sought for, to be truly convincing, would have to fit not an isolated fact, but a larger number of forms and uses. The more neatly such facts could be documented and illustrated along the axes of (a) time, (b) space (or area), and (c) the speaker's social status (in almost free variation with the level of the literary discourse where texts are at issue), the more persuasive would be the proponent's hypothesis. The approach might be – and, as a matter of fact, was tried out with impunity – on the level of conventional old-time philology, as when some cross-temporal concordance – by definition full to the brim with delicately nuanced lexical data – has been put to use for a maximum yield of forms outwardly and/or semantically varied. One thinks of succinct etymological comments parenthetically wedged into the *Thesaurus Linguae Latinae* of the five German Academies (principally Munich).

Still with regard to the broadening of the factual foundation and the built-in possibility of combining the purely identificational gambit with a more cause-oriented approach, there has been in existence, almost from time immemorial, a strong degree of curiosity about synonyms and near-synonyms among those tilling the mutually adjoining fields of rhetoric (stylistics) and didactics. If two or three lexical units designating the same object are, or should be, freely available to the educated speaker or writer, how would he be best advised to discriminate effectively among (x), (y), and conceivably, (z)? If we add to this picture the newly awakened dimension of historical competence, our sophisticated explorer (and, occasionally, even the inquisitive active user) will at once be tempted to re-formulate the previous question along a slightly different line: how was it possible that for a single seemingly indivisible concept there should have sprouted, within the same speech community, several competing expressions – (x), (y), and, perhaps, (z)? The scholar, previously exposed to such training as was imparted in the late nineteenth century, and thus familiar at first hand with various chronological layers of the given lexicon as well as with a number of dialectal varieties of the language at issue (not to forget its cognates), will tend to segregate, at the outset, the etymological transparent formations from their genetically impervious counterparts. He will then attempt to draw certain increasingly bold conclusions from the latter's record, in terms of time, *locus*, milieu, literary effect aimed at, relation to congeners, and the like. The more (near-)synonyms can be marshalled for such reciprocal elucidation, the more solid, as a rule, will be the cross-connections (encroachments, etc.) that one can expect to establish among them. Thus the copiousness and accuracy of the record, along with the semantic fineness of all brush-strokes executed in synonymic analysis, become virtual guarantees of genuine progress in etymologizing.

In this particular context, the techniques of eliciting, assembling, and projecting the data that underlie certain analyses that may be potentially rewarding for etymology are less than relevant. As early as 1895, for example, Ernst Tappolet, in a distinguished Zurich thesis on Romance kinship terms, used a profusion of French and Italian dialect dictionaries to collect the local terms for 'grandfather', 'uncle', 'daughter-in-law', and so on, preparing in the process a small dossier for each etymologically controversial cross-dialectal word; by way of support, a few cartographic interpretations of the facts thus established appeared, relegated to a supplement. Other students of the same inspired Zurich teacher, Louis Gauchat, shortly thereafter had recourse to questionnaire-style correspondence with selected informants, whose ranks did not necessarily exclude middle-class people, or even intellectuals.

Jules Gilliéron, the celebrated dialect geographer (and a revolutionary by temperament), reversed Tappolet's sequence of procedures by starting out from projections, onto geographic maps, of data observed by a trusted field-worker, Edmond Edmont, who had agreed to record, in narrow phonetic script, utterances made, preferably, by humble peasant folk in response to a cleverly devised questionnaire. Only after establishing, and making accessible, the relevant maps, between 1902 and 1910, did Gilliéron proceed to analyse a series of lexical problems in studies of varying length and technicality, among which the pamphlet (1917) and, one year later, the monograph-sized inquiry into the names of the bee (*ef, avette, mouche à miel, abeille*) rightly occupy a place of honour. Before long, Gilliéron's dramatic appeals to the repercussions of collisions between (or to threaten-ing clashes of) homophones, to false regression, to folk-etymological re-interpreation, and the like, i.e., to previously somewhat neglected (yet, by no means wholly unknown) processes in establishing, confirming, or trying to eliminate etymological equations, became familiar to every practitioner, the world over, of the art or science of etymologizing. What matters most, however, in the present context is not his notorious display of fireworks, but his preference for massive documentation – hundreds upon hundreds of meticulously localized dialect records of coeval rival expres-sions for the same concepts spread over major territories – a predilection that he and his fellow-countryman Tappolet shared, however profound the differences between their respective styles and techniques. These techniques were destined indirectly to rejuvenate etymology, even though those scholars' immediate target, I repeat, was lexicology, which was overtly descriptive and, by implication, also diachronic.

The launching of an appropriate tag for this sort of updated synonymics couched in acceptably scientific terms must be credited to Adolf Zauner, a student of Meyer-Lübke's in Vienna and, eventually, Hugo Schuchardt's successor in nearby Graz. In presenting his sensationally successful *Habilita-tionsschrift* (1902) on Romance anatomical terms, he de-emphasized the cartographic approach (for all its instantaneous impact on the reader and its sundry fieldwork paraphernalia). But he could boast among other compen-satory advantages over both Tappolet and Gilliéron, in addition to the latter's coterie of early followers, his thorough acquaintance with Gascon (Béarnais) and, above all, with Hispano-Romance. In the subtitle to his book-sized thesis, he had recourse to the newly-minted label 'onomasiol-ogy', coined in contradistinction to 'semasiology' (a term which, in those years, was a widely-accepted substitute for 'semantics'). Zauner expertly discussed the Romance progeny of scores of Latin names – recorded or safely reconstructed – for parts of the human body: *bucca, cilium, cor, cubitus, gen-iculum/-uculum, gingīua, maxilla, mola, nāsus, pectus, uenter,* etc., but in so doing he also isolated, placed mentally on a relevant map, then linked through bonds of synonymy, dozens of words of uncertain, disputed, or entirely enigmatic background, thus creating a meaningful context for further, more leisurely investigations, to be conducted pref-erably by others. The key term 'onomasiology', however, has never been fully adopted on a world scale in the end. This fiasco could have been due to the rapid decline of its nomenclatural counterpart, 'semasiology'. (Zauner's own decline in the three concluding decades of his life, 1910–40, may, sadly enough, have been a contributing factor.)

Apart from the crystallization, in several places, of sustained concern about 'l'historique du problème' and from the committed specialist's self-immersion (taken almost for granted henceforth) in the study of a given word's actual record (traceable in the parallel contexts of direct documentation, synonymy, and geographic location), one more line of curiosity became visible shortly after the turn of the century, tending to transmute the preceding period's etymological notes – often mere trial balloons – into richly developed articles and monographs. What is at issue here is the rapid rise of attention given to material civilization (German *Sachforschung*) as a constituent branch of ethnography or anthropology; that interest lent itself to smooth combining with dialectologically coloured linguistics (German *Sprachforschung*) in general, and with lexicology in particular. The resulting blend, which further lent itself to absorbing a sprinkling of information about folklore, clearly held out a promise of furthering the course of unhurried, multidimensional etymology – but at a certain price which perhaps, at the start, was not properly recognized.

In 1909 Heidelberg's prestigious Carl Winter publishing firm launched a new journal, *Wörter und Sachen*, its slant being editorially defined as 'kulturhistorisch'. It catered for several groups of experts: Indo-Europeanists, Germanists, Romanists, students of exotic cultures, and the like; this quality of cosmopolitanism was at that point almost unprecedented in the intellectual strongholds of Central Europe. The publisher made allowance for the inclusion of pertinent pictorial material: drawings, maps, and photographs. The journal heavily stressed those ingredients of a given language that unobtrusively lent themselves to imagerial representation: the names of utensils, of pieces of furniture, of containers, and the like. It offered no logical place for investigating more abstract ingredients of lexis: prepositions, for example, or conjunctions, or adjectives, or even verbs. To the extent that shape, size, and colour may co-determine the name of an object, etymological inquiries into the nomenclatural reverberations of such qualities derived encouragement from the regular appearance of such a large-format *de luxe* vehicle for advanced research and of equally sumptuous book-length supplements to it.

Since the slogan *Wörter und Sachen* effectively ruled out any appeal to conventional phonology and to the inflectional wing of morphology, as well as to syntax, calling instead for concentration on lexis, and in particular lexical semantics, it was a foregone conclusion that all facets of lexicology (including its newly defined component of onomasiology) would be heavily represented in the 1909 venture, which was spearheaded by Rudolf Meringer and Wilhelm Meyer-Lübke, together with the Germanist Rudolf

Much, the Slavicist Matija Murko, and the Finno-Ugricist J. Mikkola. But there was nothing in their programmatic message that might have guaranteed a high degree of visibility to etymology – defined as the systematic search for word origins, whether the genetic links involved were merely revised or newly identified – despite the widely prevailing climate of undiluted historicism. In point of fact, pure, uncommitted etymology, so the editorial team's manifesto declared, would at best be marginally tolerated. In reality, however, loyalty to the cause of etymology became from the start one of the rallying points for the newly recruited team and its followers.

Let us consider, as we did before, the contents of a single volume, this time of the one that opened the series, proudly announcing the inclusion of 175 illustrations (both drawings and photographs), in addition to two maps; Meyer-Lübke's name being the one familiar to us from before, we immediately notice the inclusion of two major articles from his pen.

In the first (pp. 28–39) the starting point is a given form, reduced to an algebraic skeleton (BAST-), seen initially as the kernel of a single word-family or word-clan (*Wortsippe*), with the author's and his readers' attention, which is semantically coloured, glued to the individual Romance vernaculars. The aim of the experiment is to demonstrate that, upon closer inspection, Friedrich Diez turns out to have been mistaken in operating with a single base (Greek *bastázein* 'to support'). Actually, two independent starting points must be posited, one Greek, the other Germanic, to the virtual exclusion of any contact between them that is conducive to subsequent conflation.

The second, even more elaborate article by the same author is concerned with certain varieties of threshing equipment, including their respective names (pp. 211–44). The novelty consists in the use Meyer-Lübke makes of Gilliéron's atlas, as if to counterbalance the forty graphic illustrations provided. Further guidance was proffered by Max Leopold Wagner, at that stage a mere beginner. Here Meyer-Lübke fails to attack any single etymological key issue, but, starting out, again and again, from parts of the thresher's equipment (for example, the flail) and the movements he performs (for example, treading), and taking into account even the testimonies of the Old Testament and of Classical Antiquity, he subjects to scrutiny dozens of etymological conjectures proposed by Latinists, Hellenists, Celticists, Germanists, and others. He emphasizes the tools' functions and the meaning of their labels. All in all, it is a magisterial performance.

Etymology is no less prominently represented in a whole cluster of medium-sized inquiries by Rudolf Meringer, pieces subsumed under the title 'Sprachlich–sachliche Probleme'. His fundamental concern is with nuclear meanings, often difficult to ascertain, of individual words which, once their etymologies have been securely established, can sometimes be paired off, such as Greek *spéndō* and Latin *spondeō*, which Meringer declares himself ready to associate with Latin *pendō* 'to weigh' and *pendeō* 'to be hanging' (pp. 177–81). Particularly entertaining and original are Meringer's attempts to connect etymologically German *Brücke* 'bridge' (originally 'Prügelweg über sumpfige und morastische Stellen') and *Braue* 'eyebrow', while strictly excluding the seemingly mediatory meaning 'arch' (pp. 187–92), with a parallel discussion of the reconstructible primitive meaning of Latin *pōns* 'bridge' appropriately attached to it (pp. 192–9). From lucubrations such as these, and from Rudolf Much's witty note on 'Word and Man' (in which he interprets German *Schalk* 'scamp', 'rogue', 'knave', or rather the pristine use of that derogatory word in terms of *Klotz* 'log', 'lump', 'stump', 'lout', 'clod'), one infers that certain provinces of etymological research, among them some of the visually most entertaining stretches for the analyst and his readers, formed for better or worse the very backbone of the nascent *Wörter und Sachen* approach.

A few atypical, i.e., conventionally slanted notes, all of them overtly etymological, by Matija Murko, Sextil Puşcariu, and Carlo Salvioni (on Slovene, Romanian, and a combination of Romaunsch and Lombard) appeared in smaller print as a token of their hierarchical subordination. The cross-cultural lead article, also by the indefatigable Meringer, dissected the names of primitive tools used in pounding cereals (club, pestle, hammer), compared with those devised to grind them into powder (the author contrasted the *pīnsere* with the *molere* series). Characteristically, Franz Pogatscher's exhaustive indexes to the volume fell into a 'Wörterverzeichnis' (pp. 245–57) and a 'Sachverzeichnis' (pp. 258–62). The latter referred the reader to the various tools and containers that had been paraded before his eyes. What causes surprise, in retrospect, is not so much the absence of an 'Index Nominum', i.e., a list of cited authorities, as the fact that no reliable clue was provided to the various grammatical processes and semantic phenomena which, at least concomitantly, had also constantly come up for bare mention or more incisive discussion.

It is arguable that some of the article-sized contributions to the journal volume here chosen for discussion were also, in the last analysis, clusters of notes. Even if one takes such a sceptical view, it should, in all fairness, be admitted at once that the constituent 'notes' of an article – such as those, here adumbrated, by Meringer and Meyer-Lübke – were no longer loosely arranged collections of anecdotal conjectures. They were meaningfully and often stimulatingly connected by a single unifying thread – a provocative point in need of documentation. (And, in the process, they sometimes made good reading as well.) Glimpses of dialect geography and pictorial representations of objects were, as a rule, still kept apart. Their eventual union was later to convert such studies into *objets de luxe*.

The year 1909 certainly fell short of marking the actual start of the trend here outlined; as a matter of fact, one of its prime movers, Hugo Schuchardt, either through sheer coincidence or private whim, was not at all represented (not even passively as a reviewee) in the opening volume of the journal that was to build a bridge between organized linguistics and *Sachkunde* (the branch of science dealing with inert objcts, we recall). To improve our grasp of the sequence of events we may well remind ourselves that as early as 1901 the Graz scholar had published, in a journal not insignificantly titled *Globus*, a medium-sized article concerned with the lexical implications of 'sickle and saw', 'sickle and dagger'. Schuchardt was from the outset a staunch individualist himself and, as late as 1925, an outspoken, militant champion for the cause of individualism in advanced research. He cultivated, in part consecutively, in part in a strange pattern of overlaps, several mutually complementary styles of etymological probing, so that various groups of scholars, not infrequently of different tastes and persuasions, could with almost equal justification claim him as a trail-blazer and as their immediate predecessor. The main reason for ushering him in at this juncture is the fact that, through his lengthy bipartite monograph *Romanische Etymologien* (1898–9), generously sponsored by a well-endowed Vienna Academy, he became a co-founder, if not the chief architect, of a type of leisurely and circumstantially conducted etymological inquiry in which grammatical conditions (e.g., points of morphology) and crucial facts of material civilization (i.e., correlated techniques of fact-finding) were not only coordinated with the search for certain elusive etyma, but were utterly subordinated to that search. These stubborn experiments – not necessarily always successful – with an occasionally (by no means consistently) reversed hierarchy constituted Schuchardt's claim to leadership in the field here under investigation.

Schuchardt thus remained completely immune from any suspicion that he was incapable of engaging in the more traditional sorts of historico-comparative research, in which etymological identification amounted to a routine operation engaged in for the sake of some superior (or ulterior) goal. This goal might be the establishment of all-important sound correspondences, or the tracing of itineraries for borrowings, including characteristic migratory words. In his earlier writings, he had striven to accomplish precisely that, as when, in his celebrated *Habilitationsschrift* (1870),

63

approved by a university as exacting in matters of linguistic methodology as was Leipzig in those days, he painstakingly scrutinized certain noteworthy instances of conditioned sound change in the Western Rhaeto-Romance dialect of Grisons ('Churwälsch' = 'Graubündner'), singling out for cursory, almost casual mention, practically on every page, either the Latin bases of selected words, or their French, French–Swiss, and Italian counterparts. But having demonstrated his ability to acquit himself of such an assignment more than satisfactorily, he felt free, thirty years later, to pursue etymology for its own sake – with an undeniably generous measure of self-indulgence.

The style in which Schuchardt couched the fruits of his inquiries for *Romanische Etymologien* was inimitably personal and bound to have provoked a good deal of eyebrow-raising. At the outset, he announced the inclusion, as the third part of the short series, of a discussion of French *mauvais* as an outgrowth of ancestral *malefātius*, but later refrained from redeeming his promise. As if by way of compensation, roughly one-fifth of the concluding part, reserved for French *trouver* viewed as an outcome of *turbāre* (a segment of about fifty pages), was devoted to an excursus which struck out in a completely unexpected direction. In the context of our own, inevitably retrospective discussion, such eccentricities may well appear trivial. It is worth showing, however, why the author needed eighty-one pages for stating, in the opening part, the reason for French *sage* ('wise') and its nearest cognates perpetuating *sapidus* ('tasty', 'wise'), from Classical Latin *sapĕre*, Folk Latin **sapēre*, rather than, for example, *sapiēns*, **sapius*, or **sabius*, all three congeners either documented or reconstructed.

One excuse for the seemingly unreasonable length of the venture was the sheer volume of material caught in Schuchardt's net. To demonstrate the superiority of his thinking, he felt duty-bound to do justice not only to the key-form *sage*, but to the Old French by-form *saive* as well, and to a whole galaxy of cognates (Old Provençal and modern Occitan *savi, sabi, sage*; Catalan *sabi, savi*; Spanish and Portuguese *sabio*; Sardic *sabiu*; Tuscan and Neapolitan *sapio, savio, saggio*; Piedmontese and Lombard *savi*, Veneto *savio*, Ladin (Central Rhaeto-Romance) *sabi, sabe*) to the total exclusion of Balkan Romance. The second excuse was the need that the author felt for a point-by-point refutation of rival hypotheses, on the triple basis of the record (or credibility), the patterns of form, and those of meaning; this 'negative' component of the whole runs to eleven pages. The 'positive' part would hardly have been much longer, were it not for the author's decision to insert two excursuses, one of them extra-long (pp. 17–70), in which untold side-issues were thrashed out, most of which could perfectly well have been dealt with in some different context.

At the risk of digressing, I think it opportune to acquaint the readers, at least cursorily, with the anatomy of Schuchardt's etymological workmanship. There is actually nothing sensationally innovative about the technique he adopts in the negative section of his inquiry into certain offshoots of parental *sapĕre*. In his discussion of earlier pronouncements by Louis Francis Meunier, Antoine Thomas, J. Anglade, Francesco Zambaldi, Gustav Gröber, A. Horning, and many others, then, again and again, Wilhelm Meyer-Lübke – a discussion set in the classical key of a German-style *Auseinandersetzung* – the author moves adroitly from form to meaning or in the reverse direction, discovering, somewhere along his itinerary, the proper niche for examining the authenticity and, wherever that is possible, the records of the etyma invoked. Conversely, in executing the appropriate moves to add to the credibility of his own conjecture, Schuchardt begins to take great liberties. Thus, between a terse statement (pp. 16–17) on the semantic split of *sapidus* ('tasty' vs. 'wise', 'sage') and a fairly succinct discussion (pp. 71–4) of the growth of the Romance descendants of *sapidus* 'wise' (with a side-glance at the state of affairs in Cymric), Schuchardt wedges in a whole string of digressions, and busies himself with: the spread of regular, as against analogical, *-ius* for *-idus*; the replacement of *-idus* either by *-ītus*, *-ulus*, *-icus*, or by *-us* via *-ius*; the appeal made to *rūbidus* by Plautus and a less well remembered literary figure, Symphosius; the evidence for the rise of *ruspidus*, *torquidus*, *fungidus*, *mustidus*, and *ruscidus*; and, as if all this were not sufficient, the wisdom of reading *rustum* rather than *ruscum* in Virgil.

On top of this overabundance and, consequently, imbalance of miscellaneous side-issues, the reader discovers to his dismay, towards the end of the entire venture, another, fortunately smaller, cluster of authorial reflections (pp. 74–9) on generalities (as distinct from his preceding *causerie* on generalities, pp. 1–3). Then he finds, more relevant to the topic at hand, stray remarks on the use of *sapidus* 'wise' in Alcimus Avitus and in certain Latin–German glosses, its function as a Jewish title in a certain tomb inscription, the service it lends as a cognomen in epigraphy, and its appearance – in derivative or secondary shape – in the writings of that ancient grammarian, Virgilius. The monograph ends on an interrogative note: is Sardic *scipidu*, the author wonders, by any chance a local blend of ancestral *sapidus* and *scīrī*? But even that concluding excursus falls short of clearing away the residual undergrowth, since a number of afterthoughts and data belatedly unearthed clutter up the appended Supplement (pp. 79–81).

This oddly zigzagging advance is, on balance, but an extreme instance of Schuchardt's indisputably masterly, but at the same time uniquely bizarre, workmanship. Yet, because his example, contrary to his own and to everyone else's expectations, in the end turned out to be contagious, the approach illustrated with his analysis of *sapidus* richly deserves more than casual mention. To be sure, one is free to state, from today's vantage point, that most of the embarrassing difficulties might have been smoothed out if only the author could have been persuaded to prepare two separate, if reciprocally complementary, monographs: one on the fortunes, in the daughter languages, of the suffix *-idus*; the other on the vicissitudes of the *sapere*, *-ēre* family. Hazardous as it always is to try to reconstruct someone else's thinking, especially after the lapse of so many years, Schuchardt, surely aware of the leaning of most of his contemporaries towards demoting a report on *sapidus* to the rank of a chapter or even a footnote in a monograph on *-idus*, may well have decided, in quest of originality, to attempt to reverse the trend by subordinating his dissection of *-idus* to a biographical sketch of the *sap-ĕre*, *-ēre* family.

Schuchardt's prefatory remarks read like a beautifully worded essay, but pose as many problems as they solve. His perspective is futuristic. He offers his *Romanische Etymologien* as samples of what etymological spadework stands a chance of yielding under optimum circumstances. For obvious reasons of decorum, the author stops short of elaborating on his own age and station in life. But does not the sort of research for which he volunteers to act as a spokesman presuppose an accumulated experience of, shall we, say, thirty years of continuous research (not to mention a commensurate degree of sophistication), without which no practitioner of the discipline could have moved with comparable ease and assurance through some of the most recondite corners of Classical Antiquity and modern-day circum-Mediterranean dialect speech? Also, what is ordinarily spoken of as an 'etymology' actually involves at bottom, we learn, formulas for an unavoidably complex, intricate, and, indeed, unique word history; and each such history notoriously lacks sharp edges ('verfließt ohne bestimmte Grenzen') and tends to flow or percolate into some adjacent word history. With such generous allowance made for individualism (or even for uniqueness), let me add on my own, imaginative monographs on issues in word history will easily come to resemble their counterparts in the realms of conventional history, art history, or the history of literature – a confluence which may indeed please certain etymologists. But do we not, by the same token, sense lurking here a danger of estrangement from the mainstream of linguistic inquiries, especially those into certain more 'scientifically' oriented (or, at any rate, more tightly organized) subdisciplines, such as historical grammar? Any rash adoption of Schuchardt's seductively phrased platform could thus, under an adverse set of circumstances (as, to be sure, could not have been anticipated ninety years ago) lead to an alienation, in the future, between etymology and the aggregate of the more austerely managed, less aesthetically presided-over, subdisciplines of linguistic science.

Unimpeachable, in contrast, is Schuchardt's assumption – and, simultaneously, his excuse for having supplied such liberal documentation – that a typical etymological problem more often than not falls into a bundle, or ensemble, of subproblems. Here he comes close to anticipating our present-day insistence on the likelihood of multiple causation behind most changes. Equally noteworthy is his mature philosophical view that, the farther we advance, the more our curiosity is bound to be aroused by the interplay of major forces at work ('wirkende Ursachen') behind smaller constellations of individual factors varying from case to case, and that the ultimate roots of that interplay are apt to be detected in the nature and conditioning of speakers ('in der Natur und den Umständen der Sprecher').

It may be worth reminding ourselves, emphatically, that no matter how far removed from his avowed main target – the secure classification of one almost pan-Romanic Latin adjective in *-idus* – some of the side-issues broached by Schuchardt in 1898 may appear to have been, he actually at no point strayed far from discussing exclusively linguistic data.

The latter observation no longer fully applies to the extended tail section (1899) of *Romanische Etymologien* which, we recall, had previously been reserved for a major etymological decision on a particularly moot point: the provenance of French *trouver* 'to find' (Old French *trover*, Provençal *trobar*), and their congeners or diffusional reflexes in adjoining territories. This Vienna Academy monograph runs to well over two hundred pages, and such features of the 1898 harbinger as here repeat themselves do so on a discernibly more ambitious, not to say reckless, scale. Thus, the Introduction, which is concerned with matters of principle, runs to six pages, and is as a result twice as long as its forerunner. The Supplements require the extravagant quota of thirty-two pages, and so on. Then again, the range of languages and dialects tapped is distinctly wider this time. In addition to the predictably copious Romance material (including Romanian), we stumble over a profusion of Greek, Germanic, Slavic, and even Hungarian and Basque forms, not to mention Latin proper at all its levels and in all its guises.

67

Having familiarized himself with some of the learned author's eccentricities, the reader will hardly be shocked to discover that the actual dissection of *trouver* (and also of Italian *trovare*, as well as the semantically deviant Rhaeto-Romance *truvar*) starts only on p. 54. The preceding forty-eight pages are given over to the discussion of French *gilet* 'waistcoat', 'vest', from Turkish *jelek*, and of certain words for large and small bells (*campana, nola,* **clocca*). The last-mentioned lexical type, especially in its protean by-forms (**cochlea*, etc.), gives rise to a fascinating pedigree of variant forms and variant meanings – a congeries of problems only typologically or programmatically related to the vicissitudes of *turbāre*, in which the author now dimly recognizes the ancestor of *trouver*. After agreeing to discount Schuchardt's meandering pattern of advance, the patient reader is rewarded not only by a fancy family tree of forms (p. 13), but also by tidy drawings of traditional tools and appliances: distaffs and spindles, fishing gear, and so on (pp. 39, 95–6). Only the gaudy, multicoloured maps and appropriate photographs are still missing.

The clue to some of Schuchardt's day-dreaming that gave rise to such a provocative monograph is embodied in his none-too-short Preface or Introduction ('Prinzipielles'), which he allowed to become something of a manifesto. Here one finds preempted the future programme of the *Wörter und Sachen* school of thought, except that the wording favoured by the author was slighly different: he wavered between 'Wörter und Dinge' and 'Wörter und Bilder'. Before long, these pages became the fountainhead of inspiration for subsequent followers, especially in Central Europe, of the 'Volkstum und Kultur' perspective, i.e., of the approach practising the integration of (a) pure lexicology (with increasingly heavy stress laid on nouns, especially those designating such objects as tools and containers), (b) the exploration of regional rural customs, costumes, and folk beliefs (or superstitions), and (c) finely drawn pictorial representations, alternating with supplements or companion volumes ('albums') of deftly taken photographs. Of all this pitifully little was available, even in fairly primitive form, before 1898.

In retrospect, several of the stimulating ideas here expounded and dramatized, some of them for the first time, appear sensible and have been adopted by several generations of etymologists. Close attention to meaning and to all sorts of secondary and tertiary associations rooted in 'folk-culture' is indeed relevant, and in certain instances the importance of the semantic or imagerial factor may, beyond a shadow of a doubt, outweigh that of purely formal considerations, for example, the testimony of regular sound correspondences, which, after all, can be overruled. Yet, for all his

enthusiasm, the author clearly overreached himself. A practising etymologist's private diary, in which he is beyond dispute welcome to record – for
his own exclusive use – any sort of resemblance of graphic or acoustic
contour, and the like, between two, or among any number of, lexical units,
must not be confused with the unavoidably selective presentation of just
those facts which, upon mature reflection, have been found to be of
immediate usefulness in the given, formally announced context, to the
exclusion of any display of chattiness. After all, an artist's sketchbook is not
to be mistaken for a finished drawing or painting.

Another token of Schuchardt's outlandish performance was his refusal to
grasp the unbridgeable gap between a methodological guide and a necessarily austere, self-limited monograph. While part of the overflow of his
broad ideas on etymologizing at its most haunting could indeed be illustrated with episodes of the eighteen transmutations of *clocca* adduced
(*cocla*, *cokila*, *clocia*, *clocula*, *cloca*, *cocila*, etc.), and while certain imaginative designations of 'cockchafer', 'bubble', 'tuft bunch', 'bung plug tap',
'notch of a distaff', 'to crouch squat', and also of a flower known as
'harebell' or 'bluebell', indisputably seem relevant (not to mention individual reflexes of *mūsculus*, literally 'little mouse', and of an assumed blend
of *cusculium* 'scarlet berry of the holm oak' and *cochlea* 'bell'), it is still
unclear why all these issues, inherently engrossing as they may be, should
have been subjected to scrutiny in a book-size study of the antecedents of
French *trouver*. In sum, Schuchardt must be credited with having been
among the first, if not *the* first, to have felt the need for a novel
methodology in etymological pursuits. But while he correctly sensed the
enormous difference between a grammarian's and a word historian's
approaches to analysis, he tended to exaggerate that polarization and, in so
doing, failed to go far beyond supplying some very general, attractively
phrased, ideas and certain techniques, in addition to a few esoteric and
erudite concrete applications.

Amid all these paraphernalia, exactly what was the central message of
Part II of Schuchardt's daring academy memoir? Meyer-Lübke, of all critics
then available, provided a terse, if friendly, summary of it as early as the
1901 edition of his classic *Einführung* (see §61), examining the piece in the
broader context of the ever-possible transfer of a given word from one
vocational jargon into another, or into the standard language. (Meyer-
Lübke's stamp of approval was doubly significant, since he and Schuchardt
then ranked as antipodes in most respects.) To paraphrase that epitome and
endorsement: *turbāre* (in general equivalent to 'stirring, disturbing, throwing into disorder', from *turba* 'crowd'), among fishermen meant 'hunting

about, searching everywhere, rummaging' (= German 'herumstöbern'), namely in an effort to drive the fish into appropriate dragnets – a widespread practice indeed. This activity is known among speakers of German as *pulsen*, a verb that has remained a technical term, unfamiliar to laymen. Conversely, in Romance this particular use of *turbāre* (*aquam*) won wide acceptance, except that the semantic nuance which triumphed among speakers at large in the end designated not the start of the activity at issue, but its crowning accomplishment.

Around this thought-provoking kernel of his conjecture, Schuchardt, as was his wont, wove a rich tapestry of side-studies and plain excursuses. After brushing off, in a segment of the fairly short 'negative part' (pp. 54–9) of his exposition, the candidacies of two Latin and three Germanic lexical types for the contested place of the etymon, he resolutely plunged into the advocacy of his own favourite hypothesis by removing from his path, right from the start, a few moderately embarrassing potential stumbling-blocks on the side of phonology: metathesis of /r/, alternation of /o/ and /ɔ/, use of /b/ in lieu of expected /v/ (pp. 59–68).

Only at that point, after the elaborate prelude, was discussion of the actual semantic ingredient of the many-pronged venture allowed to pick up momentum. The author abruptly turned to surveying tested imagerial sources of expressions for 'searching' and 'finding' in the languages of the world and next offered a 48-page report on the specific fishing technique and on the equipment or devices geared to it that could plausibly be suspected of being nomenclaturally involved in the complex bundle of word histories ('das Pulsen mit Trampen'). There followed a lengthy, anthropologically flavoured inventory of different makes of fishing nets. Only at that far-advanced point of intrusion into *terra incognita* did Schuchardt agree to revert to his self-imposed lexico-etymological assignment. To signal the return, there appeared a parade of individual vignettes on fourteen basic Romance designations – some of them bi- or trifurcated – for the special fishing technique and the gear peculiar to it that underlie and thus justify the local speech community's appeal to *turbāre* (pp. 125–41). In their wake one discovers comments on as many as five Hungarian and several other non-Romance counterparts (pp. 142–65). This was not all. As the procession continued, one more cluster of etymological miniatures (all in all, twelve additional vignettes, preceded by a few pages of wider-ranging remarks) focused attention on certain varieties of nets named after the fishing technique under investigation (pp. 165–81). With the end gradually approaching, the indefatigable author next regaled his readers to some mercifully succinct and, as usual, sparkling afterthoughts on suffixal derivatives and compounds within the confines of the *turbāre* family: **turb-isc-āre*, whose prongs extend into Sardic, Portuguese, and Spanish; *con-*, *dis-turbāre*, etc. (pp. 177–87). Mention has already been made of the alarmingly long and motley list of appended Addenda. The monograph lacks any Index of Words (not to mention any alphabetic roster of references), so that any irreverent reader eager to ascertain whether Schuchardt has ever bothered to assign a niche in his edifice to the faintly conceivable influence of *trou* 'hole' on *trouver* would have to reserve long and dreary hours for a search which might turn out to be frustrating in the end.

Schuchardt's 1899 monograph, which, despite its occasional faults and flaws, marked a genuine breakthrough, predetermined much that was to become truly innovative in early twentieth-century etymologizing. It afforded insights and raised problems which were conceivably more important than those that Meyer–Lübke was willing to tackle when he took cognizance of it after a lapse of three years from its publication date.

For one thing, even if it were true (as was, for a while, firmly believed) that, as regards sound shifts, each language tends to follow its own individual course (a state of affairs which, if correctly observed, might save the Romanist from worrying about sound changes outside his domain, and vice versa), semantic leaps show no signs of such severe territorial confinement, so that a student of, let us assume, Latin and Romance must not be discouraged from, or faulted for, citing near-parallels from any language (or language family) of his choice.

For another thing, etymological inquiry at its most imaginative can and, under a propitious set of circumstances, by all means should, be conducted at its own pace and for its own sake. Contrary to late-nineteenth-century belief, spontaneous etymological curiosity should not be shackled; above all, it need not be made ancillary to the compilation of a certain genre of dictionaries or to the preparation of conventionally slanted historical grammars. By the same token, the sharply pointed but, as a rule, meagrely documented etymological note, especially one that enters unobtrusively into a loosely ordered cluster of such flashes of wit (*Einfälle*, *Geistesblitze*), is apt, before long, to lose in weight and impact in comparison with the full-bodied etymological article and, above all, monograph.

Good as Schuchardt's prospects were, by virtue of the numerous real merits of his *Romanische Etymologien* (a genuine virtuoso performance) and, not least, in response to certain eccentricities, to initiate a new trend in the chosen field, he might not have produced quite such a sensation at the threshold of the twentieth century were it not for the fact that shortly afterwards Jules Gilliéron, an avowed admirer who was known for his own charisma, also became a convert to 'lexicocentricity'. Gilliéron achieved this at the expense of strict adherence to rigid loyalty to phonological evidence. Yet, unlike his Graz mentor, he applied the new, still heterodox hierarchy of values to data not exhumed by chance from texts and glossaries, but vigorously elicited from the lips of unsophisticated native *patois* speakers. While Gilliéron's shorter interpretative studies, which followed promptly upon the appearance of the opening fascicles of his major atlas venture, left no doubt as to the course he intended to steer, the crowning accomplishment of his career as analyst was clearly the impressive 1918 book, *Généalogie des mots qui désignent l'abeille* . . . . The monograph as a whole, as its author's debt to Schuchardt's ideology, has been examined scrupulously by a succession of competent chroniclers of dialect geography (including the noted team Iorgu Iordan and John Orr, in their deservedly applauded history of Romance scholarship of 1937), a situation that would tend to make any attempt at repetition here entirely otiose. But insufficient emphasis has perhaps been placed so far on Gilliéron's peculiar decision to lace his by no means brief monograph with no fewer than thirteen appendices – covering a wide range of subjects – which were allowed to occupy as many as 124 pages. Some of the issues that Gilliéron broached on that occasion indeed pertained to lexicology; their implications were both wide (concerning, for example, the collision of homonyms, or, for that matter, folk etymology) and decidedly narrow, as when they covered *essette* < *es-ep* (one of the regional designations of the bee). Others, judging from the titles at least, impinged on phonology ('Flottement *we:e*'; '*s* > *wes*') or had a morphological flavour ('suffixes masculins dans les prénoms féminins'). The tactical minutiae and the actual successes thus scored are less than relevant at this distance from those once exciting events. What matters instead is the author's resolve to abandon, in the wake of Schuchardt's unprecedented 1887–9 experiment, the old practice of subordinating etymological discoveries, as if they were little more than mere footnotes, to inquiries which were differently slanted, in an effort to try out, be it only for once, the reverse hierarchy. Precisely because of the great differences between the backgrounds, techniques, and styles of the two scholars involved, their fundamental agreement on grand strategy should not be overlooked.

The events of the years 1898–1918 have been presented here in almost disproportionate detail, because of their intrinsic significance and because they abounded in momentous repercussions (which were in large part unforeseeable). At this point they entail three afterthoughts.

First, it was certainly not Schuchardt's intention to imply that, to be respectable, all lexico-etymological studies should be planned on a cyclopean scale – a surprising consideration if one takes into account certain lengthy postscripts from his pen (consisting of replies to critics, or spontaneous afterthoughts), which appeared in learned journals, especially between 1902 and 1904. (The opponents whom he intended to convert to his approach included such luminaries as Antoine Thomas and E. Herzog.) What the author, one gathers, was eager to achieve at the turn of the century was to test the maximum of details and convolutions that an unhurried etymological discussion could entail, under favourable circumstances, such as unlimited editorial space. That unique experience, with all its ramifications, he never sought to duplicate. In the meantime, the flow of his shorter lexical notes continued unimpeded. Examples include his notes on the Spanish dendronym *madroño* and on the Sardic reflexes of Latin *ilex* 'holm oak' and *cisterna* 'subterranean reservoir for water', both written in response to an Academy memoir by Meyer-Lübke. Conversely, the professional dialect geographers, by furnishing again and again literally hundreds of forms which revolved around the same need, made monumentality almost obligatory and ended up by injecting into it a certain monotony.

Second, Schuchardt, an Indo-Europeanist by training (to be specific, a student of August Schleicher at Jena) and in addition a generalist of his own volition, raised the prestige of Romance scholarship – up to then, a stepchild – on the international arena. The role that he played in this applies in particular to his involvement in all sorts of etymological issues. In a matter of a decade or so, etymologizing in the Romance languages became a trail-blazing, downright fashionable activity. Younger Romance scholars would organize pilgrimages to his home in Graz, especially after his deliberately early retirement from teaching in 1900. Before long he became an intellectual hero.

Finally, the very definition of 'etymological *trouvaille* or windfall' (with its unavoidable ingredient of sheer luck) underwent a thorough revision in several directions. The overtones of 'sudden flash of thought', 'discovery through some lucky coincidence' began to recede into the background and almost disappeared, since etymological inquiry was henceforth compatible with long-term plans for systematic research. Moreover, the borderline between diachronic lexicology and etymology began to blur. What was needed and what invited publication in an esteemed journal was not necessarily some 'wild' conjecture that involved several unknowns, and least of all some hypothetical base manufactured *ad hoc*. The communication could perfectly well involve a more solid set of arguments in favour of a hypothesis already ventilated, even by someone else; or the reconstruction of a partially hidden itinerary of some word that had long – but until then less than persuasively – titillated the minds of far-sighted scholars. What mattered was the skilful piecing together of the mosaic of a half-concealed word history.

The impact of dialect geography on the fortunes of twentieth-century etymology was, of course, to exceed, by a wide margin, its role as abetter and reinforcer of certain ideas that Schuchardt had previously floated as so many aesthetically appealing trial balloons. True, geographic maps had been used, at intervals, before the rise of dialect geography to record any conspicuous distribution, in space, of certain facts of language. But cartographically oriented dialect geography fixed the attention of a practitioner of etymology on the areal distribution of a given word, with a typology of configurations of areas gradually emerging from the increasingly sophisticated analyses. After a while, the evidence of the area became almost as essential to the demonstration of the cogency of an etymological conjecture as the interplay of certain sound correspondences across the ages ('historical phonology'). This trend was to reach its peak in the Neolinguistic position, which carried this reshuffling to its extreme, namely to the – ultimately almost exclusive – reliance on the given areal pattern. The other direction of the impetus that dialect geography gave to etymological research was the refinement of the analyst's perception of the particular milieu (preferably rural, some theorists and practitioners argued) in which certain usages had sprouted. It is not inaccurate to contend that dialect geography, especially in its less crude shape, served as a stepping stone to present-day sociolinguistics.

In sum, the various innovations tried out by the aggressive schools of dialect geographers, in addition to the perspectives opened up by those daring reformers contributed substantially to the creation of an *avant-garde* variety of etymology which had been entirely non-existent before 1900. Schuchardt's unshakable prestige lent that genre a modicum of respectability, while Gilliéron's inflammatory message held out the promise of eagerly awaited novel techniques. Yet both scholars here cited had originally been attracted to the fold of linguistics by the drama of sound change implied by the record of sound variations. Their subsequent conversion to diachronic lexicology and, finally, to etymology proper as its logical outcome required a good deal of experience and much thinking and, as a result, an appropriate length of time. The same holds true for some of the other pace-setters of the 'new etymology', whatever the itinerary they chose for their intellectual pilgrimage.

Let us take the case of Theodor Frings (1886–1969), whose meteoric rise carried him from a Marburg doctorate, promptly earned in 1910, to a chair in Germanics (1917–27) at Bonn, fairly close to his home town of Dülken. He then moved a professorship to far-off Leipzig, and eventually became President of the Saxon Academy of Sciences. At the start, virtually nothing in the record of his accomplishments as a young investigator presaged such a course of future events. In the company of other relative neophytes and guided by a resourceful dialectologist, Ferdinand Wrede (who in turn had inherited from the actual founder, Georg Wenker, his dialectological bequest of the Linguistic Atlas of Germany), Frings prepared, for the monograph series 'Deutsche Dialektgeographie', a circumstantial treatise, *Studien zur Dialektgeographie des Niederrheins zwischen Düsseldorf und Aachen*, which closely resembled a few slightly older links of the same chain, namely thesis-style inquiries by Jacob Ramisch and Erich Leihener. Heavy emphasis was placed in all three (and in others that speedily followed upon them in the same series and displayed a strikingly similar format) on conspicuous points of phonology and morphology, usually to the exclusion of syntax, in search of isoglosses ('Linie $x \rightarrow y \rightarrow z$'). While lexical units were assembled, meticulously transcribed, lavishly glossed, and minutely localized, the last thought that might have occurred to the compilers of the word list, or of the model sentences elicited from native speakers, would have been any preoccupation with the distant extraction of those pieces (except that Leihener condescended to annotate the presence of 220 Gallicisms in his rich haul of regionalisms).

But Frings was no inferior or even average representative of narrow dialectological curiosity. In a matter of a decade or two, he rose from being an apprentice dialect geographer to the far more enviable rank of a *Kulturgeograph*, a tag which one would be tempted to equate with 'student of cultural diffusion' were it not for the indisputable fact that 'culture', in English, and *Kultur*, in German, normally have far from the same referential scope. He achieved his goals by learning early on to synthesize minutely sifted insights, by collaborating closely with an astonishing range of other scholars (not infrequently chosen on the grounds of reciprocal complementarity), and by refusing to succumb to the charm of any particular technique or giddy terminology.

Equipped with this armour, Frings, by the time he reached his midthirties, had achieved the following:

(a) He vigorously expanded the area of his active curiosity and expertise, advancing from research in *Die rheinische Akzentuierung* (1916), *Die südniederländischen Mundarten* (1921), and *Rheinische Sprachgeschichte. Ein Überblick* (1924) to inquiries into Saxon and into the rise

75

of Standard German: *Die Grundlage des meißenischen Deutsch. Ein Beitrag zur Entstehungsgeschichte der deutschen Hochsprache* (1936);

(b) He learned how to operate with the total temporal extension of the chosen language, not just with key segments, as in his *Grundlegung einer Geschichte der deutschen Sprache* (1948, 2nd edn 1950);

(c) He became immersed in the *œuvre* of an intellectual giant and generalist of the stature of Eduard Sievers (1933);

(d) He gradually moved from phonology to lexicology, a shift culminating in his decision to carve out, in collaboration with Elisabeth Karg-Gasterstädt, a dictionary of Old High German (1952–) from the piles of notes which Elias von Steinmeyer had left behind;

(e) He became interested in issues in literary history, both medieval and modern. He took as his starting point texts and salient figures of the literary scene closely connected with specific dialect areas familiar to him from previous exposure to linguistic geography. A meandering path led from two lectures *Über die neuere vlämische Literatur* (1918) to three monographic studies on the elusive medieval poet Heinrich von Veldeke (1949), reserving an extra dosage of attention for the latter's *Eneide* (1964–5);

(f) Having firmly acquired a tight control of linguistic and literary investigation, Frings, now at the height of his powers, plucked up the courage to attack broad problems of social organization, to the extent that they were reflected in lexis and older literature (*Die Brautwerbung*, 1947), or the separate impacts of Antiquity and Christendom on the crystallization of the German language (1949). In the process, an initial virtually exclusive concern with Germanics in all its manifestations began to yield ground to a preoccupation with European culture viewed as a whole: *Europäische Heldendichtung* (1938), *Minnesinger und Troubadours* (1949).

We have not yet included etymology in our purview. Now, in the early 1930s there occurred certain events which bent Frings's protean curiosity in that direction, too. In 1932, to be specific, he managed to publish a medium-sized book which was to exert major influence: *Germania Romana*. It included a powerful synthesis of early Latinisms that had percolated into the German dialects of the Rhine and Danube valleys. Almost simultaneously, he published a theoretical pamphlet on speech and settlement, ethnic by definition: *Sprache und Siedlung im mitteldeutschen Osten*. The third event was of a different nature. Largely through Frings's efforts, the industrious Romanist Walther von Wartburg became attached to the University of Leipzig. Von Wartburg was devoted to etymologizing, almost to the point of fanaticism, and the occasional collaboration between the two scholars, who complemented each other's gifts and inspirations in exemplary fashion, led to a series of increasingly pure exercises in etymological probings, with emphasis on issues in Romano-Germanic lexical and, broadly, cultural symbiosis. Paradigmatic examples include one piece on German *Hees*, French *haise*, and German *Heister*, French *hêtre* (1937), and an elaboration on that article, in response to hostile criticism, the following year. When Walther von Wartburg, soon after that, moved away from Leipzig, Frings continued to cultivate etymology on his own, as in his study of the words for 'willow' (1963), an example of Romano-Germanic symbiosis. All lexical and etymological pronouncements by Frings bear the stamp of his early spadework in dialect geography.

The unusual and impressive instance of Frings's almost simultaneous espousal of two causes at first glance as disparate as etymology and literary research may provide the right opportunity for ventilating the issue of a possible hidden link between the two. To begin with, the case here mentioned is not as isolated as a casual observer may be inclined to assume. Let us take the astounding record of inquiries into the provenance of the Spanish and Portuguese verb *tomar* 'to take'. After renowned etymologists of the calibre of Schuchardt or Meyer-Lübke, had fooled around with unconvincing points of departure (Germanic **tômjan* or onomatopoeia – the noise allegedly produced by a falling object), it was a major literary scholar, namely Pio Rajna, who in 1919 drew the philologists' attention to Latin *autumāre*, a hypothesis soon after endorsed by a consummate etymologist, namely Jakob Jud. Whether the choice of *autumāre* 'to affirm, assent, aver' actually represented the last word in this protracted controversy or should yield right of place to *aestumāre* 'to estimate, esteem' (either etymon, to qualify for that role, must be assumed to have suffered a deep slash of aphaeresis), the salient point in this context is that this conspicuous achievement was made by a pure literary scholar, not by chance by a philologist who, like Gustav Gröber, managed to straddle linguistic and literary expertise. One is, of course, free to argue that literary studies, in the Age of *Quellenforschung*, required on the part of their practitioners such fine knowledge, even down to minutiae, of older languages as to have made it possible for the more gifted among them to hit occasionally (better still, almost accidentally) on some avidly sought lexical source as well. But this is not the whole story, since vexing issues in, let us say, phonology and inflection did not excite or inspire literary savants to the same extent.

The reasons for the affinity, then, must lie deeper. In part, they are due to the fact that certain words have a haunting biography or a range of disquieting connotations that have already been on the minds of major

77

literary figures even before the advent to prestige and influence of strict linguistic science. Thus, Arturo Farinelli surely was not the first expert who became interested in the tortured history of Spanish *marrano* 'crypto-Jew', but the sources to be consulted and interpreted for such a study called for the skill of a pre-eminently literary scholar. A combination of flair for literary insights and talent for linguistic analysis stood Carolina Michaëlis de Vasconcelos in good stead when she attacked the problem of Portuguese *saudade* 'nostalgia' (from older *soidade* 'loneliness'), while general familiarity at first-hand with the colonial period of Hispano-American history (including its literary sources) lent special authority to Pedro Henríquez Ureña's inquiries into such exotic words, imported from Spain's overseas possessions, as *tomate* and *patata*. From this point we are free to go one step further and to state that individual growth, rather than mere obedience to 'laws', or conformity with them, is what best characterizes the convolution of a typical etymological problem as much as it does the configuration of a characteristic literary piece or issue.

True, the average prospect of a lexical study that is apt to attract the attention of an imaginative and many-sided literary scholar is one that dangles before his eyes the chance to disentangle a series of semantic or functional shifts to the exclusion of complete etymological unknowns. Thus, in grappling with the vicissitudes of *persōna*, a Latin word of Etruscan parentage, Hans Rheinfelder, at the start of his career, obliged Romanists by discussing nominal Portuguese *pessoa* vs. (pro)nominal French *personne*, as well as Anglicists by virtue of the attention he paid to English *parson*; but his sole etymological decision was the genetic separation he advocated of *per-sōna* from *sŏn-āre*. In the past, incidentally, most literary scholars have viewed their brief periods of concern about etymological 'riddles' as unique marginal experiences, preferably not to be repeated. One paradigmatic example of such a recoil has been María Rosa Lida de Malkiel's tacit retreat from etymologizing after her not entirely successful bout with Classical Spanish *arpado* as used in the fixed phrase *arpadas lenguas* (1951).

As this last example most eloquently demonstrates, one consequence of the sporadic trespassing of certain literary historians on etymological territory has been the appearance of extra-heavy documentation, something unprecedented in the last century. By a strange convergence of tastes and styles in the presentation of corroborative evidence, the hundreds upon hundreds of dialectal forms of a given lexical unit that a present-day dialect geographer has learned to toss in when faced with puzzling situations have been matched, as regards sheer weight, by an often equal number of tell-tale passages from ancient texts that a connoisseur of fine literature is in a position to produce. In either context investigators have learned to work with extra-heavy documentation, the like of which no earlier explorer picked from the ranks of conventional historical linguists could have visualized in his wildest dreams.

Not surprisingly, *avant-garde* ideas about priorities in etymologizing fell short of meeting with the same degree of enthusiasm in all quarters. Most controversial among Gilliéron's innovative thoughts were those that revolved around his stiff opposition to practically all earlier practices and assumptions. In the ranks of his direct followers one finds those who became enthusiastic about the novel technique of interviewing or data-elicitation via field-work, in addition to the cartographic projection of the material gathered. Of greater concern to us is another group whose members were interested in Gilliéron's flat rejection of the regularity of sound change as the prime mover in matters of language evolution, as well as his insistent, indeed strident, demands for closer attention to be given to such phenomena as folk etymology, the reactions of the speaker to the collision of homonyms, and false restoration (or regression).

Easily the most devoted of his students was the Edinburgh professor John Orr (1885–1966) who, towards the end of his life, collected into books a scattering of essays (one of them in dialogue form), articles, and notes written at a much earlier date. Orr was a medievalist by training and was thus hardly predisposed to engage in a style of research favoured by social scientists, such as recording neatly transcribed utterances. Having been exposed, from the start, to the sort of imaginative writing that fiction is expected to represent, he was visibly enchanted by the anecdotal flavour of certain word biographies and derived pleasure from debunking not a few pretentious reconstructions made by rigid Neo-grammarians. He thus came to represent, in the English-speaking world, the witty approach to etymologizing, a very hazardous pose to strike.

Most of Gilliéron's followers, however, overrode their mentor's prejudice and leaned toward reconciling old-style and new-style etymological methodology, against the dual background of the steady improvement of interview techniques (for example, through the inclusion of urban dwellers) and of the creation of increasingly sophisticated pictorial records (for example, by the addition of photographs and drawings). This holds, above all, for the two highly successful Swiss Romanists Karl Jaberg and Jakob Jud (stationed in Berne and Zurich respectively), who insisted that they themselves and their advanced students be perfectly familiar with the undiluted medieval dossier of each word viewed through a powerful dialectological lens.

Some workers, after temporarily developing a lukewarm interest in Gilliéron's approach to issues in word history, allowed their erstwhile response to cool off. Two paradigmatic examples of such a metamorphosis

79

were Ernst Gamillscheg and Leo Spitzer, both students of Meyer-Lübke in Vienna shortly after the turn of the century. These two, upon their return to their homes after a brief sojourn in Paris, combined their efforts in studying the reflexes of a group of semantically connected phytonyms in regional Gallo-Romance: *Die Bezeichnungen der Klette im Galloromanischen* (1915). Soon after, Spitzer, without interrupting his general concern with etymological lucubrations, nevertheless veered off in directions entirely at variance with Gilliéron's doctrine, while keeping up his loyalty towards Schuchardt. Gamillscheg, as late as 1928, i.e., almost immediately after Gilliéron's death and his own move from Innsbruck to Berlin, published a booklet (*Die Sprachgeographie und ihre Ergebnisse für die allgemeine Sprachwissenschaft*), in which, after deftly replacing costly maps by equally, if not more, effective monochromatic sketches, he pleaded for the cautious acceptance of lexically centred dialect geography as an adjunct to, if not outright substitute for, straight historical grammar. Had Gamillscheg been sufficiently inspired to make generous use of such inexpensive sketches in his own French etymological dictionary (completed that same year), that dictionary, which is known under the acronym *EWFS*, might have acquired a distinctive feature that would have set it off to advantage against certain rival undertakings, and so demonstrated with unprecedented graphic eloquence the close ties that bind individual word histories (surely not only in French) to recurrent patterns of areal distribution. Unfortunately, on that occasion Gamilischeg missed such a chance of a lifetime.

If we extrapolate from certain writings by Schuchardt and from the sort of lexicocentric atlas project launched by Gilliéron, that the ideal of massive documentation is a major prerequisite for skilful etymologizing, then the answer to our prayer will be the monumental dictionary of, principally, individual dialect forms or, better still, a sort of concordance recording whole utterances. A bold and exceedingly laborious experiment along these lines (but not, I hasten to add, one that is entirely persuasive in retrospect) was conducted, over a period of about half a century (c. 1920–70), by Walther von Wartburg, a native Swiss Romanist whose slightly chequered university teaching career took him from Lausanne via Berne to Leipzig and Chicago and, finally, to Basle. His brainchild which I have alluded to here, namely the *Französisches etymologisches Wörterbuch*, was to go through numerous mutations, but at least the opening phase of its tempestuous growth invites a survey at the present juncture.

The low-key start to the author's academic career hardly presaged anything sensational or controversial. His Zurich doctoral dissertation (1912), which he himself viewed, with his teacher Louis Gauchat's blessing, as being semantically oriented, even though others may have leaned towards calling its bent onomasiological, was pan-Romanic in scope – a good omen, and one step ahead of Tappolet's monograph on kinship terms. It dealt with expressions for 'blindness' and other forms of defective sight. This topical choice, indeed, involved an excellent start, from which the youthful author could have advanced with ease to explore expressivity, since most such qualifiers as 'deaf', 'lame', 'hard-of-hearing', 'hunch-backed' contain ingredients of phonosymbolism. However, the author's next venture showed no move in that direction. It involved a distinctly shorter, more concentrated piece, issued by the Berlin Academy in wartime (1918), conceivably with a delay, and revolved around the Romance names of the sheep – a domestic animal which was exceptionally well represented in the relevant rural households. An excellent exercise in zoonymy, and planned on the same scale as the preceding piece, but endowed with less potential for further growth, it testified to the author's improved skill in presenting with commendable stringency material which was copious to the point of overflow.

Organization began to loom as more important than inspiration. Less than four years after the restoration of peace in Europe the opening fascicles of Vol. I of Walther von Wartburg's *Französisches etymologisches Wörterbuch* began to run off the press. But the over-optimistic author clearly miscalculated the work's total cumulative length. The entries were so long, and subsequently so increased in sheer extension, that a reader, whether casual or committed to a certain engagement, was confronted with a string of full-sized, formulaically phrased etymological articles, rather than a mere succession of dictionary entries. The articles, let me clarify at once, were marked by the subordination of conjectures and discussions to assortments of impeccably accurate data, checked and counterchecked for their precision and dependability. The pattern favoured by a then still youthful author in his mid-thirties was an instantaneous success, not least on account of one weighty circumstance of which, at that point, no close observer was unaware.

In the aftermath of a stinging military defeat, etymological scholarship, as practised in Central Europe, became cluttered up by bitter and lengthy con-troversies, virtually amounting to attempts at mutual extermination, fought out by certain contenders for the privilege of leadership. Ernst Gamillscheg, Josef Brüch, and Leo Spitzer were for years among the most vociferous and ruthless participants in that infighting. Lengthy etymological articles, for a while, seemed to be written with the sole purpose of publicly demonstrating the rival's inferior logic and equipment. Walther von Wartburg, in contrast, displayed, first and foremost, the methodically assembled record. He initially laid heavy stress on the testimony of dialect glossaries (of which he concomitantly compiled a useful catalogue), but later gave increasingly more liberal allowance for atlas attestations, for the private preferences of conspicuous literary figures (without disregarding the leanings of anonymous medieval texts), and for affirmative statements, as against spells of silence, by pioneering lexicographers. (Of course, by tacitly breaking up the given word's semantic spectrum and derivational–compositional edifice, the author from the start campaigned unobtrusively for the, to his mind, most plausible solution of the underlying etymological problem.) Next came a matter-of-fact listing, in chronological progression, of the various etymological pronouncements caught in the compiler's net, with, as it were, only a minimal interspersion of calmly stated editorial caveats. Finally, the author, with commendable detachment, not to say composure, would present his own reconstruction of events, which, with the passage of time (starting in the 1930s), might gradually increase to a full-length column or even an entire page, and would consistently remain free of any polemic overtones.

As a powerful antidote to certain briefly prevailing misdemeanours this approach, for a while, seemed excellent. However, after having effectively served its purpose, and after having found at least one late imitator, namely Max Pfister, this method in the end lost much of its initial appeal. In the long run, it tied etymology far too tightly to ambitious, time-consuming data-collections conducted on a massive scale; and it tended to conceal the most cogent, often crucial arguments – those of special concern to theorists – by burying them under unwieldy aggregates of bare forms, as if forms alone were invariably the decisive factor in cases of doubt. The quality of finesse in unavoidable reconstructions was gradually crowded out altogether. Towards the end of his life, with time and energy running out, von Wartburg called in a number of collaborators, picked from among former students and junior colleagues, and entrusted to their care entire volumes. Not all of these heirs, understandably, worked with the same zest as the founder of the project or managed to maintain his level of interpretation, since the pervasive structure of the undertaking, on balance, reflected someone else's taste and way of thinking.

One more technique for sharply increasing a meticulously researched corpus of documentation and for tightening, as a reward for all the labour invested, the network of etymological conjectures was demonstrated by Paul Aebischer (born in 1897, and hence junior to Jaberg, Jud, and von Wartburg), from the mid-1920s until the 1950s. After that date the

French–Swiss scholar veered away with dramatic suddenness from his earlier preoccupations (which had also included anthroponymy and toponymy on an almost pan-Romanic scale) and plunged into intensive research in medieval literature, stressing both its Romance and Nordic components. Anticlimactically, not to say ironically, a representative collection of his finest articles written in the earlier key, i.e., addressing etymological questions, made its appearance at a shockingly late date, almost post-humously in 1978.

Aebischer's originality was rooted in his selecting for private research only the most salient lexicological questions, with or without etymological overtones. (We can safely disregard in this context the position he temporarily held with the influential Bureau des patois de la Suisse Romande, where he was encouraged to practice the art of studiedly slow data-gathering.) He concentrated on the prehistory and stratification of challenging individual words, e.g., *rūga*, literally 'wrinkle, crease in the face', to the extent that it qualified for the designation of a 'street' (French *rue*), or of that celebrated pair of Hellenisms, *thius* 'uncle' and *thia* 'aunt' (cf. Spanish *tío, tía*; Italian *zio, zia*, etc.), which in certain provinces crowded out their Latin counterparts, *avunculus* and *amita*. Or he focused on the territorial distribution of the dendronyms *sabūcus* vs. *sambūcus* 'elder-tree'; or else on the variant forms of another Greek word transplanted onto Romance soil, namely *amygdala* 'almond'. A few significant or intriguing proper names were likewise caught in his net, e.g., *Hispān-us* vs. *-iscus*, as were a very few grammatical and derivational morphemes, witness his studies in the vicissitudes of *-ora* and *-ārius*. Aebischer's principal originality lay in his almost blind reliance on the testimony of charters (in preference to the evidence of literary texts), overwhelmingly preserved in copies, or copies of copies alone. To that extent, Aebischer simply applied to etymology the earlier insights into phonology of Erik Staaff and Ramón Menéndez Pidal; territorially, he was particularly at ease in Italy.

This style of microscopic inspection of the available record can, in isolated instances, produce splendid results. Unfortunately, Aebischer gratuitously weakened the potential impact of his painstaking studies by certain intellectual caprices. Also, the wisdom of almost completely disregarding literary attestation, even where it happens to be within reach, eludes most readers. His inquiries into the names for 'uncle' and 'aunt' (in addition to a parallel investigation into the palaeo-Romance names for 'cousin') would have gained from being assigned places inside a wider-ranging study of Romance kinship terms, which went beyond the scope of Tappolet's venture. The study of the *-ora* plurals might have been imaginatively linked with the so-called 'unstressed suffixes' *-aro*, *-ara* (and their variants) in Luso- and Hispano-Romance, and so on. Aebischer's excessive individuation of lexico-etymological problems places him at the exact opposite pole from the, at present, more fashionable structuralist slant of thinking.

The last potential benefit to etymology that came with the rise to influence of 'classical' dialect geography and of the *Wörter und Sachen* approach was the experimental elevation of the areal patterns of distribution of rival words to a higher level of relevance than any other consideration admissible in diachronic analysis, including the previously all-powerful evidence of regular sound correspondences. This radical step is usually associated with the extremist doctrine of the Neolinguistic school of thought, conceived and launched by a small group (which included G. Vidossi and U. Pellis) of Italian 'glottologists'. Its founding father was Matteo Bartoli, and its last and easily most militant proponent (in particular during the ten years or so that he spent at Princeton) was Giuliano Bonfante.

As a result of his pioneering research in Dalmatian and his excellent knowledge of circum-Adriatic Latinity (and also of Romanian), Bartoli – a comparatist ever since the days of his close association with Wilhelm Meyer-Lübke in Vienna – developed a special flair for 'Eastern Romance' and, in the process, discovered some arresting lexical resemblances between Balkan–Romance and Hispano- (or Ibero-) Romance. Let us choose a single eloquent example, the word for 'beautiful, handsome'. Deriving, on the one hand, in Portuguese *formoso* (originally *fremoso*), in Spanish *hermoso* (initially *fermoso*) and in Romanian *frumos* from ancestral *fōrmōsus* 'shapely', and, on the other, in French *beau/belle* (originally *biaus*, *bel/bele*) and in Italian *bello*, from parental *bellus* 'pretty, cute', the two forms of the word represent the flanks vs. the centre of a single edifice, as it were. Translating this state of affairs into the language of temporal sequences, Bartoli next argued that any consensus of the lateral or marginal zones (as the Iberian and the Balkan peninsulas indeed are *vis-à-vis* Rome) represent the earlier phase, while the central zone, namely the aggregate of Northern and Southern Gaul and Italy, serves as the mouthpiece for the later phase of essentially the same process. In this instance, philological evidence indeed happens to be available to make it plausible that the predominance of *fōrmōsus* anteceded the reign of *bellus*. Moreover, the etymologies of the two contenders happen to be transparent (the former is a derivative from *fōrma*, the latter is an offshoot of *bonus/běně*). Using such relatively simple relationships as his unobjectionable starting point, Bartoli before long began to draw unwarrantedly bold conclusions in the case of etymologies and grammatical features of a lower degree of translucency, and to operate with other schemata of territorial distribution. In addition, he hastened to make a bold leap from Romance to Indo-European as a whole, and in the end to exotic language families as well, so that his ambitions became less and less realistic. The Bartoli–Bonfante platform came in for sharp criticism, for example, from Robert A. Hall, Jr in North America, and was tacitly rejected on the European continent as well. However, applied in its more reasonable form, the extra dosage of attention paid to areal distribution did benefit etymology, for example, in the case of such peculiar lexical units as Latin *afflāre* (literally 'to blow or breathe on', then, as a term of hunting, perhaps with an allusion to hounds, 'to hit upon, find'): witness Portuguese *achar*, Old Spanish *fallar* (> mod. *hallar*), and their South Italian counterparts. Using an utterly different starting point, Menéndez Pidal, at a distinctly later date (in 1954), also discovered a strong affinity of Hispano-Romance with South Italian, a point which can be used as an independent argument of considerable weight in etymological debate.

Discussing etymological procedure in terms of rival assumptions, competing methods, and alternative techniques can be both profitable and enjoyable (not least because these considerations indeed lend themselves to neat description), as long as one remembers that, after their subtraction, there still remains, as a rule, an untapped residual element – namely the irreducibly unique identification formula itself, which in general does not so easily yield to one's hankering after tidy classification. By making use of circumlocutions, we are at liberty to affirm that certain scholars are endowed with enviable detective faculties and an almost instantaneously working flair for felicitous identification, while some of their peers, of otherwise comparable merit and, in particular, equally commendable erudition, are sorely lacking in such mental equipment. Leaving details to psychologists, we can confidently assert that etymological talent, inborn as it may be in the last analysis, lends itself to substantial improvement through tireless practice, observation of the performance of others, and willingness to learn from mistakes, including one's own.

To revert to the actual period under discussion, there can be no comparison between Menéndez Pidal's gropings at the turn of the century and even his improved skill in compiling, a decade later, the etymologically oriented *Cid* glossary, on the one hand, and, on the other, his magisterial elaborations on the original version of Meyer–Lübke's etymological dictionary (1920). Most historical linguists are fairly realistic about their own aptitudes, paying special attention to that elusive ingredient we call inspiration, and tend to espouse the cause of etymology, or to shy away from it, on the basis of that preliminary self-assessment. In this particular respect, the contrast between Karl Jaberg and Jakob Jud, who were compatriots, approximate contemporaries, and even partners in at least one major venture, could hardly have been stronger, as one notices at once in scanning their respective bibliographies.

The talented and versatile etymologist (a human type that Jud personified in exemplary fashion) will easily be tempted to experiment with varying formats and different approaches, adjusting the resources called upon, with appropriate elasticity, to the configuration of the particular problem under study. Because, for certain pending problems, the moment of decision or arbitration simply may not have arrived yet, a scholar of Jud's persuasion will flatly reject the genre of an etymological dictionary, which might force him to pronounce prematurely on a number of rebellious questions.

As a beginner, Jud focused his attention on a number of words serially tied together, as is true of certain numerals (1905), or on nouns whose histories lend themselves to particularly dramatic presentation through the instrumentality of dialect geography, for example, French *poutre* '(wooden) beam', French *aune* 'alder', and North Italian *barba* 'uncle' (1908, 10). But he also concerned himself with unusual patterns of nominal declension (1907) and, right at the start of a succession of distinguished book reviews, allowed himself to be dragged into the discussion of etymological issues posed by I. A. Candrea and O. Densuşianu in reference to Latin/Romanian lexical equations across the ages, by a challenging map ('to saw') of the French dialect atlas, and by J. Gilliéron and J. Mongin's stimulating response to that provocation. He also turned his attention to P. E. Guarnerio's attempt to delve, via an archaic text, into an Old Sardic dialect (1908f) and to Max Leopold Wagner's distillation of a phonological system from data garnered in Southern Sardinia (1908g). The selection of problems of possible appeal to one's own thinking can thus start with thumbing through a dictionary of word-origins, the scrupulous examination of one map, the philological interpretation of a text, or the scanning of a sophisticated historical grammar. One cannot ask for an exhibition of greater variety and elasticity!

Until his death in 1950, Jud remained virtually protean in selecting the right pretext, size, style, and slant for airing his etymological hunches, and the quest for the right 'etymology' occasionally included not the kernel, but, for a change, a difficult-to-grasp, teasing derivational or compositional feature of the lexical unit at issue. Even among the last and easily more elaborate of Jud's experiments in this direction, not all turned out to be equally persuasive; I have elsewhere stated my reservations about the extraction of the triad French *mensonge*, Italian *menzogna*, Spanish *mentira* 'lie' and the reverberations in the vernaculars of *opus est/est opus* 'it is necessary' (cf. Old French *estovoir*) that he proposed in those years. But even a partial defeat, at the hands of a scholar as gifted and compelling as was Jud, is apt to contain grains of truth of sufficient value to vindicate retroactively his almost reckless investment of time, energy, and enthusiasm in this sort of etymologizing for its own sake, not just to fill minor gaps in the edifice of knowledge. Soon after the start of his career, Jud almost triumphantly announced and exemplified some of the goals and modes of the 'new etymology' he personified so well (1911–12). Later he strove to influence younger scholars by example more than by precept, a hazardous decision in the long view.

An entirely different climate, whether intellectual or emotional, surrounds Karl Jaberg's *œuvre*, which stretches from 1901 to his death in 1958, and beyond, given the availability of certain posthumous publications. As one scans the definitive list of his scholarly pronouncements (1965), in addition to the various indexes meticulously carved out from that list by S. Heinimann, one quickly realizes that experiments in straight etymological identification were few and far between among his writings, that they fell short of ranking as sensational, and that the author scrupulously subordinated those that he happened to make to other, more general or more abstract, concerns and considerations. In scrutinizing the titles of his scattered monographs and shorter papers, one looks in vain for any that appear to tout the discovery of some exciting etymological connection. To be sure, Jaberg was interested in striking semantic changes and, even more, in concatenations of such changes, as when he contributed, in the testimonial volume in honour of Ernst Tappolet (1935), a real gem of a zoonymic inquiry: 'Wie der Hundedachs zum Dachs und der Dachs zum Iltis wird'. He developed genuine curiosity about onomasiology, offering to a journal which he had co-founded, by way of initial encouragement, a miniature history of the Romance verbs for 'to begin, start' (1925). In the wake of Meyer–Lübke, but concentrating deliberately on a single small area (to wit, the Romaunsch-speaking section of the canton of Graubünden), he inventoried, as early as 1922, the labels for local techniques of threshing and for the tools put to use for that purpose. Expanding on his own early pamphlet on dialect geography (1908), which was geared exclusively to Gallo-Romance conditions, he delivered, in 1933, three lectures at the Collège de France and eventually collected them into a single, finely polished book (1936), in which areas of form or meaning and the possibilities of their cartographic projection were examined with special attention to newly constructed maps of Italy. In most of such instances, and no doubt in a great many more, the wisdom of establishing certain etymological links overlooked by earlier generations of explorers was, incidentally, brought up, but the novelty of these valuable additions to the earlier fund of etymological knowledge was deftly played down. The same holds for three of Jaberg's last sparks of enthusiasm: his crusade for the acceptance of sound symbolism as a major force in the transmutation of languages (witness his separate inquiries into the names of the swing and those of the sling), his concern with the folk names of diseases, and his self-immersion in problems of serialization, paying heightened attention, in a cross-linguistic perspective, to numerals. At every step Jaberg, a mature scholar by now, clearly was in a position to correct, even delete earlier etymological assumptions and to propose superior substitutes – services that he indeed performed, but in a tacit, discreet way, as a self-understood commitment within the broader framework of diachronic lexicology.

To use a single, simple formula capable of doing justice to all these tentative innovations (and no doubt to others germane to them), which were equally characteristic of the first half of this century, what was accomplished in the end was the highly successful transfer of etymology from a modest place in the domain of historical grammar (principally diachronic phonology) to a prominent position in the newly opened-up field of lexicology, at its most arcane and sophisticated. What, until approximately 1900, was little more than a residue of intellectually piquant word histories, involving minor and minuscule episodes that apparently could not be presented through the instantaneous application of straightfoward sound correspondences, in other words, an aggregate of extended footnotes to truly important events, almost overnight became a semi-autonomous discipline, which had a strong appeal to enthusiastic researchers whose imagination, responsive to the challenge of individual concrete situations rather than to the appeal of abstract schemata, refused to make them first-rate phonologists, grammarians, or syntacticians, but did elevate them to the rank of leading etymologists.

It is not sheer coincidence that, in presenting the advent of this new era, we have depended heavily on the record of research in Romance quarters. Just as the postulate of the regularity of sound change had initially been established by a close-knit, highly motivated group of militant Indo-Europeanists, who gathered in Leipzig in the 1870s and 1880s with Romanists, Semitologists, Amerindianists, etc. following suit as best they could, so the crusade for the new dignity and aspired-to semi-independence of etymology was chiefly spearheaded by Romance linguists, who used newly launched linguistic atlases as their rallying points.

As nearly always happens under such an exciting set of circumstances, there were involved in this movement both hotheads and moderates. Some joined it after having previously demonstrated their ability to do creditable research under the old set of premises, and thus strove for a reconciliation of the old and the new. Others recognized in the rhetorically announced 'revolution' an excuse or a pretext for neglecting, even forgetting about, any prior knowledge. Societies and journals began to be founded to serve as mouthpieces and outlets for the new set of beliefs and preferences. Certain pioneers were declared martyrs, not to say saints. The names of sceptics and agnostics became unpronounceable in some quarters; and individual instances of unfairness and misjudgement can easily be identified in critical retrospect.

One readily grows aware of several variants of this reallocation of etymology within the total edifice of socio-spatio-temporal linguistics. As regards place, the previously practised allotment of a given form to a certain language or dialect (and, by implication, to an obvious *locus* or habitat of its speakers) during those years began to be rivalled by the intensive study of migratory terms (*Wanderwörter*). In that style of research the investigator, who was concerned with the transfer of lexical items from, let us say, Language x to Language y (whether or not these were closely related), could usually afford the luxury of ignoring the ultimate provenance of practically the entire lexical inventory of x, but obligated himself, by the terms of his 'contract', to focusing on a more or less closely defined sector of the lexis of y, which was suspected of harbouring words of unusual or atypical extraction. One speaks of a closely defined sector where the process of percolation is best, or solely, observable in one neatly delimited cultural (or semantic) domain, for example, in names of garments, among hunting and sporting terms, in military or nautical vocabulary, among chromonyms, and the like. Assuming that one cares to include certain categories of proper names with the rest of the vocabulary, those can indeed be taken into account. It is, for example, arguable that the spread of *Kitty*, *Dotty*, and the like among Russian mid-nineteenth-century aristocrats ran parallel to the temporary adoption of words like *fashionable* in that same milieu.

The details of the plans for research undertaken by any individual scholars, or teams of scholars, so inclined have varied from case to case. An ambitious book venture, such as the study of Turkish nautical terms of Italian and Middle or Modern Greek origin, launched by Henry and Renée Kahane and happily brought to conclusion in collaboration with Andreas

Tietze (1958; manuscript completed in the Spring of 1954) could have sprung into existence in response to the challenge emanating from a few preceding small-scale etymological explorations; or its writings may have been stimulated by certain overlapping satellite studies; or else a residue of etymological inquiries into certain particularly rebellious or recalcitrant case histories may have followed upon its completion (as a rule no information is expected from authors on such private choices).

Whatever the anecdotal biographies and bibliographic details may be, it is a fact that the first half of the present century witnessed a sharp increase in both the number and, preponderantly, the quality of inquiries into lexical migration (a genre of research less than frequently experimented with before) and that, as an inalienable part of such major, long-term commitments, countless individual etymological issues were reformulated and, in many instances, satisfactorily solved. Here are a few examples, chosen at random, of article-, monograph-, or vocabulary-sized studies of this sort. They concern such discernibly foreign 'strains' as: Italianisms in Egyptian Arabic (S. Spiro, 1904); Arabisms in Portuguese, Spanish, Catalan, and Sicilian (A. Steiger, 1932); Italianisms in Turkish (C. Tagliavini, 1940) and in Spanish (J. H. Terlingen, 1943); Gallicisms in Dutch (M. Valkhoff, 1931); Neo-Hellenisms in Serbo-Croatian (M. Vasmer, 1944); Italianisms in French (B. E. Vidos, 1939); Palaeo-Hellenisms in Occitan (Walther von Wartburg, 1952); and Hispanisms in Italian (E. Zaccaria, 1927). The attribution of credit is more complicated in the case of Italian nautical terms in Modern Greek, since Renée Kahane (Kahane, 1938) followed in the wake of D. C. Hesseling's much earlier and broader-gauged study. All of this does not begin to take into account the dictionaries of foreignisms, descriptive or, more frequently, programmatic, in which German scholarship, for transparent reasons, specialized.

Lexicologically, rather than phonologically, underpinned search for word origins may also hinge on successful periodization, to the extent that the skilful division of the whole mass of data into layers adjusted to time levels goes hand in hand with the acquisition of vitally needed secondary skills. To discuss judiciously lexical units found in Old English, the etymologist in charge must be at ease in the entire Palaeo-Germanic domain, moving with assurance through the labyrinths of Gothic, Old Norse, Old High German, and Old Saxon (=Old Low German) material – a heavily loaded programme for a lifetime of research. A candidate for expertise in Middle English, especially Chaucerian English, may settle for a lighter programme of self-immersion in comparative Germanics, provided that this is compensated for by a thorough familiarity with Old French in all its shades and ramifications (and, via Old French, with Romance as a whole). The student of modern, i.e., post-Elizabethan, accretions to English lexis, especially its overseas (including former colonial) varieties, urgently needs prior exposure to the indigenous tongues of India and Pakistan, to the language patchwork of the Near and the Middle East, as well as South Africa and tropical Africa, and to the maze of North America's autochthonous languages (although familiarity with colonial French, Spanish, and Dutch, as well as with the languages of nineteenth-century New World immigrants from Scandinavia and Germany unquestionably will also be a major asset in ascertaining the descent of any regionalism of dubious ancestry). Since no researcher, not even one endowed with a knack for virtuoso performance, can be expected to be on equally familiar terms with all layers of such an avalanche of forms, it follows that a typical set of etymological issues affecting English, to yield impressive results, needs to be tackled by a team of at least three differently specialized experts. A distant model was provided, as long ago as 1932, by the two Parisians Antoine Meillet and Alfred Ernout, who agreed to examine, in an etymological vein, every Latin word family from two mutually complementary angles, first, as a member of the Indo-European family (with reference to that family's groundwork) and, second, for its own sake, with increased attention paid this time to its Latin and even Romance superstructure.

The factor of time level is closely interwoven with the matter of documentation, specifically its volume and its degree of trustworthiness. As the investigator develops growing curiosity about the deepest layers of language in a given area, spurred on in his quest for lexical antiquities by all sorts of relics (genuine toponyms, oronyms, and hydronyms, ingredients of microtoponymy, for example, names of caves and rocks), he begins to operate with languages of the distant past, whose phonology and grammatical structure are not only practically unknown, but, still worse, stand virtually no chance of ever being pieced together.

Among the ensuing uncertainties, one can distinguish three degrees of obscurity. The European substratum language (overlaid by some Indo-European tongue, typically, two to three millennia ago) may itself have been Indo-European, judging from its cognates. It may, for example, have belonged to the once exceptionally widespread Celtic subfamily. In that case the margin of doubt may remain relatively narrow, inasmuch as the longer-surviving, hence better-known, Celtic languages (for example, Irish, Manx, Welsh, Breton) throw sufficient light on the entire subfamily to allow analysts to judge the plausibility of a new conjecture concerning a congener not directly accessible to observation. Alternatively, the closest Indo-

European language invoked by the proponent of such an etymological hypothesis may have been extinct for, let us say, two thousand years, but has at least left reliably reconstructed records; Osco-Umbrian seems to be a case in point. The third situation, and the one that deserves to be called the least advantageous strategically, involves a language (or a language family) which is neither directly accessible, nor obliquely imaginable via cognates that are extant or, at least, securely pieced together.

While cautious scholars like Jakob Jud recognized the marginal legitimacy of such etymological issues, which we are least equipped to cope with (characteristically, in the year 1946, he devoted a lengthy article to *Reliktwörter*, i.e. 'residual Romance words' that somehow got stuck in territories overrun by the Alemanni, but only a three-page note to pre-Romance ingredients of the lexis of Alpino-Lombard and Rhaeto-Romance dialects, by way of comment on an inquiry conducted by Norbert Jokl), other scholars went much further in this type of extra-hazardous etymological inquiry. The roster of such dare-devils includes: a number of Italian 'glottologists', chiefly Vittorio Bertoldi, dedicated student of phytonymy; Ramón Menéndez Pidal, especially in the concluding decades of his crowded life (witness his 1952 collection of toponymic explorations); and, above all, Johannes Hubschmid, whose peculiar bent, ever since the early 1940s, has been aptly described by Kurt Baldinger (1982), a scholar of an entirely different persuasion in his own research programme.

We must here confine ourselves to this brief statement, because the current of etymological thinking at issue embodies an extremist position, involving as it does exaggerated optimism regarding reconstructibility.

Espousing likewise the cause of lexically oriented etymology and relying also on the additional boon of very heavy documentation (part of it sometimes cartographically recorded), some scholars have been guided less by considerations of space (area) or time than by the selection of recurrent meaning as a common denominator. I am referring here to the celebrated onomasiological approach, which burst into bloom around 1900, then suddenly underwent a sharp decline between 1950 and 1960, and has been resorted to ever since only at rare intervals. Even though onomasiology need not be dependent on the ready availability of dialect atlas maps, there can be no doubt about the mutual support that dialect geography at its peak and onomasiology during its half-century of flowering were lending one another.

The field worker, by showing each of his informants the picture of, let us say, a squirrel, in an effort to elicit from him or her the local designation of that little rodent (known for its queer looks and bizarre movements), collects a splendid array of, possibly, dozens or scores of carefully transcribed vernacular labels. To be sure, not all of these tags conceal unsolved etymological problems; in all likelihood, only a small minority does so. Moreover, the author of the monograph (typically, a doctoral candidate) who is at work on the names of the squirrel will hardly feel constrained to supply the missing etymology (or etymologies), although the temptation to do so will be very great and society's rewards for having managed to do so may be overwhelming. The point is that knowledge of the exact area where the etymologically elusive lexical unit happens to prevail serves more often than not as an etymological eye-opener. Also, microscopic inspection of the record, with special attention paid to receding variants, is apt to lead to the chance discovery of some long-concealed variant, which at long last offers the eagerly awaited solution, as when *colmena* ('beehive'), in Spanish, leads one nowhere, although it is on almost every speaker's lips, while the discovery of dialectal *cormena*, a long-overlooked by-form (or so it seems), immediately clamours for an appeal to ancestral *crūmēna* 'purse, bag', with the further possibility of *colmar* 'to heap up, fill to the brim', *colmo* 'heap, crown', and yet other words which have deflected the descendant of *crūmēna* from its straight course.

Since we are concerned here with the trends of research which were fashionable in the first half of the present century and the genre now under discussion had its boom precisely during those five decades, we are fortunate in having at our disposal Bruno Quadri's Zurich dissertation (inspired and supervised by Jakob Jud): *Aufgaben und Methoden der onomasiologischen Forschung* (1952), except that Quadri, having raised and successfully answered a long series of pertinent questions, was apparently unable to foresee, let alone to explain, the rapid decline of a genre of research which still enthralled and held spellbound his generation of young European explorers.

A mere onomasiological inventory of cross-dialectal and, equally useful, cross-linguistic synonyms can be highly relevant to the etymologist. Thus, to revert to the names of the squirrel, German *Eichkätzchen* (lit. 'oak-tree kitten') and Russian *belka* (literally 'whitie', i.e., 'animal whose fur has a white spot' – seen from a hunter's perspective) seem straightforward enough, but the development in Romance and, in its wake, in English has been extremely complicated, as a quick glance at the onomasiological index unobtrusively appended to the revised dictionary (1930–5) by Meyer-Lübke (pp. 1187–1200) will show at once. One discovers traces of false identification with some other animal, allegedly similar in some respects (*glīs* 'dormouse', *nītēla* 'small rodent', *uīuerra* 'weasel'); there are also vestiges of borrowing from some other language, above all, from Greek: *skiūrus/* *skūrius* (which underlies French *écureuil*, with English *squirrel* representing its northward prong; Aragonese *esquirol* qualifies for the position of its southward, trans-Pyrenean outpost). Other etyma have been characterized as, basically, onomatopoeic: **kosja*, or as hints of the animal's striking tail: *rāpum* 'turnip, knob, *tail', or as references to the conspicuous position of its body: *prōnus*, or as evocations of its motley colour pattern: *varius*; in *nītēla* a blend of the word for 'splendour' with the designation of some ill-defined species of a small mouse (dormouse?) may have occurred. Thus the etymologist who runs into yet another, still unidentified name of the 'squirrel' will instantaneously know approximately what to expect. It will hardly come as a surprise to learn that Meyer-Lübke, on the same occasion, recorded twenty disparate sources for 'lizard', and twenty-four for 'owl'; but it is, admittedly, a matter of astonishment that the same inventory should list twenty-one starting points for words which, at a certain evolutionary stage, came to designate in Romance an animal seemingly as unexciting as the donkey.

Understandably, the degree of lexical variegation stands in a direct ratio to the fascination that certain onomasiological problems have exerted on etymologically alert scholars. If one is to rely on Bruno Quadri's statistics (which have the year 1950 as their chronological limit), four scholars had by then busied themselves with the names of the squirrel, eight with those of the lizard, and no less than fifteen with those of the insect 'ladybird' (*Coccinella septempunctata*). These numbers include Romanists, Germanists, and, possibly, a sprinkling of experts in other domains as well.

In the half-century here under scrutiny, historically oriented research concerned either with lexical semantics (previously also known as sematology or semasiology) or with its converse, namely lexical onomasiology (or synonymics), invaded also, in accelerated tempo after 1920, the extensive domain of Germanics, including the various evolutionary phases of English. In his aforementioned monograph, Quadri appends a rather thorough examination (pp. 212–49) of the record of Germanicist research relevant to his principal survey of Romance accomplishments along that line, identifying the centres of research responsible for that vogue in Germany, Austria, Switzerland, The Netherlands, Belgium, Scandinavian countries, and (on a disappointingly meagre scale) the English-speaking countries. He identifies the scholars who were chiefly in charge of this development at that stage – in part through their own efforts, in part by supervising student dissertations: H. Falk, G. G. Kloeke, H. Polander-Suolahti, R. Hotzenköcherle, Paul Kretschmer, E. Schwarz, S. Singer, J. Trier, Francis A.

Wood, P. Zinsli, and many others. What Quadri, whose bibliographic prowess exceeds, by a wide margin, his analytical finesse, fails to accomplish, is to define the various styles of research selected by the practitioners of this method and, even more relevant, to segregate, for easy consultation, any etymological discoveries – whether incidental or intended from the start – that may have emerged as by-products of the entire current.

One recognizes the appeal the authors at issue made to this method – once 'modernist', at present *passé* – by the titles they chose, or were persuaded to adopt, for the finished product of their works: 'The names of . . . '; 'The Maple-Tree . . . ' or 'Parts of the body . . . '; '(The) designation(s) of . . . '; 'Verbs denoting locomotion'; 'The terminology of the realm of . . . '; 'The Geography of phytonyms . . . '; 'Words semantically akin to . . . ' (= *'Die Sinnverwandten . . . '*); and several variations on these. A fine-meshed cross-cultural investigation into the purely etymological yield of their converging research efforts (to the extent that diachrony, especially reconstruction of the concatenation of past events, was at all aimed at by those authors), remains, I repeat, to be undertaken.

The triple emphasis placed here so far on (a) an *avant-garde* style of early twentieth-century exploration, (b) choice slices of Romance lexical material that attracted attention, and (c) the Central European tradition and peculiarities of scholarly endeavour, must not be allowed to produce the impression of a certain inevitability, as though there had not existed, at the crucial moment, tempting alternatives to these three interlocking patterns of highly motivated commitment. To become duly sensitized to at least one viable alternative it suffices to examine the role assigned to etymology by Antoine Meillet and by a few leading members of his once highly influential Parisian circle of language historians. By way of random selection of a suitable specimen, let us dissect, then reassemble, some representative portions of Vols. XXVIII and XXIX of the tone-setting annual *Bulletin de la Société de Linguistique de Paris*, which correspond to the years 1928–9 and thus jointly mark the peak of the inter-war period.

From Vol. XXVIII we shall pick the master's own piece, actually an ensemble of four short semi-independent notes, 'Observations sur quelques mots latins' (pp. 40–7), the illustrative lexical units being: *salūs* 'health, welfare'; *propinquus* 'near, neighbouring'; *dīcere* 'to say'; and *aperīre* 'to open' alongside *operīre* 'to cover (over)'. This composite item will be flanked by a concise Old Iranian (specifically, Sogdian) note from the pen of Émile Benveniste, already recognizable as the heir apparent (pp. 7–8), against the background of a medium-sized article by M. Cohen, which is entirely different in its coverage and styling, since it concerns itself with problematic ties between somewhat nebulous entities, such as the Mediterranean cultural sphere and even a family of Oceanic languages (pp. 48–62). Vol. XXIX promises to enrich our dossier to the extent that it contains a fairly typical article by Meillet, rich in etymological implications, on the Indo-European lexemes for ordinal numbers (pp. 29–37). It was accompanied by a relatively long piece on two Latin near-homonyms, *cernō* 'I separate, discern' and *crēscō* 'I grow', contributed by Alfred Ernout (pp. 82–102). Michel Lejeune's note on Ancient Greek πρῶτος (pp. 117–21) also qualifies for consideration, while M. Cohen's divagations on migratory words in Semitic and adjacent territories (pp. 132–7), once more, strike one as being least germane to the central line of advance. Benveniste's, Ernout's, and Lejeune's shares in this volume (at least those that have so far been identified) certainly lend themselves effortlessly to bracketing with the two magisterial contributions by Meillet, the undisputed leader of the group.

Apart from such pervasive features as expository and phrasal elegance, in addition to intentional parsimoniousness of documentation, precisely what are the salient features of the Meillet School's approach to everyday etymological practice?

To begin with, the term 'etymology' itself and its offshoots are used sparingly (and virtually never in the titles of articles and notes). The items in question are offered, less ostentatiously, as contributions to diachronic lexicology. By implication, the pieces hold out no promise of presenting any radical revision of existing knowledge as regards the starting point of a given lexical trajectory. Although the quest for the ultimate ascertainable origin of a given word is, typically, aimed at, the course that word took in mid-career or some other significant feature of its growth (for example, its varying distance from congeners, its territorial spread, the shrinkage of its use) may just as cogently serve to justify the writing of the note.

Even though the lexical items chosen for closer inspection may have been removed from any section of the given lexis, it so happens, again and again, that in addition to their lexico-etymological weight they are also grammatically significant. Any trend toward driving an irreversible wedge between historical grammar and etymology has thus been blocked from the start. As a matter of fact, it sometimes becomes a point of sheer expediency to decide whether a problem of this kind should be treated under the rubric of phonology (or morphology), with the subordination of its lexico-etymological kernel to grammatical considerations, or whether the reverse hierarchy should be allowed to prevail. But even where the issue basically remains confined to lexicology, as with *cernō/crēuī*, the particular episodes of two narrow-meshed word histories, after having been duly singled out for leisurely analysis, must in the end lend themselves clearly to subordination to general diachronic lexicology – if necessary, one of the future rather than of the present.

Thus, Ernout concludes that the threat of (near-) homophony can lead to two polar opposites: either the elimination of one (of necessity, the weaker) of the two contenders – a loss that may be limited to sections of the paradigm – or their tendential merger through semantic rapprochement. Reduced to this simple formula, the results of the experiment lend themselves to cautious application to other languages and even language families (they might, for example, have advantageously underpinned the study presented independently in *Language*, 55, 1–36 a half-century later). As an accomplished historian, Ernout readily admits that there were additional forces at work within the chosen corner of the field (namely, the pressure of certain Greek models, in particular on *concrētus* and *concernō*, to the extent that the habits and references of the educated were involved); yet, he hastens to add that the basic contours of the dilemma which faced the crowd of speakers of Latin were not thereby diluted or distorted.

Meillet's own paper on Indo-European lower ordinals (1–10) is far more highly concentrated, and displays the same pattern of inextricable interweaving of etymology and historical grammar (with a distinctly heavier stress placed, for a change, on phonology than on morphology), except that here the great powers of serialization and of analogy (the permeating influence of cardinals on corresponding ordinals, with an additional role assigned to distributives) assert themselves. One further dimension is the areal characterization of Latin and Celtic, on the one hand, and of Indo-Iranian, on the other, as marginal or lateral zones within the given family ('extrémités du domaine indo-européen') apt to have given shelter to archaisms. And the entire highly sophisticated discussion is crowned by the newly gained insight into 'abnormal' (i.e., unlevelled) forms serving as the best available clues to the otherwise elusive stage of pristine Indo-European. Each single form (with those for '6.–10.' discussed ahead of those, more recalcitrant to analysis, for '1.–5.') is examined as a separate issue in etymology (or word history), with the refined machinery of Indo-European comparativism at its most intricate pressed into service. But, finally, a single inflectional, i.e., grammatical fact is borne out when the author superimposes upon one another the individual lexical sketches, to the effect that the *-to-* suffix, as in Greek *hékatos* 'tenth', is late and secondary if measured by the yardstick of its chief rival, the *-mo-* suffix, as in Latin *dĕcimus*.

97

The preceding four shorter pieces by Meillet lend themselves to similar characterization. Apropos the Latin abstract *salūs*, Meillet demonstrates that even an authoritative partial answer to pressing etymological queries can be useful, provided that the experienced etymologist knows exactly where to draw the line between the domain of the known (or knowable) and that of the unascertained. He makes it clear why *salūs*, designating as it does an active force viewed in a religious context, is a feminine noun, and casts a bridge to the adjective *saluus*; but he confesses his inability to solve the mystery of *sānus*. As regards *sollus* 'totus et solidus', he voices his disbelief, on phonological grounds, in a widely accepted conjecture, and identifies ways and means for cicumventing it, but stops short of reaching any decision. The note on *dīcere* offers no new etymology at all, but strengthens our earlier grasp of the word's filiation by laying heavier stress on its affinity with *iū-dex* and *in-dic-āre*, and by calling attention to the paradigms of its cognates.

Meillet's success in developing a pleasing personal style for his etymological research must not be rashly misinterpreted as a token of disinclination on his part to take into account and, where appropriate, to applaud studies conducted elsewhere in a radically different key. Thus, apropos the vignette on *aperīre/operīre* (in conjunction with *pariēs* 'wall'), he fell back on decisions reached by Leumann, Meringer, Müller, Niedermann, Persson, Schulze, Sommer, and Trautmann, a phalanx of foreigners steeped in a different tradition of scholarship, against whom he cited only his teacher Bréal. Then again, in coming to grips with the vicissitudes of *propinquus* 'nearby' (and its semantic opposite *longinquus* 'distant'), he cast about for support from Brugmann, Leumann again, and Solmsen.

Among Meillet's disciples already mentioned above, one detects varying degrees of approximation to the recommended model. Émile Benveniste, already at that juncture rivalling his teacher in the art of pithy presentation, allows a Sogdian Buddhist term, reducible to **βarxār*, to come to life, likening its ambit to that of Sanskrit *vihāra* 'sanctuary'. For his virtuoso performance two printed pages are sufficient to survey the local record of toponymy and oronymy; to extricate himself from a misleading conjecture of his immediate predecessor Gauthiot; to expand the evidence by introducing Old Armenian data previously overlooked; to toy with the possible agency of expressivity; to inject a few drops of poetics (through allusion to Middle Persian *farxar* 'blissful abode' abounding in lyrical poetry) and, for good measure, of the history of Oriental religions. To watch an etymological inquiry so carried out becomes a source of aesthetic pleasure, doubly so because one suspects no concomitant loss of rigour.

Possibly a shade less sparklingly worded, Michel Lejeune's compact study of Greek πρῶτος 'first' derives its attraction from the author's skill in welding the search for an acceptable etymon to a discussion of certain problems in ancient numerology, including (a) mankind's long inability to realize that one should start counting from 'one' rather than from 'two', and (b) the consequent schema of suppletion prevailing in the erratic relationship of 'one' to 'first', throughout Indo-European and far beyond its bounds. At that point Lejeune balances purely linguistic against non-linguistic, i.e., broadly cultural considerations, knowing exactly where to stop. The documentation proffered, apart from its accuracy, is varied, but light. Quick glances are cast at Finno-Ugric and Romance (specifically, Romanian), but the centre of gravity is not allowed to shift in any rival direction from Palaeo-Indo-European, especially from its arsenal of prefixes. General linguistic measurements are taken, but the commitment to one particular sector of the globe remains firm.

Not for nothing did Meillet, Ernout, Benveniste, Lejeune, and their peers have rather sparing recourse sixty years ago to the classificatory tag 'etymology', ordinarily preferring to see themselves cast in the roles of lexicologists. Their articles and notes, indeed, could not by any means, through simple acts of routine inflation or compression, have been transmuted into entries in a typical etymological dictionary (even though, ironically, two among them were later to embark on, of all things, such a protracted venture). An honestly conceived etymological dictionary remains, by definition, a reference work, despite all and any latitude of embroidery. Conversely, an etymological note or article is meant to be read, judged, and appreciated for its own sake, multidimensionally as it were, not in narrowly informational terms. It invites flashes of thought on methodology and thrives on judiciously rationed generalizations. It need not be lacking in style.

Any confrontation, as regards the handling of etymology, of the influential Meillet School in Paris with the practices of Central European linguistic science almost sounds like giving credence to reports about national varieties of scholarship. Such reports or, worse, postulates must be firmly met with scepticism. After all, France boasted, among the incarnations of her tradition of etymological learning, an Antoine Thomas (already referred to here at an earlier juncture), who certainly did not think, write, or teach about etymology in the same key as Meillet and his followers, while such protagonists of Central European erudition as the Neogrammarian Meyer-Lübke and the anti-Neogrammarian Schuchardt, though tactful in eschewing personal clashes, were in sharp disagreement with each other in practically all matters concerning etymology. Moroever, were one to insist seriously on a French (or French-style) approach to etymological analysis as being irreconcilably opposed to a German (or German-style) approach to the subject, then one might finally be forced to admit, albeit only facetiously, that the sole escape from such baneful limitation would be for a practitioner either to be a Swede writing in French on issues in Romance etymology (like Gunnar Tilander, principally as unrivalled connoisseur of medieval hunting terms), or to be a versatile Austrian capable at all times of dashing off witty, but superficially researched lexical notes either in his native German or his nearly-native French, as Leo Spitzer is known to have done from before World War I to long after World War II.

This would, then, amount to being caught in a blind alley, an experience doubly perilous because, through a strange and, all told, sad twist of circumstances, not a few major early twentieth-century cultures committed to their own, entirely respectable brands of linguistics fell short of developing any truly distinguished tradition of etymological inquiry. It gives me little pleasure to admit that the United States of America and British Canada formed one such culture throughout the first half of the present century, despite the availability of a few talented, but severely isolated 'loners', who, as if to complicate matters, chose to specialize in highly esoteric languages. David S. Blondheim (at Johns Hopkins University) specialized in Old Judaeo-French, and William A. Read (at Louisiana State University) specialized in the Caribbean melting-pot of diverse languages and cultures. Since neither, despite their zest and stupendous erudition, proposed a new style which lent itself to generalization or ventilated any fresh, challenging theory, their activities produced only a pathetically limited echo.

It is singularly depressing to report that Edward Sapir, for all his dazzling versatility, not only treated etymology as a stepchild in his otherwise deservedly influential series of essays, *Language, an introduction to the study of speech* (1921), but, in the recent informal estimate of an expert as thoroughly grounded as Yves Goddard, turned in a less than satisfactory performance in etymologizing Indian lexical material. These disappointments cannot be counterbalanced by Sapir's loosely connected attempts, made in the concluding years of his life, to etymologize a scattering of words connected with the Ancient Near East.

Opinions have been divided from the start, and continue to be so, on the merits of Edgar H. Sturtevant's 'Indo-Hittite Hypothesis', a matter of no direct concern to us here. However, students of Ancient Anatolian who are indisputably authoritative and, in addition, demonstrably friendly to the late Yale scholar, in assessing the global value of his accomplishments, have privately singled out etymology as the single most vulnerable spot in his record. Not surprisingly, Sturtevant's *Introduction to linguistic science* (1947) treated etymology only obliquely.

Through the prism of certain chapters in Leonard Bloomfield's long-revered book *Language* (1933), especially of Chapters 19 and 22–7, experienced readers could observe the admired author's occasional brushes with etymological issues. The more naïve readers, who viewed themselves as militant followers of Bloomfield's doctrine in the 1930s and 1940s, did not extract from the book they assimilated with such fervour the impression that etymology continued to be a valuable discipline, worthy *per se* of heightened attention. (As a neophyte, however, no doubt under the influence of his Chicago teacher Francis A. Wood, Bloomfield had zestfully practised the craft of etymology.)

The unfavourable balance produced by all these mutually corroborative trends was reinforced when converts to linguistics, from coast to coast, turned to the one European generalist who was most influential in the New World during those decades: Otto Jespersen. Danish linguists, however meritorious in other respects, have lacked any marked penchant for advanced research in etymology.

In this section we have so far succeeded in circumventing the difficulty of taking into due account the special genre of the etymological dictionary – with a few exceptions (Ernout and Meillet, Walther von Wartburg). Strictly speaking, there exists no rigid division between a monograph (article, note) and the dictionary designated to explore word origins. For one thing, not a few scholars, before embarking on a book-sized project in this domain, value chances to experiment with more modest undertakings. Thus, Murray B. Emenau's *Dravidian etymological dictionary*, written in collaboration with Thomas Burrow (1961), was preceded by a long series of short-to-extended etymological papers, dealing, it is true, for the most part with Sanskrit. For another thing, there exist several intermediate subgenres. Thus, especially before the watershed date of 1950 (chosen here somewhat arbitrarily), an exceptionally thorough glossary compiled to accompany a text in an ancient or medieval language would easily become an exercise in controlled etymologizing. The Hispanist can cite examples ranging from Menéndez Pidal's almost legendary edition of the *Cid* epic (1908–11) to George Sachs's commendable edition, which is particularly strong on the etymological side, of a thirteenth-century veterinary treatise (*El libro de los caballos*, 1936).

Despite all these indisputable facts and arguments, individual research efforts in etymology and etymological reference works, including those prepared by reputable experts, display no perfect mutual compatibility. The one-volume dictionary marked explicitly as etymological, which aims at being both handy and authoritative, will, as a rule, offer under any entry a single hypothesis declared correct by implication, without bothering to identify the *locus* and date of its original presentation (or 'discovery') or the name of its earliest proponent, even though it may want to qualify the fragmentary identification thus conveyed by some such attenuating adverb as 'doubtless', 'probably', 'possibly', 'hardly'. Of course, the lexicographer is also free to attach to the word at issue some such alternative label as 'of uncertain origin' or 'of dubious authenticity'. The discriminating reader's obvious expectation is that the given author's professional reputation virtually guarantees his having scrupulously examined the entire dossier of the word under consideration and of its offshoots, including (a) the actual record and (b) the various, often mutually contradictory, explicative hypotheses. This two-way policy, on the part of author and reader, applies to a not inconsiderable number of familiar mid-century ventures, including Juan Corominas' *Breve diccionario de la lengua castellana* (1961) (characteristically ushered in by a far more voluminous work from his pen), C. T. Onions and his two associates' *Oxford dictionary of English etymology* (1966), Giacomo Devoto's *Avviamento alla etimologia italiana; dizionario etimologico* (1966), no less than to Bruno Migliorini and Aldo Duro's distinctly earlier *Pontuario etimologico della lingua italiana* (1950), the *Dictionnaire étymologique de la langue française* compiled by the 'Larousse team' (H. Dubois and H. Mitterand's 1964 revision of Albert Dauzat's dictionary, traceable to 1938), and to many others, of undeniable value to laymen and advanced workers alike. Only in a small minority of such compact dictionaries, for example, Wilhelm Meye-Lübke's *Romanisches etymologisches Wörterbuch* (1911–20, 1930–35), or in Ernst Gamillscheg's *Etymologisches Wörterbuch der französischen Sprache* (1926–8, rev. 2nd edn 1966–9), or else in Alois Walde's *Lateinisches etymologisches Wörterbuch* (1905–6, 2nd edn 1910; later revised by J. B. Hofmann, 1938–54), are the names of the discoverer (or of a pioneering endorser) of the recommended solution explicitly revealed, the voices of prominent critics, sceptics, and dissenters identified, and the reasons succinctly stated for the author of the given reference work having aligned himself with one school of thought in preference to all others, or having volunteered an entirely new solution. One readily imagines the difference in the treatment of such genetically 'troublesome' French words as *aller*, *avec* (Old French *avuec*), and *trouver* between those two neatly contrastable categories of etymological dictionaries.

The situation is further complicated by the fact that there developed in certain societies (including that of North America) a certain split between the taste and scale of values of 'advanced linguists' and those of the citizens at large. Advanced linguists opted for a highly technical re-arrangement of the science entrusted to their care and, overwhelmingly, placed cogent descriptions of observable facts above inspired reconstructions of events. As a result, the status of diachronic linguistics was pathetically weakened; in particular, the prestige of etymology, including any serious historical study of proper names, was relegated to the very rear, or fringes, of the discipline. Indeed, they came perilously close to being expelled from the grounds of organized scholarship. The reading public at large, however, reacted differently. There continued to make itself felt a strong demand for easily assimilable guides to the origin of both lexical units and proper names, and since that demand could no longer be satisfied from above, as a result of the withdrawal of potential first-rate purveyors of knowledge, the gap was filled by dilettanti, of varying degrees of seriousness.

It is only fair to draw a dividing line between Ernest Klein's unquestionably studious, if perhaps unoriginal *Comprehensive etymological dictionary of the English language* (1966–7) and Joseph T. Shipley's more successful than distinguished writings, including his *Dictionary of word origins* (1945, 2nd edn 1969) and *The origins of English words; a discursive dictionary of Indo-European roots* (1984). It is equally important not to confuse Shipley's level with such exercises in uninhibited entertainment as Charles Earle (alias Tom) Funk's triad: *A hog on ice and other curious expressions* (1948); *Thereby hangs a tale. Stories of curious word origins* (1950); and *Horsefeathers and other curious words* (1958). Also, only a completely humourless observer would be troubled by a successful writer and literature professor, like George R. Stewart occasionally deviating from the straight and narrow path and writing a bestseller like *Names on the land. A historical account of place-naming in the United States* (1945, 1958). What Klein, Shipley, and Funk shared was their disinclination to engage in technical etymological spadework, and Stewart leaned towards the same attitude. No minutely flawless inquiries, in research papers checked, tested, and approved by professionals, accompany these attempts to win approval from a lay readership. And the – not unexpected – consequence of such a hazardous imbalance can be a piece like Funk's Preface (1940) to Reider T. Sherwin's book, whose title alone sounds like a joke: *The Viking and the red man. The Old Norse origin of the Algonquin language*.

One conspicuous difference, then, increasingly visible after 1920, between the monographic exploration of challenging etymological riddles and the brisk manufacturing, on the assembly line, as it were, of etymological dictionaries consists in this: the publication of the former in specialized series, journals, and bulletins remained under the tight control of fellow-scholars, a state of affairs normally carrying with it a guarantee of professionalism. The production of the latter was, in many environments, in the hands of 'free enterprise', and dictionaries of this sort, a lucrative business venture from the start, unfortunately tend to be the more profitable for the publisher the less satisfactory they are on the technical side.

3

The second half of the twentieth century

In the forty-year period surveyed in this concluding section of our venture (1950–1990), etymology can be seen steering a strange course, as if its practitioners and its beneficiaries were sometimes working at cross-purposes; in addition, irreconcilably conflicting ideas all too often prevailed inside each group. There are few exceptions from this trend towards diversification at almost any cost. One rare universal is the fact that a single, particular genre of etymological guide is at present clearly doomed to rapid disappearance (not least for economic reasons), namely the dictionary of word origins in Language X expounded in Language Y (assuming, of course, that both X and Y are major living tongues). The nearly-extinct type of lexicographic compilation here hinted at is exemplified by Max Vasmer's meritorious work on Russian and Ernst Gamillscheg's on French, each phrased in German, in conformity with an old tradition. To be sure, there was published a revised translation into Russian, by O. N. Trubačëv, of the former, and a slightly expanded second edition of the latter made its appearance in the original garb without, it is true, producing any stir outside Central Europe. Yet, the more characteristic course of recent events can be illustrated by the fluctuating fortunes of Walther von Wartburg's incomparably more ambitious and influential venture, which concerns Gallo-Romance lexis as a whole, and more. At the outset the monumental project was undertaken as a venture to be worded in German, and was so continued, when the author moved from Lausanne to Leipzig. Next, the Romanist agreed to produce a concise, single-volume counterpart, in collaboration with a Paris-based colleague, Oscar Bloch – this time, a reference work couched in pleasing French. Finally, the concluding volumes of the original series, issued posthumously by Walther von Wartburg's intellectual heirs, started making their appearance, under the tutelage of

France, and written entirely in French, with a French-trained scholar, J.-P. Chambon, assuming full responsibility for the von Wartburg archive at Basle. This abrupt switch may rank as a shade opportunistic, or as inescapable, or even as tasteless, and the successors of the equally excellent Tobler–Lommatzsch dictionary of Old French, worded in German, have found a sponsor who fortunately allows that undertaking, not entirely etymological in slant, to continue sailing under the old flag. But Max Pfister's etymological dictionary of Italian, and Bodo Müller's of Spanish, both demonstrably launched after 1950, though innovative in few ways, are clearly progressive in this one respect: in the retreat of German from a role which to many has seemed contrary to logic, economics, and nature. Obviously, the situation is wholly different where dead languages, such as Latin, Greek, and Sanskrit, or entire language families (for example, Indo-European) or little-known, or else exotic tongues, like Basque or Breton or Vietnamese, are involved.

The various national communities of scholars' active concern with etymology, measurable along several axes (not always easily compatible), and each readership's, each public's response to the challenge of that discipline after the mid-century point show their own sets of peculiarities. In the Russian sector of the former Soviet Union, for example, a special learned journal, with the unequivocal name *Ètimologija* emblazoned on its cover, has sprung into existence, a state of affairs rich in implications. The earlier record of Italy was distinctly weak, even in regard to that country's own standard language; Robert A. Hall, Jr's 1941 bibliography, for example, lists, apart from a sprinkling of transparently dilettantish experiments, only two noteworthy older florilegia of etymological notes, from the thoroughly respectable pens of Napoleone Caix (1878) and Giovanni Flechia (1876–8), in addition to the indisputably modest, even weak, full-sized etymological dictionaries by Enrico Levi (1914), Ottorino Pianigiani (1907, 2nd edn 1937), and Francesco Zambaldi (1889, 2nd edn 1913). As the gaps between the dates of the respective first and second editions show, the educated public's demand for such book ventures seems to have been mild rather than passionate throughout those decades. But from the middle of our century a radical change in supply and demand becomes clearly perceptible. There appear, to begin with, entirely respectable introductions to the art of etymologizing, first by that seasoned veteran Vittore Pisani (1947, 2nd edn 1967), later by the distinctly younger Alberto Zamboni (1976). Equally if not more important, one observes a real mushrooming of etymological dictionaries, practically every one of them original, interesting, and reliable in its own way. The series stretches from

Bruno Migliorini and Aldo Duro's intelligently selective *Prontuario etimo-logico* (1950), a clear-cut success with lay readers (3rd edn, 1958; 4th edn, 1964), through Carlo Battisti and Giovanni Alessio's somewhat bulky *Dizionario etimologico italiano* (5 vols., 1950–57), D. Olivieri's 1961 edn of a 1953 original, and Giacomo Devoto's *Avviamento alla etimologia italiana* (1966–7), to Manlio Cortelazzo's and Paolo Zolli's superbly researched *Dizionario etimologico della lingua italiana* (5 vols., 1978–88).

The situation in the United Kingdom is by no means easy to describe through a simple formula. In series inherited from earlier periods, such as the venerable *Publications of the Philological Society*, lexicology, in general, and etymology, in particular, have continued to eke out their modest existence unimpaired, balanced by an equal share of attention accorded to word-order as a chapter of historical grammar (for example, D. G. Pattison, 1975) and to other studies diachronically slanted (for example, P. M. Clifford, 1973). In series greatly invigorated after World War II, such as the universally appreciated annual digest *The Year's work in modern language studies*, the critic responsible for each individual language and literature domain, be he an I. González-Llubera, a John N. Green, an S. Ullmann, or a R. Wright, will ordinarily bracket lexicology with etymology in his straightforward report, keeping his private preferences under control. From an encyclopedia (or *Grundriß-*) type of multi-author venture, such as Rebecca Posner's and John N. Green's not so distant four-volume brain-child, *Trends in Romance linguistics and philology* (1980–82), literature had to be excluded by definition and philology was subordinated to linguistics; but one discerns not a trace of a discouraging or condescending attitude towards the study of word-origins, as is obviously also true of Posner's earlier large-scale report, *Thirty years on* (1970; see Iordan, 1937). But the feeling that etymological curiosity and skill represent something definitely old-fashioned, *passé*, a quaint orientation reconcilable, at best, with John Orr's odd scale of values but not with a modernist, progressive view of language research traceable, in the final analysis, to Saussure's *Cours de linguistique générale*, has become visible in the pattern of editorial prefe-rences of deliberate *avant-garde* periodicals such as Britain's impressive *Journal of Linguistics*.

Let us pick, at random, one concrete example presumably illustrative of what was in the air as the third quarter of this century was approaching its end. The second number of Vol. X of the aforementioned tone-setting journal (issued in September 1974) contained a combination of four original papers (two articles and two notes), in addition to a profusion of book reviews of varying size, including a twenty-page 'blockbuster' by an

107

American contributor, Charles J. Fillmore, stationed at Berkeley: a healthy ratio by all means, at first glance. Of the original pieces three dealt with syntax and one with phonology, as might have been fully expected given the trends and events of that well-remembered decade. The critical appraisals busied themselves with book-length publications on a wide range of stimulating and perfectly legitimate topics, including, in alphabetic order: aphasia; cognitive processes; communication and interaction; experimental psychology; inflectional morphology; intonation; literary stylistics; paraphrase grammar; phonetics in linguistics; phonology set in various keys; reference grammar; semantics; sociolinguistics; the speech of primates; stratificational analysis; syntactic theory (besides syntax in generative garb); typological genetic linguistics in a generative framework. The voice of pragmatics alone was apparently still missing in that chorus. But where, amid this wealth of offerings, could one plausibly expect to find a niche, however modest, for etymology, the identificational operation *par excellence*? The last glimmer of hope was the discovery, among the books assessed, of an unassuming anthology compiled by James M. Anderson and Jo Anne Creore. It was titled *Readings in Romance linguistics* and had been issued two years before. Yet, as the by no means hostile reviewer, M. Harris, pointedly remarked, etymology was specifically excluded from the programme of the compilers, 'since to permit . . . adequate coverage would have required considerable increase in space'. Interestingly, of the two co-editors of the journal, sponsored by a newly launched dynamic association of British linguists one, on the strength of his record, was committed to diachronic research.

We shall do well to keep in mind the relevant date as, possibly, the all-time low in the esteem in which a preponderantly youngish crowd of British linguists and of their closest foreign friends held etymological probing. The paradox consists in that the same country, just a decade or so earlier, had wisely patronized, in an Oxonian framework, Thomas Burrow and Murray B. Emeneau's trail-blazing comparative *Dravidian etymological dictionary* (1961, with a battery of significant sequels) and soon thereafter made available the helpful and handy *Oxford dictionary of English etymology* (1966), the work of a trio, namely C. T. Onions, G. W. S. Friedrichsen, and R. W. Burchfield. As a matter of fact, a later experiment planned and supervised by Burchfield alone (1987), shortly before his retirement, leads one to expect further reverberations of that project. Has etymology of late tended to become, in the United Kingdom, a privileged pasturing ground reserved for independent-minded individuals and extra-small teams of mature researchers?

The recent fortunes of etymological inquiries on North American soil have abounded in contradictions, not the smallest of which has been the fact that it has of late been demonstrably feasible to get a major, time-consuming etymological project approved by society (witness James A. Matisoff's *Sino-Tibetan etymological dictionary*, sponsored and staffed by the Berkeley Campus), as against the transparent unavailability of space in front-line journals for monograph-sized articles on the subject. Exoticism, contrary to expectations, also helps; yet, one of the most meritorious (and, one hopes, successful) ventures among the latest crop has been the English-oriented *Barnhart dictionary of etymology* (1988). Repeatedly, one gets the impression that etymologists are bracketed, in the estimation of educated laymen, with straight lexicographers rather than with *bona fide* linguists, a classification which borders on the absurd, because students of word origins, though concerned with lexis in diachronic projection, need not in the least commit themselves to the production of wholesale reference works; also because experts in historical phonology and morphology are helpless without the constant flow of support from the headquarters of practitioners of word-identification.

The confusion whose symptoms we have just exemplified did not arise at the mid-century point; it has much older roots. After the pioneer William D. Whitney had extolled the virtues of etymological insights in almost ecstatic terms (1867, 1875), the long-influential textbooks by Leonard Bloomfield (1914, 1933) and Edward Sapir's series of spellbinding essays (1921) barely mentioned it at all except by implication or incidentally. The paradox within the paradox consists in this: as a rank beginner (1911), Bloomfield, as we have seen moving in the footsteps of his teacher Francis A. Wood (who, of course, never swerved from that traditional path) had indeed made attempts to cultivate etymology for its own sake, but hastened to abandon that sort of inquiry for the sake of more 'scientific' pursuits, whereas Sapir's flickering concern with word biographies (and, inescapably, with word origins) became recrudescent the more he swerved his attention from a long-trodden path of Amerindics towards Semitic and Palaeo-Indo-European. Yet, these finer points eluded the attention of the crowds of New World students whose curiosity about linguistics began to warm up after 1940.

However, these twists do not exhaust the complexity of the situation that has crystallized in the United States, from coast to coast, over approximately the last half-century. Because, while the near-consensus of tastes of American-born explorers went one way, not a few intellectuals among the newcomers were bringing with them to the shores of the Western

Hemisphere a radically different standard of preferences. In the Hittite field, the decision of Jaan Puhvel, an Estonian by birth and early upbringing, to bank on a larger-scale etymological dictionary of Hittite (1984), seems to represent a case in point. In the Romance domain, strong leanings towards unhurried etymological excavations before long became perceptible in the far-flung ensemble of writing by the ménage Henry and Renée Kahane (residents of the USA since 1939, but frequent travellers to Europe), who not so long ago obligingly collected the finest among their scattered writings in three sturdy volumes. The two elements of novelty in the spadework of this exemplary team consisted, first, in the imaginative combination of Greek (including its Byzantine variety) and Oriental (particularly Anatolian Turkish) with Latin-Romance lexical ingredients, and, second, in the exceptionally broad humanistic foundation of their glottological scholarship. While that kind of miscellany doubtless can be scrupulously indexed, it will never amount to a dictionary, perhaps fortunately so. The point is that, on the European continent, the quest after etymological knowledge – as a glance at the Italian scene has taught us before – had not been eroded around 1950; and since some European scholars so preconditioned and later transplanted onto American soil succeeded in recruiting students of indisputable American authenticity, the pendulum, in part, began to swing back.

The hard-core younger Indo-Europeanists, primarily (among them Calvert Watkins at Harvard and Eric P. Hamp at Chicago), and secondarily, a handful of enthusiastic and undaunted comparative Romanists offer, then, a virtual guarantee of continued in-depth etymological inquiries, despite the extra difficulties produced by the necessity to heed the separate testimonies of a steadily increasing aggregation of languages, and by the many obstacles that continue to stand in the way of any unified theory, which, once formulated, might make etymological analysis more fashionable.

Let us take as our concluding instance of a national scenario, as concerns recent or current commitment to etymological investigation at its most advanced, the example of post-war Germany, flanked by other German-speaking countries. Given the exceptionally deep roots that etymological curiosity, for centuries, had struck in Central European soil, no one was surprised to see Manfred Mayrhofer present, as early as 1953–80, a concise etymological Sanskrit dictionary (*Kurzgefaßtes etymologisches Wörterbuch des Altindischen*); nor is it astonishing, in that environment, to see the same scholar at work on a Sanskrit grammar – a duality of commitment traceable to the classic tradition of Jakob Grimm, Franz Bopp, Wilhelm Meyer-Lübke (and, before him, Friedrich Diez), and the like.

Now the existence of a firm tradition offers both advantages and drawbacks. On the positive side of the ledger, one detects the same availability as before of human resources willing and sometimes eager to compile all sorts of etymological dictionaries, vocabularies, glossaries, and mere word-lists. One also detects the same zest and endurance for long-drawn-out spadework, the same degree of will-power and self-effacement required to continue work initiated and programmatically circumscribed by one's predecessors (with this task now, at intervals, assigned to foreign colleagues, as was the case with Winfred P. Lehmann's recent revision of the third and final edition of Sigmund Feist's *Vergleichendes Wörterbuch der gotischen Sprache*), also, the same readiness of private publishers or learned bodies to endorse or sponsor such ventures. Finally, one notes the availability, in high-level journals, such as *Kratylos*, of adequate editorial space for publishing extensive, minutely detailed assessments, some of them concerning a dictionary as a whole, while others are allowed to concentrate, through a microscopic lens as it were, on individual fascicles: witness Klaus Matzel's recent attempt (1989) to devote thirteen pages of mostly small print to Vol. I (*A–Bi*) of Albert L. Lloyd and Otto Springer's *Etymologisches Wörterbuch des Althochdeutschen*, published just the preceding year. With thoroughness, even if it is achieved at the cost of slowness, being the watchword, one is not amazed to see just the first two fascicles of the letter A of Rolf Hiersche's *Deutsches etymologisches Wörterbuch* (1986) converted into objects of independent critical attention. Supporting evidence of continued (as a matter of fact, growing) loyalty to this time-honoured genre of research, which at present preferably sails under the fashionable flag of 'Historische Wortforschung', can be readily supplied on any desirable scale. Suffice it to mention here, entirely at random, the *Etymologie der hethitischen Sprache* (one of several such overlapping projects) initiated by Heinz Kronasser and now successfully concluded by Erich Neu (1962–6, 1987). This project, incidentally, exemplifies the new genre of 'tentative or preliminary etymological dictionary'. As regards the triumph of the label 'Historische Wortforschung', as a cautious substitute for the slightly outworn 'Etymologie', suffice it to cite the case of the 'Brüder-Grimm-Symposion zur historischen Wortschöpfung' (Marburg, 1985), a conference whose fruits were made known by Reiner Hildebrandt and Ulrich Knoop the following year. Alternatively, one is free to speak of 'Studien zum Wortschatz' (for example, Wolfgang Meid, 1987).

One less attractive feature is the continued inability of the (otherwise meritorious) German-language school of etymological probing to draw an incisively sharp line between:

(a) solid etymological work of intended use for fellow-specialists alone, with exhaustive documentation of every single occurrence of the words under study, and with due mention of every previous hint or statement made by earlier analysts; and

(b) equally respectable work divested of such apparatus (and even of any claim to original discovery of minute facts), but imposingly original in its organization and the perspectives that it opens, also endowed with a refreshingly high degree of readability.

Thus, Friedrich Kluge's classic, *Etymologisches Wörterbuch der deutschen Sprache*, which, on the scale of sheer accessibility, used to be compared to the Grimm brothers' masterly collection of folk-tales and to Konrad Duden's guides to correct orthography, has beyond dispute been improved in countless details by its successive revisers, including Walther Mitzka (1967, 1975), but has, in the process, lost much of its original verve and assimilability. Here, a few other countries, including France (due to the energetic revision of Albert Dauzat's pre-war venture by Jean Dubois and Henri Mitterand) and the United States (by virtue of the already mentioned experiment staged by Robert K. Barnhart and his collaborators) seem to have moved ahead of Central Europe.

The individual word study conducive to an etymological restatement (as distinct from a dictionary of word origins) continues to flourish in Central Europe, but is these days seldom engaged in with an *élan* remotely comparable to what one could confidently expect to find before, especially in the 1920–50 period. This recoil from a conceivably excessive vogue looks like a symptom of temporary fatigue or, worse, disappointment and gives the impression of being somehow connected with a nearly simultaneous retreat from three positions, each one until recently blessed with enviable potentialities of brisk and aggressive advance, and all three neatly profiled in Central Europe's tradition of scholarship:

(a) onomasiology (or historical synonymics) planned from the start as exactly the reverse of diachronic semasiology (akin to present-day lexical semantics); its assignment was to concentrate on rival expressions for the same concept – usually a noun in overt preference to any other form class (for example, 'The Designations of 'Uncle' and 'Aunt' in Language X');

(b) Dialect geography practised in a dynamic key, which examined the moves of individual words, or commonly used itineraries, across space and, by implication, time. It specialized in the causes of the extinction of certain doomed words (for example, those damaged by the hazards of erosion or homonymy) and in the rise of suitable substitutes for them, with constant attention to increasingly intricate dialect maps, collected in special atlases; and it stressed selected features of rural life, again with an emphasis on nouns; and

(c)   Concurrent study of lexicology and material civilization, predominantly synchronic but with the ever-present possibility of extension into diachrony. It entailed almost mandatory concentration on the vast repository of nouns (for example, tools and containers), to the near-exclusion of pronouns, adjectives, and, above all, verbs.

Since the more modern currents of linguistic thinking, rightly or wrongly, lean towards a heavy stress on various categories of pronouns and verbs as the classes most rewarding for inquiries into syntax, which currently enjoy such a vogue, there has gradually threatened to develop a divorce, even on German soil, between all guises of modernism and etymological traditionalism, however recherché.

Experience shows that etymology is engaged in most effectively when paired off with some other, collateral interest, a combination which prevents reckless scattering of attention and gives etymological inquiries a more 'structured' appearance. This lesson has by now been learned on either side of the Atlantic. In Germany's 'cultural sphere', the period of space-filling conjectures recklessly assembled, in the quarterlies, under the rubric 'Etymologisches', has definitely – and fortunately – become a thing of the past. The combinations, whether topical or methodical, are not meant to last forever; we have just watched the decline of three of them. More durable has been the alliance of (a) standard etymological operations and (b) inquiries into the rise and spread of proper names, whether anthroponyms and zoonyms or toponyms, oronyms, and hydronyms. As a matter of fact, the borderline between the two domains, where it has been drawn at all, seems entirely artificial. Consequently, high-level studies in proper names, more characteristic of the academic environment of Germany than of other countries, have continued to make their appearance and have preserved their relevance to etymological practice and theory. (Cf. Wilhelm Eilers' 100-page study of the Near Eastern oronym *Demawend* (1988) and the literature cited in the somewhat older collection of Ramón Menéndez Pidal's Hispanic toponymic investigations (1952); or, on a monumental scale, Manfred Mayrhofer's and Rüdiger Schmitt's multi-volume *Iranisches Personennamenbuch* (Vol. IV, by M. Alram, 1986).)

Another increasingly close connection has developed between word- and name-history, on the one hand, and, on the other, the history of settlements

(*Siedlungsgeschichte*). The hazard here lies in the possibility of political overtones and even of hidden claims when the author belongs to one of the participants in a territorial conflict. The risk, of course, lends itself to tight control: there may be some wisdom in subordinating these kinds of reports on contact-through-conflict to the general history of lexical diffusion, also known by its older labels as 'loans' and 'borrowings'. Such analyses offer the perfect backgrounds or starting points for etymological investigations, and German scholarship has acted wisely in refusing to abandon them. A major step forward taken of late has been the selection of maritime zones as focal areas for such purposes as the analysis of lexical infiltration, witness T. Hofstra's study (1985), characteristic in this respect, of protracted contacts between Finnish and German in the Eastern Baltic.

Having so far observed a string of clashes and contradictions in the latest zigzag course followed by advanced etymology in several countries, we would almost be disappointed to discover nothing of the sort in one of the homelands of the discipline at issue, namely Germany. And, sure enough, there has of late crystallized a new and hazardous genre, which it seems safe to dub 'etymological counterdictionary' (Malkiel, 1986, used greater restraint in mentioning an 'aberrant style of etymological research'). The spokesman for it has been Harri Meier, no youngster at that stage, and he has managed to recruit a whole crew of inexperienced followers.

The prototype of this novel genre was harmless enough. Important etymologica, abounding in fresh data, new techniques, and illuminating solutions of age-old 'riddles', have for a long time tended to provoke unrealistically lengthy critiques, sometimes followed by authors' rebuttals. Thus, in the Romance domain, Gustav Körting's uninspired compilation (1891, 1901, 1907) received far closer attention, especially in Italy, than it actually deserved. The thing to do, for a book reviewer who is both imaginative and judicious, is to vindicate his opinion by examining under a powerful lens a randomly selected slice of, let us say, ten or, at most, twenty pages of the book under scrutiny. Seventy years or so ago, some over-zealous critics started to exceed such a reasonable quota by a frighteningly wide margin. Among Hispanists alone, the original edition (1911–1920) of Wilhelm Meyer-Lübke's pan-Romanic dictionary produced a single superb review article from the pen of Ramón Menéndez Pidal, a slightly overextended sequence of instalments of Américo Castro's interesting comments (still a journal article in the aggregate); and Vicente García de Diego's book-length running commentary. The last-mentioned critic's excuse (had he been called to order) might have been that his 200-page book, basically, was an enfilade of factual addenda, elaborations, and corrigenda extracted from a storehouse of peninsular dialectal data which he had patiently accumulated over the years, without actually proposing many entirely new solutions. The next act of the comedy was an experiment staged by Leo Spitzer, a many-sided Austrian scholar and critic, who had meanwhile been transplanted to Baltimore. Américo Castro's philological edition (1936), spiced with crisp etymological remarks, of three late fourteenth-century Latin–Aragonese glossaries, was subjected to line-by-line scrutiny in several consecutive volumes of an overseas journal. Spitzer was so sophisticated and many-sided, and knew so much about ancient, medieval, and modern languages that the reader was willing to go along with his invariably witty (and sometimes persuasive) counter-proposals. Riding this vogue of success, Spitzer, almost a decade later, repeated the trick apropos of Juan Corominas' original etymological dictionary of Spanish, in four volumes (1954–7).

Again, one was inclined to forgive Spitzer his eccentricity in haphazardly ventilating a great many etymological conjectures by way of mere 'Geistesblitze', without any independent laborious collection of raw data or of earlier hypotheses (Corominas' museum, although well-equipped with such information, was obviously far from complete). Eventally Meier, lacking any excuse for this bizarre *modus operandi*, applied such objectionable methods to the book-length sifting, in excess of 200-pages long (1984), of the Corominas-Pascual venture, an expansion of the earlier dictionary by the former writer alone, aimed to occupy a total of six volumes. Meier offers the barest minimum of arbitrarily chosen fresh data; unfortunately, his book bristles with new (and, almost invariably, untenable) 'Einfälle'. The sceptical reader gains the painful impression that a detour has here been tried out. While hesitant to fall back directly on a Körting-level degree of superficiality, one of our contemporaries has cleverly circumvented the difficulty by giving free rein to his roaming imagination via the cloak of counter-proposals nonchalantly tossed off, and ranging from *A* to *Z*.

The widely discrepant records of recent commitments to etymology elsewhere could easily be discussed in comparable detail, no doubt at the risk of some monotony. But, in all likelihood, there exist equally noteworthy dividing lines among traditions, not necessarily drawn along the borders that happen to separate national cultures. Thus, in the English-speaking community of scholars it has become customary to include derivational and even inflectional morphemes among the entries, on a par with the bulk of lexemes taken into account. The *Barnhart dictionary of etymology*, for example, makes a point of discussing, under the entries *en-* and *-en*: (a) a weakly perceptible prefix *en-* (variant *an-*) inherited from Old French, as in *enchant, anoint*, making some allowance for its intensive function in *enclose, enfold* (var. *in-*); (b) a weakly detachable prefix *en-*, of hazy connotation, found in Hellenisms, as in *endemic, energy, enthusiasm*; (c) a suffix, of Germanic provenance, serving to extract verbs from adjectives and nouns, as in *black-en, flat(t)-en, soft-en*; (d) a suffix, often obsolescent, of the same origin, forming adjectives from nouns, as in *ash-en, wood-en*; (e) a suffix that qualifies for coining past participles, for example, *brok-en, fall-en*; and (f) an element residually used in the formation of certain plurals, as in *brethr-en, ox-en*, and, through conflation with a *-re* plural, *child-r-en*.

The somewhat older *Oxford dictionary of English etymology*, overwhelms its reader with, fundamentally, the same kind of information, except that it dwells far more on Old English and Middle English usages and spreads out richer collections of examples. Also, it mentions the seventh use of the same morpheme of which a single trace has survived into contemporary English (*vix-en*), namely the use of *-en* to mint feminine from masculine nouns, as anciently *gyden* 'goddess' from *god*, including such abstracts as *hæften* 'custody' or *ræden* 'arrangement'.

The editors responsible for the second (revised) edition of the unabridged *Random House dictionary* seem to be in agreement in principle, except that their favoured pattern of functional segmentation comprises five categories, including diminutive *-en*, as in *kitt-en, maid-en*.

Now, this tradition turns out to be almost totally alien to Romance scholarship, whatever the environment in which it is being practised. True, Wilhelm Meyer-Lübke, in both versions of his comparative dictionary (1911–20, 1930–35), still presented a short separate entry *re-* (§ 7102), chiefly because stray attempts had been made, in certain daughter languages of Latin, to grant a measure of autonomy to that erstwhile prefix. Ernst Gamillscheg, as a student and loyal follower of Meyer-Lübke, agreed, in his etymological dictionary of French (1926–8, 1966–9), to list separately *dé-* and *re-*, i.e., characteristic prefixes; but he excluded the *-ons* of *av-ons* and the *-u* of both *ten-u* and *touff-u*, i.e., suffixes of all sorts inflectional and derivational. Juan Corominas, in his counterpart for Spanish (1954–7), went one step farther and altogether discarded *re-*, making an ill-advised leap all the way from *razzia* to *reacio*. True, most Romance prefixes also function as adverbs or prepositions and thus do come up elsewhere for incidental mention; but this advantageous status stops short of applying to most, if not all, suffixes. The answer to the threat of a lacuna is then, apparently, the insertion of a diachronically slanted concise treatise on derivation in the total edifice of the given dictionary venture, along the lines tried out by the nineteenth-century Hispanist Pedro Felipe Monlau, whose etymologicum was repeatedly re-issued in Argentina half a century ago (1941, etc.).

In reaching their perfectly defensible decision the Romance scholars were no doubt merely following in the footsteps of Diez (and, in the last analysis, those of Grimm); but they were inexplicit in justifying their position, which amounted to bracketing all details of word-formation with historical grammar (specifically, with morphology) rather than with straight lexis, and became lax about explicating any underlying theoretical considerations. Thus, Joseph M. Piel, when invited to revise and bring up to date his teacher Meyer-Lübke's *Wortbildungslehre* (1921), excellent for its time, confined himself to appending a long series of minor details (1954), a policy which explains, at least in part, the cool, not to say hostile, reception of his efforts by disillusioned younger critics. An otherwise experienced and well-informed Gerhard Rohlfs, this time apparently undecided as to where to insert his discussion of Italo-Romance prefixes and suffixes, finally appended it to his analysis of syntax in the concluding volume (1954) of his otherwise well-structured *Historische Grammatik der italienischen Sprache und ihrer Mundarten*. Max Leopold Wagner, with his thinking conceivably riveted to his forthcoming etymological dictionary of Sardic, then in an advanced stage of preparation (it was to appear posthumously, in three volumes, 1957–64), produced, in 1952, a hastily written *Historische Wortbildungslehre* of that same language, which he knew so well, a manual that contributed little to grammatical insights, but, at least, neatly segregated borrowings from the native stock of insular words and not infrequently inventoried up to fifty or sixty derivatives involving a single suffix, i.e., confused lexical with grammatical information. Henry and Renée Kahane, after straddling etymology and suffixation as late as 1948–9, thereafter wisely decided to concentrate on the former.

More thought-provoking, perhaps, than any further elaboration on the subject of blurred dividing lines between subdisciplines is likely to be a quick look at a gradually arising new variety of etymological inquiry, characteristic of the academic microcosm after the two World Wars: to wit, the extension of etymological curiosity to neologisms rather than to ancient lexical deposits. Conceivably by the time a side-effect of the general recession, after c.1920, of traditional excitement about the classics, the long mandatory study of secondary level of Latin and Greek – *qua* languages and *qua* carriers of a peerless cultural heritage – began to sink on both sides of the Atlantic, this shift had a dire effect on the mainstream of historical linguistics, i.e., of the discipline to which etymology was an ancillary. While being itself a university-level subject of study and research, that speciality was nevertheless geared to its devotees' preliminary familiarity with Latin and Greek as the two mutually complementary pillars of our grasp of Antiquity. Ironically, while fewer enthusiasts could thus afford to warm to the prospect of future careers as classicists, as Indo-Europeanists, or even as palaeo-Romanists, the respective programmes of advanced study were becoming more and more complicated, through the ceaseless discovery of new languages and dialects.

In such a climate of opinion and preference, the prospects for continuity and improvement were few and slim indeed; and it took a 'desperado' like the German–Swiss investigator Johannes Hubschmid, in the 1940–60 period, to declare, or insinuate, out of sheer stubbornness, as it were, that he, a versatile Romance etymologist by training and initial inclination, found the building of lexical bridges from medieval and modern dialect speech, such as Gascon or Sardic, to Latin insufficiently fascinating for his spadework and the interpretations based thereupon. Apparently, for a Romance word to whet his appetite, he expected to recognize, however dimly, at the other end of the lexical corridor some pre-Latin (for example, Celtic) or, better still, some downright pre-Indo-European (for example, Iberian) base – despite the disproportionate size of the hazards taken in such identificational exercises across millenia (and, in addition, over distances of thousands of miles). Witness the eloquent titles, here mercifully abridged, of such characteristic studies from his pen, inquiries extending from 1949 to 1960, as: *Praeromanica. Studien zum vorromanischen Wortschatz der Romania* (focusing on the Franco-Provençal and Occitan dialects of the Western Alps); *Alpenwörter romanischen und vorromanischen Ursprungs* (i.e., Alpine words either of Romance or of substratal stock), 1951; *Sardische Studien. Das mediterrane Substrat des Sardischen* (certain pre-Romance, 'Mediterranean' ingredients of Sardic are here connected with Berber, Basque, Eurafrican, and Hispano-Basque), 1953; *Schläuche und Fässer* (the lines of lexical borrowing here stretch from Anatolian Turkish to European and from Turkish-Caucasian to Iranian), 1955; *Mediterrane Substrate* (with special consideration of Basque and of West–Eastern lexical connections), 1960. Clearly, in this kind of exploration etymological curiosity and intuition reign supreme, since there remains virtually nothing else to look into. But at what price in loss of realism has this aim been achieved!

If Hubschmid's *œuvre*, which apparently came to a virtual standstill a quarter of a century ago, represents in its exaggerations a sort of overreaction to the general retreat from antiquarianism, as it had flourished before 1914, the new developments, luckily and somewhat unexpectedly, offered realistic alternatives to any exclusive infatuation with but hazily recognizable prehistoric languages. When the new-style genre of linguistics journals, divorced from earlier concentration on Antiquity, sprang into existence, designed to capture the attention of the modern-language teacher at college level, one could have expected their respective editors, contributors, and reader-subscribers to have attempted to rid themselves of any ties to 'old-fashioned' etymology, concentrating instead on phonetics, stylistics, and the like. This holds for *Die neueren Sprachen* in Germany (1893–1943, and 1952–); for *Moderna Språk* in Sweden (1906–); for *American Speech* in the USA (1925–); for *Le français moderne* in France (1933–); for *Lingua nostra* in Italy (1939–); and no doubt for numerous other similar journals.

What actually happened, however, was something entirely different and not readily foreseeable. The founding editors of the aforementioned journals (and of several others, sloped in the same direction) – Albert Dauzat in the case of *Le français moderne*, Bruno Migliorini in the context of *Lingua nostra* – were erudite but flexible persons, thoroughly trained in the ways of traditional etymologizing (witness their respective etymological dictionaries), but unconventional enough to turn their eyes and ears to alternative possibilities, more in tune with the post-war *Zeitgeist*. Instead of, unimaginatively, declaring etymology antiquated, as has indeed been done of late in certain opportunistic quarters on either side of the Atlantic, they leaned towards encouraging something truly new: the application of the old technique and method to the large reservoir, for the most part left untapped, of currently observable neologisms. These, to be sure, included some linguistically noteworthy scientific terms pieced together by scientists from the nearly inexhaustible resources of authentic Greek and Latin. Understandably, much heavier emphasis was placed, however, on new, 'colourful' slangy words which were gradually seeping through from some directions that remained to be ascertained. As a rule, their arrival on the scene could easily be dated with the help of newspapers, announcements, radio broadcasts, television messages, tapes, gossip columns in newspapers, informally overheard conversations, performances of (musical) comedies and farces, and the like. There certainly was no dearth of primary sources. Lists of colloquial 'mistakes' deserving to be weeded out, compiled by purists or pedants with an entirely different aim in view, also provided excellent fuel for the neo-etymologists.

It almost goes without saying that enterprising editors of new-style journals (and contributors whom they managed to recruit) were not the only priests of the spreading cult. Certain freewheeling scholars, endowed with special aptitudes for this kind of data-gathering and analysis, readily chimed in. One example was the Frenchman Pierre Guiraud (of the University of Nice), distinctly better-known through his many-pronged corpus of publications than through the limited fruits of his teaching. Migliorini, on the other hand, had a deservedly strong following. He derived added strength from occupying a chair at Florence not of 'glottologia' (an appointment that might have enticed him to divide his time and energy between Indo-European and comparative Romance), but of 'Storia della lingua italiana' – an appointment (the first in this subject) that literally invited a division of his leisure time into more conventional and more innovative approaches.

The point of the entire movement was that it could, minimally, aspire to satisfy the 'etymological hunger' of educated and sophisticated, but unspecialized readers (lawyers, doctors, college teachers, enlightened businessmen, tourists, for example), i.e., persons who could never be prevailed upon to delve into, let us say, Hieroglyphic or Cuneiform Hittite, or into Tocharian B, by giving them a chance to familiarize themselves with exactly how the tracing of individual words to their origins works. As the potential maximum yield one could single out the analyst's confidence that, at least, a few younger readers thus stimulated could eventually be persuaded to turn their attention to the serious, professional practice of etymology.

Scattered traces of such thinking are visible in the sporadic attempts made, in good taste, by present-day weeklies and monthlies of wide appeal to reserve a page or two of each issue for exercises in 'neo-etymology', couched in an easily assimilable, non-technical, but nevertheless tasteful style. Even the keyword 'etymology' is then, as a rule, avoided, as being possibly conducive to, or redolent of, undesirable pedantry. The column or page in question can, for example, be discreetly titled 'Among the new words'. One remarkable experiment along this line has, for example, been imaginatively conducted in the United States by the nationally esteemed *Atlantic Monthly*, a very establishmentarian periodical normally far removed from the *avant-garde*.

Let us see how the scholars here somewhat arbitrarily brought together actually operate to arouse their readers' dormant curiosity. The *Atlantic*'s shrewd expert Craig M. Carter knows how to cut a path with a well-honed knife through the jungle of studies engaged in by serious linguists, but forgets not for one moment that he has agreed to address and enlighten a huge crowd of non-professionals – ideally, all the habitual readers of the well-established monthly (presumably in the neighbourhood of half a million adults), practically all of them laymen so far as technicalities of linguistic analysis are concerned. Therefore he basically offers them a bit of entertainment rather than a dull sermon or a cogent demonstration.

Being in charge of 'word history', as the concluding section of a typical 180-page large-format issue of The *Atlantic* is titled, he will dutifully acknowledge a single source via the habitual obligatory subtitle: 'Etymologies derived from the files of the *Dictionary of American regional English*' (a respected venture still in process of publication). Other sources likely to have been consulted are, as a matter of policy, never identified, even though upon occasion one finds hints of divided opinions, splits which testify to Carter's having, at least, tried to rummage around for some conclusive explanation.

The three-column page offers just sufficient space for ventilating three or four usually disconnected lexical issues, if one takes into account that same number of accompanying pictures (not, or not yet, cartoons). A graphic illustration, in this context, dwells not on the crucial stage of the development envisaged, but on some recent phase that one can safely expect to titillate the average American subscriber's thirst for knowledge via amusement. Thus, the November 1990 issue concerns itself with (*inter alia*) *bonanza*, as applied, chiefly in present-day Nevada, to a rewarding kind of farming cleverly suggested by the illustration adjoined. Every imaginable effort has been made not to fatigue the potential reader (or, for that matter, the typesetter): Greek *malakós* 'soft', *malakía* 'softness' (i.e., the ultimate sources) appear in Latin script, without the requisite accent marks; **bonakía*, the hypothesized counterpart of *malakía*, is relieved of its asterisk, which would have overtly marked it as a reconstruction; while the label 'euphemistic' is withheld from the substitution of *bon-* for *mal-*, after the latter's witty reinterpretation as a member of the *malus* family. Not a single word is wasted on the replacement of the (semantically empty) terminal segment *-akia* by the fully-fledged suffix *-antia*, although there happens to be in existence a book-sized monograph of the twin suffixes *-antia* and *-(i)entia*, written in English and published by a California university press over forty-five years ago. The pivotal stress shift does not come up for mention. In sum, these sacrifices are indeed heavy, but apparently are deemed sufficient to provide in the reader's mouth for the expected salivation. Hence the urgent need for some 'kick-off' statements, such as the anecdotal opening remark that there at present exists a television series so named, or, equally sensational, that a US senator recently called one provision of the 1990 Civil Rights Act a 'lawyer's *bonanza*'.

Far more complicated is the history of the phrase (*to be*) *snarky*, which in Britain is tantamount to 'to be irritable, short-tempered' and in the United States rivals '(to be) elegantly stylish'. Part of the difficulty resides in homonymy or near-homonymy. Ultramodern American English *narc* 'narcotics officer' must be kept out of the family tree, while the name of the

121

imaginary animal *snark* (Lewis Carroll) turns out to be a portmanteau word formed from superposition of *snake* on *shark*. Carter brushes off any possibility of influence from that direction, although he is not above toying with the off-chance of some mild lateral pressure from *nark* 'unpleasant, quarrelsome person', (British slang) *narky* 'ill-tempered, irascible', originally 'informer'. Fundamentally (so he reports), *snarky* belongs with *to snark* 'to snore, snort', a sound-imitative verb of Germanic ancestry with cognates in Scandinavian and German. With so many admitted uncertainties besieging us, why bother to introduce the unwary readers to such a stumbling-block without, in the process, wasting a single word on the habitual expressive or phonosymbolic dimension of the word-initial consonant cluster *sn-*? The motivation or relevance of the choice has not been withheld. Jim Henson (a locally famous entertainer) reportedly once said of his best-known Muppet, Kermit the Frog: 'He's a little *snarkier* than I am'.

These two examples suffice to provide an illustration of what middlebrow (actually low-brow) etymologizing can amount to. Alas, one discovers an even less appetizing variety on the entertainment page of one's neighbourhood daily newspaper. Here, even any harmless façade of professionalism becomes totally invisible. Thus, on the back page of a typical issue of the *Oakland Tribune* (to be sure, not the equal of the *New York Times*), etymological riddles are inconsiderately squeezed in as an ingredient of a tasteless pot-pourri of comics, horoscopes, crossword puzzles, announcements of television programmes, cryptoquotes, questions and answers on bridge-playing, horse sense columns (a pastime at which a player can score a number of points for correct answers to assorted 'silly' questions), and similar amusements (intellectually unrewarding as a rule, if not downright banal). Platitudinous cartoons and, in the their sequel, colourless public notices are occasionally allowed to appear on the same newspaper pages.

At the opposite end of the scale of possibilities characteristic of the New World's present-day *mores* one discovers, in an early-1989 issue of *American Speech*, John and Adele Algeo's truly high-standard piece, 'Among the New Words'. And, if one is eager to advance one step farther in the direction of serious, organized scholarship with an etymological tinge, one can indeed find representative specimens of such work in a 1988 issue of a strictly philological periodical, namely the University of Georgia's *Journal of English Linguistics*, as when Mary E. Clark and Brian D. Joseph try to vindicate the (controversial) derivation of English *bum* 'buttocks' from *bottom* by assuming its migration from child language into adult speech by combining historical evidence with direct observation of their own two-year-old son David's baby-talk.

It is correct and feasible, then, to amalgamate one's separate impressions of the layers of the present-day American scene into a single composite picture. That projection ranges from (1) the truly serious attitude of a chosen few interpreters towards their assignment, involving lexemes that are (a) either fairly new (but long left unrecorded) or were (b) actually introduced not all that long ago, through (2) semi-scholarly analysis misleadingly disguised as sheer entertainment to (3) completely, almost cynically trivialized treatment, pretending that a playful attitude is called for in coming to grips with such problems.

A palpably different climate of opinion has, until recently, at least, prevailed in France where, side by side with unimpeachably conducted experiments traceable to the historicist legacy of Antoine Meillet and his school, there also developed a heterodox school of thought ordinarily associated with the name of Pierre Guiraud (1912–83). If one agrees to call Guiraud's fierce independence of mind, combined with a phenomenal capacity for hard work, his obverse side, then a certain capriciousness and arbitrariness in matters academic and no doubt personal constituted the corresponding reverse. He rapidly developed into a loner, was prevented from making, in Paris, a career commensurate with his talent and promise, and had to content himself with thirty years or so of teaching at the University of Nice, i.e., at a considerable, not to say prohibitive or punitive, distance from the crucially-important capital. (An erratic attempt he made in 1952 to establish himself in the Netherlands, at the University of Groningen, seems not to have led him very far, either.) With few avid or demanding students knocking at his door, he had plenty (perhaps an excess) of leisure, which he used to produce a frightening number of textbooks, not all of them of uniformly impeccable quality. In the end, his slim introduction to Old French (1967), ironically enough, gained by being revised by a younger, but more rigorous scholar, G. Zink. But his etymological inquiries turned out to be truly interesting and original, not only topically but also by virtue of their methodological heterodoxy. He fell short, I repeat, of assembling any school of sympathizers or followers. Recognition came late – at first, surprisingly, from England (witness the four pages that Rebecca Posner, in 1970, reserved for an appreciation of his 'new and fascinating insights into language dynamics' in her report *Thirty years on*, that well-remembered supplement to Iordan–Orr's *Introduction to Romance linguistics*). He received no testimonial volume except posthumously (1985), and its editors, C. P. Bouton, E. Brunel, and L.-J. Calvet, were little known outside the precincts of Nice. Nevertheless, there could be no doubt that he became a major experimentalist after 1967, the publication date of his *Structures étymologiques du lexique français* (a second edition was arranged for by Paul Robert's associate Alain Rey in 1986). There followed his possibly weightiest and most ambitious venture, the *Dictionnaire érotique* (1978), which has completely replaced Auguste Scheler's earlier venture issued under an assumed name. Finally, the *Dictionnaire des étymologies obscures* (1982) rounded off his attempts to tread this risky and treacherous ground, except that the most memorable contribution to the aforecited *Hommage* (1985) is rumoured to have been Guiraud's posthumous 'inédit': 'Encore des étymologies obscures', ten concentrated pages devoted to the vicissitudes of twenty-one words with initial '*h* aspiré'.

One cannot measure Guiraud's performance as etymologist by the same yardstick that is commonly applied to the accomplishments of a Wilhelm Meyer-Lübke or a Walther von Wartburg, not to mention, in the ranks of Indo-Europeanists, such practitioners as Alois Walde and Johann Baptist Hofmann. Of the more than forty books that he wrote, rarely if ever in collaboration with others, not one deals, programmatically, with a language (living or dead) other than French, or even with French envisioned in some thought-provoking combination with other languages, even though foreign tongues, to be sure, may constitute unobtrusive parts of the background material, as indeed they inescapably must in a venture slanted in the direction of *Les mots étrangers* (1965). Other doubts arise as one discovers, in scanning Guiraud's imposing bibliography, his uncanny skill in dashing off, in breathtakingly rapid succession, one book-length synthesis after another, in a rather disorientating sequence: at first, a pamphlet on the sources of the rhyme (1952); next, somewhat longer treatises on stylistics (1954) and on the statistical method applied to the study of languages (that same year, and a return performance in 1959); then, slender books on semantics (1955; rebaptized 'semiology' twenty years later); on grammar and on the learned vocabulary (both in 1958, despite the wide disparity of the two topics); finally, on syntax (1962), on Old French and on Middle French (the following year: two separate, parallel ventures), and on versification (1970). Almost inevitably, a bystander's initial impression is that of a chain of *travaux de vulgarisation*, some of them admittedly successful as publishing ventures (as had been, before Guiraud, certain books by Albert Dauzat, written agreeably enough for a public of laymen and neophytes). But while this series of books and booklets, and Guiraud's involvement in some other side-issues, e.g., in the lexical corpus of certain writers, did little to consolidate his reputation among serious specialists, certain other books from his pen, step by step, circumscribed his more sharply silhouetted bent, indeed, talent, for straight etymological inquiries. His eventual penchant for 'etymologies obscures' and his inquiries into the provenance and vicissitudes of racy, scurrilous, or erotic words were adumbrated by his sole authorship of writings such as *L'argot* (1956), *Les locutions françaises* (1961), *L'étymologie* (1964), and, in 1968, *Patois et dialectes français*, side by side with *Le jargon de Villon ou le gai savoir de la Coquille*. The more resolutely Guiraud decided to veer away from his earlier concern with the vocabularies of, for example, Corneille, Racine, and Valéry (a preoccupation highly characteristic of the 1950s), the more daringly he could plunge into the exploration of murky etymologies, almost in the wake of an earlier nonconformist, namely Lazare Sainéan.

Sound symbolism, starting with the speculations of the ancients (especially Plato), was destined to play a major role in Guiraud's thinking, and he felt more at ease, upon his own admission, with contemporary theorists and practitioners (like O. Jespersen, R. Jakobson, and Émile Benveniste) who had made generous allowances for it, than with certain disciplinarians who were narrow-minded enough to question its agency or to leave it unmentioned. Guiraud, flexibly enough, stood prepared to operate with multiple causation: a given form, he felt, could represent a compromise of sorts between some other processes, better studied but all too often marginalized (a blend, a suffixal derivation, a borrowing, to cite three disparate possibilities), on the one hand, and, on the other, onomatopoeic orchestration. (From the dialect geographers he inherited a certain predilection for small-sized 'interpreted' maps.) Thus, in his *Structures étymologiques* he assembled 180 clusters of Modern French words (all in all, over 400 lexemes) presided over, as it were, by a *T-K*, or, better still, a *T-R-K* skeleton, an assertion which did not exclude the high probability that most of them boasted normally shaped ancestral forms traceable to neatly individuated etyma. But the *T-(R-)K* feature came close to acting as a sort of common denominator, as a shared dominant peculiarity, and must not be rashly eliminated from consideration when the analyst trains his lens on an ensemble that comprises items extracted from heterogeneous, not to say haphazardly arranged, sources, such as standard dictionaries, *argot* glossaries, dialect vocabularies, maps torn from linguistic atlases, Old French, Old Provençal, and Modern Occitan data collections. Interconnecting, then, lexemes extracted from disparate sources, and likely to exhibit a variety of meanings which are at first glance difficult of reconciliation (*tac*, *taque*, *taquer*, *attaque*, *attaquer*, *taquée*, *taquoir*, *taqu-et* [*-ette*], *taquot*, etc.), Guiraud, all obstacles notwithstanding, believed to have recognized certain common denominators: 'Le protosémantisme', he remarked, 'l'idée initiale qui supporte l'ensemble, est celle de 'frapper', sous les alternances *taquer*, *tiquer*, *toquer*. (*Structures*, p. 74.)

Guiraud himself classified the case of *T-K* as one of two instances of onomatopoeic structures that had come to his attention, the other being one of 'labialized roots', which also presupposed, as its main pivot, a pattern of biliteralism, *B.B.-*, *P.P.-*, *F.F.-*, *B.F.-*, *P.F.-*, with nasalization of one or, less frequently, two of the vowels involved, representing the counterpart of the aforementioned infixation of the *R* into the *T-K* architecture; specifically, BOB- either directly or obliquely suggests or, at least, connotes a show of 'arrogance, presumption, display, overbearing manner'.

In an effort to launch what he called 'structural etymology' and to mark off several 'morphosemantic fields', at least in his native French, Guiraud, by the time he reached maturity of age and experience, transcended the domain of onomatopoeia, examining such processes as tautological and advocative compounding as two examples of morphological structures. He also examined: the naming of spotted (furs of) animals and correspondingly chequered (plumages of) birds, in addition to arrays of zoomorphic metaphors, as so many illustrations of semantic structures; pseudo-suffixal derivation and onomastic metonymy as instances of paronymic structures; the aforementioned morphosemantic fields (for example, analyses of the colloquial verb *chiquer*, of the French designations of the 'cat as a pet', and collisions of homonyms, a classic), as well as certain 'semic structures' (for example, folk taxonomy: the leap from phytonym to zoonym) as topics inviting heightened attention. The book culminated in a concluding 22-page chapter, theoretically nuanced, which epitomized salient problems and methods of structural etymology. The limited attention the author was lending to medieval forms, as he himself may have realized, obviated any need for systematic appealing to the comparative method on a generous scale.

The author was well aware of the modernity of his stance, as defined, after some zigzagging, a quarter of a century ago, and stressed this modernist attitude through unhesitating (excessive?) use of a plethora of newly minted technical tags. He was also conscious of the fashionable predilection of certain contemporaries for well-defined areas of meaning, such as chromonyms and kinship terms, but hastened to declare such favouritism incompatible with the tenets of any truly even-handed structuralist philosophy. He admitted the affinity of his own thinking to experiments conducted by ten other younger would-be innovators, but found their new semantics too strongly modelled on the pre-existent pattern of newly-emerging phonology. Conversely, his prime intention, he averred in the Introduction to his 1967 synthesis, had been to balance semantics against morphology in synchrony and diachrony alike, throughout the mutually overlapping domains of lexical and etymological probings.

In a critical vein, one is free to observe that Guiraud was attracted not only to genuine neologisms, but to many words which had reached a level of prominence over the last three or four centuries. He was a good listener and an assiduous reader endowed with a splendid memory; dispassionate interviewing, in a social-science framework, was of lesser appeal to him. He enjoyed wading through the by-ways of lexis, picking lexemes from the gallant writings of certain eighteenth-century authors, thus stumbling over taboo words and over lame, more or less ephemeral replacements for them. His self-immersion in 'obscure' etymologies therefore amounted, in part, to inquiries into spontaneously or artificially 'obscured' word histories. He attempted, probably in vain, to reconcile his infatuation with modernism with a strong aversion to the Saussurian belief in the arbitrariness of the linguistic sign.

Bruno Migliorini's long commitment to the cause of etymology in a few respects resembled Guiraud's extended advocacy and in many ways differed radically from it, starting with the fact that from his early thirties almost until his very late seventies Migliorini (1896–1975) was consistently a very successful man in matters academic. Of direct relevance to his eventual espousal of the cause of etymology after some false starts (for example, his concern with artificial languages) were the topic and the slant of his first major publication (1927), which aroused immediate attention in several quarters, not only inside Italy: *Dal nome proprio al nome comune*. By observing, within the total range of Romance languages and dialects of all periods, recurrent shifts from proper names to common nouns, the author of the c.300-page monograph at once established himself as an anthroponymist, an etymologist, and a versatile student of lexical semantics, all three applied in diachronic perspective, not to mention the seductively pleasing tone of any disagreements with certain predecessors, a level of tone which clashed with the bitter sarcasm characteristic – precisely in those years – of not a few contemporaries (Ernst Gamillscheg, Josef Brüch, Leo Spitzer, to cite just three names) similarly excited by etymological unknowns.

But that was merely the start (except that the author made a point of reverting to the subject-matter attacked and the approach practised in a lengthy supplement included in a generously revised and expanded second edition, 1968). Fifteen years later, in polishing to a fine sheen the eighth edition of Alfredo Panzini's *Dizionario moderno delle parole che non si trovano nei dizionari comuni*, Migliorini found a splendid opportunity for concerning himself (in collaboration with A. Schiaffini) with the ensemble of foreignisms and neologisms. Interestingly, in 1963 he had a chance to reissue as a separate book distributed by the publishing firm his listing of 12,000 newly coined (or newly introduced) words.

The year 1945 gave Migliorini one more fillip for strengthening his etymological prowess, this time from the side of dialect research. With some help from Ulderico Rolandi, he rejuvenated, in launching its second edition, the *Vocabolario romanesco* by Filippo Chiappini (1836–1905). Shortly thereafter (1947) he made an experiment with instilling new strength into the inescapably etymological bent of the treatise *Della fortuna delle parole, libri due*, by the pioneer Giuseppe Manno (1786–1868). The time had now arrived to join forces with a younger colleague, to be specific, with Aldo Duro, in issuing a sort of preliminary or cursory etymological vocabulary of Italian, one that provided answers to queries but lacked discussions. That venture was crowned with major success, not least among laymen, on account of the authors' commonsensical attitude and the refreshing simplicity of their presentation: *Prontuario etimologico della lingua italiana* (1950; 4th edn, 1964).

Common to all of these meritorious undertakings, differently slanted as they were, was an ineradicable element of fragmentation; the author regaled his readers with albums of polished, sophisticated miniatures or vignettes. In the masterpiece of his mature age, *Storia della lingua italiana* (1960; 3rd edn, 1961), Migliorini examined unhurriedly – and, for a change, entirely on his own – layer after chronological layer of the entire growth of the edifice of Standard Italian, the same way as Ferdinand Brunot and his successor Charles Bruneau had narrated the history of French and Rafael Lapesa had pieced together the chronicle of Spanish (but with less attention to minute details than the former 'team', yet somewhat more specifically than the latter investigator, at least in the earlier versions of his venture). Migliorini's book, translated into, at least, two world languages, embedded scores of etymological equations in some kind of meaningful context, catering more to the taste of language historians than to the preferences of straight historical linguists (i.e., the champions of historical grammar); and there was an engagingly even distribution of editorial space and expertise among the Middle Ages, the Renaissance, and modern times, down to the twentieth century, with the barest minimum of attention accorded to prehistory, under the pretext of exploring nebulous substratum languages. The margin of reconstruction, chiefly in the etymological bricks of the edifice, had been reduced to a modicum, to the advantage of readers chiefly concerned with language as a tool of fine literature.

When Migliorini's *magnum opus* appeared, his star was at its zenith, and repercussions of his feverish activities were felt in many quarters. His brief tenure of a professorship of Romance Philology at Fribourg (1933–8), which had enabled him to establish contacts with such giants of Swiss-style etymological research as Karl Jaberg, Jakob Jud, and, more sporadically, Walther von Wartburg, had come to an end. He was now firmly entrenched, for almost three long decades (1938–66), at the prestigious University of Florence, occupying a chair newly created and expressly reserved for him, as Professor of the History of the Italian Language. Radio, television, enterprising publishers, and several influential newspapers were at his command.

Migliorini indeed lost no time in displaying extraordinary energy, almost invariably crowned with success, upon firmly establishing himself in Italy. From editor-in-chief of the *Enciclopedia italiana* he rose, we recall, to the position of founding editor (with more moral than actual support from Giacomo Devoto) of modernist *Lingua Nostra* (1939–) and became, under a difficult régime, president of the Crusca Academy (1949–64). From contributing fine articles to influential journals, foreign and domestic, he switched to publishing, in astonishingly quick succession, a whole phalanx of books and booklets – on balance well over thirty – allying himself, more and more frequently, with younger partners who were presumably picked from among the best of his former students (F. Chiappelli, Gianfranco Folena, but also Carlo Tagliavini). One cannot help noticing a certain scattering of initiative and industriousness: introductions to spelling, to lexicography, to linguistics, to the history of Italian; confrontations of today's and yesterday's languages; inquiries into the relation of cultural history and language growth; textbooks for secondary schools; reconstructions of the chronological sequence of the major events; semi-formal *causeries* about the Italian language, viewed in various perspectives; preparation of concise anthologies of Old Italian texts; disquisitions about the most appropriate pronunciation to select for didactic purposes (Florentine or Roman?). Migliorini's practicality and realism are visible everywhere, even though not all the projects upon which he embarked appear, in retrospect, to have been equally worthy of the attention of a major figure. It is interesting to observe how, as time went by, Migliorini's knack for word biographies – a deeply ingrained talent – broke through more and more; witness, for example, his 1968 venture: *Profili di parole*, the harvest of a septuagenarian. For a while, however, the bent for etymologizing (sleuthing with a Spitzerian knack for surprises) was effectively held in check by other, perhaps more respectable lexicological exercises.

There may be some point in disclosing the strategy Migliorini resorted to in an effort to discuss present-day neologisms by analyzing his two books, mutually complementary, on twentieth-century Italian – books which he published, with excellent timing, at the threshold of the protracted Florentine period of his career. *Lingua contemporanea* appeared, as a supplement volume to the aforementioned journal, *Lingua Nostra*, in 1938 (i.e., technically slightly ahead of the opening issue) and became available, five years later, slightly retouched, in a third edition. The companion volume, *Saggi sulla lingua del Novecento*, saw the light of day in 1941, while the second edition, superficially revised, made its appearance the following year, and was destined to reappear on the book market, to everyone's surprise, as late as 1990, in more elegant garb and ushered in by a very substantial introductory essay (over ninety large-format pages), from the pen of the best-qualified critic, the author's influential heir Ghino Ghinassi. The two books here being jointly assessed are, strictly speaking, collections of learned essays for the most part previously published in tone-setting journals, such as *Archivio Glottologico Italiano*, *Archivum Romanicum*, and *La Critica*, and, in part, had already been reviewed by authoritative critics, foreign and domestic, including Leo Spitzer and B. A. Terracini; or else they involve public lectures, unless they echo contributions to earlier testimonial volumes. Whatever the set of circumstances, a distance of several years enabled the author to lend each one a welcome last finishing touch. The typographic standard of either book venture was very high, and appended word indexes effectively bracketed both collections.

What sort of Italian, socially speaking, was the author aiming at? In one of the two prefatory notes he made it unmistakably clear that his principal, indeed only target, was not (unlike the preference of most preceding linguistic analysts) the spontaneous speech of some group of natives, for example, villagers, but the normal, or average, written idiom of the educated middle class, with the scrupulous exclusion of dialectal (rustic) variants. Other styles were marginally taken into account, but only to the extent that they served the same layer of the Italian public. Additional languages, upon occasion, were taken into consideration for contrastive purposes, but not necessarily because they were close cognates. Twentieth-century French, to be sure, received its proper share of attention, but the voice of Spain made itself heard only at rare intervals, while references to contemporary German and English caught the reader's eyes at every step.

Sixty years ago, an educated (but not necessarily erudite) Italian could be credited with some knowledge of the classical tongues, so hints of Latin and Greek prototypes are visible everywhere, in undiluted shape; and the apparatus of the footnotes bristles with bibliographic details, sparing no weak-kneed reader.

Etymological issues come up everywhere for incidental mention or discussion, but they have been cleverly subordinated to scrupulous examination of broader problems, which appear less 'petty' to the uninitiated person. Here Migliorini displays a quota of mild indifference to phonology and inflection (not to mention syntax, of subordinated relevance in a lexicological context), but instead exhibits striking enthusiasm about the two traditional pillars of Romance word-formation: affixation and compounding, especially in their innovative rather than antiquarian aspects. Thus, the *Saggi* (i.e., 'Essays') begin with a long, brilliant piece (pp. 7–54) on 'prefixoids', a term minted by Migliorini himself (who was rightly known as an inspired word-smith) to designate certain opening segments of artificially coined compounds, such as the *aero-* part of *aeromobile* and the *radio-* ingredient of *radiodiffusione*. It might be rewarding to check Migliorini's findings, polished to a fine sheen but necessarily confined to present-day Standard Italian, against the possibly conflicting evidence of, for example, contemporary Spanish before giving his thoughts an unqualified stamp of approval.

Here are a few more illustrations of the content of the book. An originally medium-sized article on the vicissitudes of the prefix *super-* in present-day Italian, here generously expanded (pp. 55–89), is fascinating for the inclusion of its rivals (some, but not all of them, congeners): alongside *sovra-, sopra-, sor-* one also encounters *stra-, oltra-/oltre-, arci-, iper-*, which the author judiciously compares among themselves, then assesses in relation to German *über-*, remaining fully aware of the two competing patterns of lexical polarization: *sopra-/sotto-* vs. *super-/sub-*. The next piece, on the thriving suffix *-istico* (pp. 90–133), has also, as a result of elaborations, become three or four times longer than its modest 1931 prototype. The trajectory of the heavy compound suffix is compared with those of its lightweight counterparts *-ista* and *-ico*, in terms of relative usefulness. Once more, intermittent comparison with courses of events in neighbouring languages becomes unavoidable and actually serves to season the presentation of the main issue.

These samples suffice to show the thrust of Migliorini's most characteristic and conspicuous scholarship of those years. He was a cosmopolitan at heart, at a juncture when it was in Italy politically difficult and, for a while, even dangerous to be one, and he recognized, ahead of most contemporaries, the inalienable value of a respectable scholar's concentration on modern rather than on antique or medieval lexis. In particular, he cherished the revival and sophisticated transmutations and use of ancient derivational tools in a modern, technologically dominated environment. Though addicted, at least in these two volumes, to the systematic exploration of present-day conditions of derivation and compounding, he refused to become a fanatical follower of such theorists as demand the merciless extirpation of historical considerations from all and any analyses slanted in the direction of description, i.e., of synchrony.

While Migliorini did not consistently adopt in other writings the approach here sketched out and was perfectly familiar, from the start, with the more traditional ways of conjectural etymologizing, the choices he made around 1940 show him passionately addicted to the study of neologisms, giving only collateral and incidental attention to the inalienably etymological components of the complexly structured issues. The contrast with the heterodoxies of Pierre Guiraud, a prisoner of the vernacular, could not have been more dramatic.

A slightly later stage in Migliorini's thinking and preferred *modus operandi* in the context of short and medium-sized word histories is reflected in those articles and notes (originally channelled through newspapers) which he eventually collected in the miscellany *Profili di parole* (1968), an appropriate sequel to the midway point along that line of dignified popularization, *Lingua e cultura* (1948). The readership aimed at was still the same, and the level of presentation remained unaltered; but most of the items focused upon were now neatly isolable individual words rather than arrays of similarly shaped formations, so that any supportive collateral material, unannounced in the chapter headings, was unobtrusively relegated to the background. Thus the pretext for discussing *glamour* (pp. 100–1) was the triumph of that allegedly untranslatable Anglicism in sophisticated Italian mid-century speech. The author reveals nothing new to students of English by contending that *glamour* is a descendant of Old French *grimoire* 'magician's guide', itself traceable to *(ars) grammatica* (even though some readers might have preferred him to posit a blend of *grimoire* and *gramaire*). The author's margin of originality consists in his knack for surrounding this bit of dry factual information with allusions to near-parallel sense-developments observable in the see-sawing performances of other 'esoteric' words, such as Italian *carattere*, French *charme/ charmer* (let me here toss in the remark: also absorbed by English), Italian *incanto* and its satellites as well as *fascino/fascinare* and *malìa* 'enchantment' (in addition to its offshoots).

Another note, even more concisely worded (pp. 222–3), lays bare the reverberations, in older North Italian and French microtoponymy (*Foxhall*, *Waux-hall*, *Facsàl*, and the like), of English *Vauxhall*, with special reference to the famous amusement park located there. The value of this curious witness to Continental Anglophilia (and even Anglomania) might, incidentally, have been enhanced through inclusion of Russian *voksál*, generally used to this day for 'railway station'.

While studies of this sort deal mainly with intricate processes of borrowing, diffusion, and semantic adaptation rather than ultimate extraction, central issues of word origin also come up for occasional distillation, among them the celebrated controversial question of the descent of *barocco* (pp. 21–34), an Italian word whose history abounded in international repercussions.

Migliorini's styling of such lexical cameos fell short of revolutionizing the exploratory strength of etymology, but definitely invites comparison with the previously described approach used by, for example, the contributor(s) to *Atlantic (Monthly)*. An abyss separates the original investigator who – strictly by way of a sideline – also knows how to enlighten (and, incidentally, to entertain) hurried and less specialized readers from the amateur, or worse, the would-be professional entertainer in the realm of etymology.

A flair for generalization and forceful distillation are hardly characteristic features of Germany-style scholarship, so one is unlikely to look for bold experiments with 'neo-etymology' in Central Europe (although the waves of neologisms of the National-Socialist era, including those rooted in abbreviations, have indeed been inventoried). Perhaps one should here briefly mention the ambitious venture that goes under the (not unequivocal) name of *Der Große Duden*, sponsored by the Mannheim Centre for Lexicography. The relevant activities, started in the 1930s, reached their all-time peak in the 1960s and are ultimately traceable to the turn-of-the-century pioneer, Konrad Duden, a master of standardization and 'correctness' of spelling and grammar. Whereas in the typical dictionaries of our century the various crumbs of information provided – rather heterogeneous, not to say disparate at that – tend to make the individual entries uncomfortably crowded and require the use of excessive abbreviations, the Mannheim team intended to disentangle the knots. This goal was achieved (or, at least, aimed at) through isolation of the typical components, or strains, of the entries as ordinarily presented. Special medium-sized volumes, assigned to the care of responsible experts, were organized for pronunciation, spelling, synonymy, syntax-and-semantics, pictorial representation (where appropriate), status as a foreignism or an assimilated borrowing, stylistic nuances, etc. of the lexemes at issue. One such facet of the total picture thus emerging was the provenance of the given word. For bits of etymological information, a separate volume was reserved, titled *Etymologie. Herkunftswörterbuch der deutschen Sprache* (1963), entrusted to the care of Paul Grebe, a middle-of-the-road man rather than an avant-gardist. The information poured out is, obviously, more elementary and offered in less sophisticated terms than in the various consecutive revisions of Friedrich Kluge's classic.

In the standard dictionaries of German destined for a large market, etymological information has been retained, perhaps as a matter of respectability, but is now being offered in calculatedly discreet dosages and, as it were, incidentally. Thus from Alfred Schirmer's 1960 revision (=7th edn) of Hermann Paul's magisterial *Deutsches Wörterbuch*, the curious reader can ferret out hints of pre-classical and even medieval, as well as strictly regional, use. But Proto-Germanic, not to mention Proto-Indo-European, reconstruction has been ruled out as a matter of principle, even though it would continue to be relevant in an etymological dictionary of Old High German, of Gothic, or of Old Norse (all of which belong on the shelf of a research library).

On balance, the various attempts undertaken on both sides of the Atlantic to shelter, or even to fan, the lay public's residual interest in the ultimate provenance (as far as it is ascertainable) of individual words and names is not devoid of interest and deserves the creative, advanced scholar's sympathetic attention; but no real remedy seems to have been devised so far. The general trend of events, at least among laymen, runs in the direction of simplification rather than complication, and curiosity about, as well as knowledge of, dead languages (or older stages of living languages) will continue to be on the wane, unless such language study demonstrably serves to bolster the theory of glotto-diachrony.

The fact that certain innovative stimuli as well as certain techniques of simplified presentation have been tried out, roughly since the middle of the century, in a number of countries and in a variety of intellectual climates (all this in a transparent effort to restore or rejuvenate lay curiosity about etymological riddles and relationships), may not have been devoid, one hopes, of a modicum of intrinsic merit. Above all, that fact is symptomatic of an unmistakable malaise surrounding etymological pursuits in the concluding half of the present century. This uneasiness – be it interpreted as embarrassment, impotence, discomfort, indifference, or else active defiance – invites dispassionate analysis. As a matter of fact, it deserves two-layered dissection, since the position of sophisticated etymology *vis-à-vis* rival linguistic disciplines seems to be as much at stake as are the legitimacy and intensity of less specialized curiosity about the origins or starting points of lexemes – a curiosity which is moored to the total fabric of late-twentieth-century culture on either side of the Atlantic, at least as can be observed in the West.

Etymology, still much admired by experts two generations ago, appears of late to have been banished altogether from certain influential head-quarters, for example, editorial offices of key journals, the planning centres for choosing the topics of meetings, and similar nerve centres of active scholarship. In typical academic environments, an intelligent present-day student of linguistics will before long unfailingly notice that he is not being encouraged to put this subject on a par with, let us say, phonology, prosodics, morpho-syntax, lexical or syntactic semantics, pragmatics, psycholinguistics, or even poetics. Etymology no longer enters into mainline linguistics, except obliquely via diachrony, and the mere mention of it is redolent of irretrievable past enthusiasms, of something quaint, rather than of truly relevant present-day concerns and the common interests of keen minds.

The reasons for this fairly rapid loss of status, even among otherwise fairly balanced specialists, who are by no means one-sidedly *avant-garde*, are, *grosso modo*, these (enumerated in a loose sequence):

(a) The general prevalence of synchronic over diachronic commitment among most younger front-line researchers, a bent rationalized in many different ways; a tendency, perhaps, that, *inter alia*, may ultimately reflect the gradual banishment of 'dead languages' from secondary-school and collegiate curricula (or, at least, the trivial-ization of their continued study);

(b) The absence, from most etymological lucubrations, of any tightly phrased theory that might invite sharply pointed and, as a result, truly appealing and rewarding discussion, paying full attention to gener-alities;

(c) The gradual loss of esteem, among tone-setting intellectuals, for certain once highly prized national schools of thought or revered regional academic traditions known to have, decades ago, granted a place of honour to etymological probing. This re-assessment has a bearing on the once very prestigious Central European, especially German, philological scale of values, as a consequence of certain misapplications of etymological evidence in that part of the world;

(d) The network of alliances on which etymological research seems to rest and to thrive, for example, archaeology and mythology, plus the study of ancient or rural material civilization. It seems more advantageous and certainly more fashionable to many moderns to establish closer rapport with mathematics, logic, cognition theory, statistics (including probability theory), and kindred disciplines;

(e) The high degree of subjectivity transparent in etymological pronouncements, a margin of arbitrariness which threatens to degenerate either into unforeseeable caprices, or into all too predictable prejudice: ethnic–racist, aesthetic, religious, socio-cconomic, broadly cultural, and the like, sometimes to the extent of ruling out any fruitful dialogue. In the past, certain etymologists, while temporarily amusing readers through the resultant bickering, have in the end been digging their own graves by undermining the seriousness and detachment of marginally admissible debates;

(f) The growing realization, on the part of observers, of the sheer number of factors involved and the complexity of their patterns of intertwining in the procreation of a given lexeme. While the Neogrammarians, approximately a century ago, somewhat naïvely assumed that all that truly mattered in trying to ascertain the obfuscated ancestry of a word was the accurate application of certain highly reliable sound correspondences ('phonetic norms or laws'), contemporary practitioners judiciously recognize the typical intricacy of studies in lexical identity and continuity.

Here is one example of a relatively simple imbroglio. Florentine *casa* looks and sounds like a replica of Latin *casa*, although it is semantically distinct ('house' vs. 'cabin'). Spanish *casa* makes a similar initial impression of rectilinearity, which in the end turns out to be faulty, since Old Spanish /kaza/ brusquely interrupts the smooth connection between ancestral /kasa/ and virtually identical modern Spanish /kasa/, thus illustrating a zigzag rather than a straight-line movement. Portuguese *casa* looks exactly like its Latin, Italian, and Spanish counterparts, but its first *a*, stressed, and its second *a*, unstressed, make radically different impressions on the ear. French *chez* displays a switch to an entirely different form class (noun > preposition), a shift for which Spanish dialect *en ca' de*, literally 'at the house or home of', has duly prepared the few familiar with it for the French-style development. In addition, *chez* exhibits, along with the acquisition of a new meaning, an unforeseeable loss of the final vowel, also a change of inherited /k/ to /š/ via /č/ and of one /a/ to /e/ via diphthongal /je/, etc. Such instances of multiple causation produce the need for increasingly detailed and convoluted accounts in preference to deceptively elegant formulas;

(g) The continued growth of a formidable competitor. For a long period of time elaborate word indexes appended to historical grammars (or elevated to the rank of heavyweight *Registerbände*) have served as succinct substitutes for independent etymological dictionaries – as was true, at the start of this century, of Wilhelm Meyer-Lübke's comparative and of Friedrich Hanssen's Spanish grammars (1890–1902, 1913). The trend has continued into more recent periods, gaining force; witness the concluding volume of the mid-century venture by Gerhard Rohlfs (1949–54), less so, of Tekavčić (1972), so far as Italian is concerned. This remark holds, as a rule, for the entire range of phonology and for certain privileged sectors of morphology (primarily derivation), but distinctly less so for syntax; it presupposes comparability of time depth in our accounts of grammar and of lexis. Alphabetically arranged word indexes designed to accompany synchronic semantic projections of structural rules and lexical material, such as Karl Jaberg's and Jakob Jud's priceless posthumous guide (1960) to their *Wort- und Sachatlas* of Italy and Southern Switzerland, obviously do not qualify for this subsidiary service;

(h) A defensible tradition demands that any proponent of a new etymological solution of some long-vexing 'mystery' pass in review, with a critical eye, most or, if this aim is at all attainable, all earlier explicative statements on the problem. No such demand is pressed with comparable strictness where a point of grammar is at issue;

(i) The expensiveness of certain auxiliary tools (for example, of accompanying maps, rarely used in grammatical investigations; also, of drawings and photographs, especially where designations of certain objects, for example, those of tools or containers, are involved; ultimately, of pedigrees, minutely accurate transcriptions and meticulous transliterations of certain records) tends to make the publication of an etymological monograph a real budgetary headache, for the most part unparalleled, at least on such a scale, in the production of an etymological dictionary. The net result of these circumstances and, possibly, of yet other conditions, similar in essence, is the gradual, but relentless isolation of modern-day practitioners of etymology, who tend to form sects, often riven by internal dissension;

(j)   There has also occurred a parallel estrangement between etymology and the philologically flavoured production of older texts. While Wendelin W. Foerster's glossary (including its revised version by Hermann Breuer) that accompanied the corpus of Chrétien de Troyes' romances that he undertook to publish aimed to list not just lexical items, translating each one into German, but also the relevant etyma, such an approach would appear anachronistic at present. Ramón Menéndez Pidal, sailing in the wake of his German masters, adopted it (indeed, expanded it) in his magisterial edition of the *Cid* epic (1908–11) and, on a selective scale, in his polished, if much shorter, presentation of the well-known dialogue, *Elena y María* (1914). But, in revising his *Cid* venture (1944–6), he excused himself from re-working the Glossary as a whole, even though individual lexico-etymological points were taken up, with expected skill, in the Supplement. While glossaries of varying degrees of *détaillisme* continue to be a desideratum in the presentation of texts and chrestomathies alike (witness Lucien Foulet's vocabulary compiled to match J. Bédier's masterly reconstruction of the *Roland Song*), their compilers, with the rarest of exceptions, at present tend to dispense with etymological comments. In the New World, Jeremiah D. M. Ford, in providing etyma for the vocabulary of his *Old Spanish readings*, went with the times (in 1911). Henry B. Richardson, by supplying them in 1930 for Juan Ruiz and, after joining a team of three other scholars, at the mid-century point, was already behind the times;

(k)   One factor not yet adduced in this ensemble of obstacles is the staggering number of units for whose exploration the subdiscipline at issue has tacitly assumed full or partial responsibility. The phonologically trained analyst, in bringing his special skill to bear on a given language, is likely to end up with, perhaps, twenty-five autonomous phonemes. If variants produced by position (stress) or contiguity to other sounds are to be included in one's estimate, he arrives, conservatively, at a low three-digit figure for the number of sound units ear-marked for being taken into account. The contingents of grammatical morphemes, both inflectional and derivational, differ a good deal from one another, depending on the general character of the language under consideration and on the favoured method of counting such units; but the aggregate will very seldom exceed a few hundreds. Over against this basically wholesome modesty of available resources stands the number of word families that can be pressed into action in a representative European language. It is bound to run into thousands, while the sum of individually isolable lexemes, correspondingly, may reach tens of thousands. As a result of this glaring disproportion between the sheer sizes of conglomerates of phonemes (or morphemes) on one side, and, on the other, those of lexemes, the experienced phonologist or grammarian is in a position to perform elegantly executed leaps from one projection of his favourite classificatory theory to a possibly superior alternative in a matter of weeks or, at most, of months; whereas the parallel labours of an etymologically inspired lexicologist, ineradicably plodding on account of their slow rhythm, may require years of concentrated data-gathering and data-ordering, be it carried out by one individual or by a well-sychronized team, with or without the help of instruments.

Another facet of this difficulty is the painful decision whether imported, learnèd, exotic, and comparably marginal elements of lexis which are clearly recognizable as such (for example, English words introduced by transparently antique prefixes, like *archi-*, *hyper-*, *proto-*, borrowed from Greek, or *extra-*, *infra-*, *inter-* / *intra-*, *pre-*, *praeter-*, *subter-*, *super-* / *supra-*, and *tra-*, *trans-*, all extracted from Latin) deserve attention in the etymological dictionary of a late-twentieth-century language. The problem is by no means new – as a matter of fact, it is traceable, in a straight line, to Humanism and the Renaissance – but has, of late, been made far more acute than before through the ceaseless influx of thousands upon thousands of scientific neologisms. Also, it exists not for English alone, despite the particular hospitality formal English has shown to such newcomers. Italian is replete with them, too, and certain etymological dictionaries of Italian have gone very far, not to say unreasonably far, in paying attention to them. This holds for the five volumes of Carlo Battisti and Giovanni Alessio's mid-century venture and, on an even more generous scale, for Max Pfister's overabundant collection of entries, which is still in the process of compilation. Such lexemes, to be sure, deserve to be recorded and their rise may justifiably be dated, but this sort of information, to be potentially useful, belongs in an all-embracing thesaurus of the given language (or in a special compilation of Neo-Hellenic and Neo-Latin usage) rather than in an English or an Italian etymologicum, unless the foreignism has somehow managed to infiltrate and influence the host language;

139

(1) Against the backdrop of modern-day conditions of life, the 'pure etymologist', unpleasantly enough, runs the risk of adversely impressing the community of scholars to which he inescapably belongs as a belated romantic, a sort of straggling daydreamer and intuitivist who is out of tune with his rationally organized and smoothly functioning academic environment – one intent on brewing a strange mix of data amassed with overextended, fanatical patience and of solutions (conjectures, 'theories') unaccountably arrived at, whose abandonment, even under the pressure of cogent counter-arguments, he may stubbornly resist to the bitter end. He is free, of course, to avoid making such an unfavourable impression by shrewdly balancing etymological against more soberly conducted grammatical inquiries in his total programme of creative research. For a long period of time and until fairly recently, successive generations of flexible, versatile scholars did, or, at least, aimed at doing, precisely that: witness the bibliographies of Franz Bopp, Carl Darling Buck, W. F. Edgerton, Antoine Meillet, August Schleicher, Edgar H. Sturtevant, and Joseph Vendryes, among leading Indo-Europeanists; of Jakob Grimm and Hermann Paul, among celebrated Germanists; of Friedrich Diez, Wilhelm Meyer-Lübke all the way to Max Leopold Wagner, Gerhard Rohlfs, and Vicente García de Diego, among respected Romanists; etc.

But this test of his intellectual pliability is what today's 'pure etymologist' may want, above all else, to avoid. Juan Corominas (also known as Joan Coromines), for example, who has superbly embodied this type of idealized purity in the sustained scope and tone of his pre-eminently etymological research over a period of, at least, half a century, has engaged in a chain of inquiries that bear increasingly eloquent witness to such progressive stiffening of self-confidence.

Upon scrutinizing Corominas' voluminous record of publications, one discovers that, after an auspicious start at Barcelona (evidenced by a Pyrenees-oriented monograph on a dialect spoken in the Upper Garonne Valley as a doctoral dissertation, 1931 and a re-examination of Arabisms in Hispano-Romance, after attendance at Jakob Jud's Zurich seminar), he switched, in the wake of his temporarily enforced transfer to western Argentina (Mendoza) in the early and mid-1940s, to such topics as 'Some semantic features of Argentinian Spanish' (free translation), 'New Spanish [and Portuguese] etymologies' (a cluster of seven notes), 'New-World contributions to pending issues' (a constellation of three notes, all three etymologically slanted), 'Problems still awaiting a solution' (again an etymological triad), all three items traceable to the years 1941–2. A second series of 'Etymological Studies', this time marking a simultaneous attack on twenty-one less than closely related issues, was followed by a 'Harvest of Vulgar Latin' (a chain of nine etymological vignettes, brought to bear on as many as thirteen isolable questions), of 1942–4 vintage. Then came a third bouquet of topically disconnected etymological cameos, this time eleven, flanked, for once, by the inclusion of a newly edited short Old Catalan text which was not, to be sure, deprived of, at least, an etymological glossary, all three items falling under the chronological rubric '1943–5'. This is not all. Alongside the pieces just enumerated, which Corominas deftly placed in his own journal, he squeezed a 115-page monograph of etymological *bric-à-brac* (whimsically titled 'Indianorománica'), entertainingly enough presented, into three instalments spread over a 1944 volume of an even better-established Buenos Aires quarterly. And, surpassing his own earlier achievements, he came to the shores of the United States with another, similarly titled miscellany in his hands, as a welcome gift (1947–8) to an impatiently waiting California journal editor!

The one-sidedness and resultant monotony of this self-immersion, to the point of near-exclusiveness, in etymological controversies is obvious. So is the author's resolve to inundate the book-market, from then on, with one monumental etymological dictionary after another, with practically no adequate intervals reserved for other categories of linguistic or philological probing (except for the long-delayed edition of Juan Ruiz's early fourteenth-century text). Milestones along this path include a four-volume dictionary (1954–7), overtly etymological, of Spanish, which the compiler somewhat arbitrarily and out of context called 'Castilian' (with a Supplement appended to Vol. IV), a six-volume partial revision and expansion, intended to cover the ensemble of 'Hispanic' dialects, likewise viewed exclusively in the etymological perspective (c. 1980–90), and an even more ambitious multi-volume dictionary of Catalan, an undertaking concluded in 1991, once more, predictably, etymological. (For the last two projects the ageing author collaborated with a large number of younger colleagues, apparently reserving for himself all crucial decisions and the stylistic colouring of the whole.) While the *Breve diccionario etimológico* was, one gathers, meant to represent a mere by-product of such feverish activities, its three nearly identical versions actually make it the most manageable and readable of these ventures, not least on account of a welcome absence of polemics.

What matters in the present context is the oft-observed fact that such a high degree of feverish concentration on the minutiae of etymological riddles provoked the author's almost complete neglect of what was meanwhile (1930–90) going on in other branches of linguistics, both Romance and general, with the inevitable result that these huge edifices of lexicological guesswork are not infrequently thrust on the archaic, pre-structural, and hence highly vulnerable, foundations of phonology and morphology. To be sure, there is no dearth of incidental phonological and grammatical asides (often polemically spiced), scattered over his overextended discussions of controversial proposals advanced by others. But this is not the sort of imaginative performance by which his prowess as a student of historical grammar can safely be judged. He will go down, in the annals of scholarship, as a one-sided investigator excited by the adventures of risky word biographies at the expense of any new grammatical insights;

(m) A number of additional vexing problems have arisen from present-day societal pressure on the practitioner of etymology. If he is prudent enough to remain satisfied with elucidating individual cases of lexical filiation, or small clusters of such cases, he may be relatively well off. At worst, he may be – somewhat cynically – advised to avoid the use of 'etymology' in the title of his note or article, on account of the hypersensitivity of certain journal editors to many younger readers' aversion to this key word, which of late has indeed tended to become controversial. At least, he will feel protected from any pressure to release the results of his inquiry before he has slowly reached some mature and defensible conclusions.

Thus, in the year 1951 a single American journal, namely *Language*, published three overtly etymological pieces. The Sinologist Roy Andrew Miller focused attention on the provenance of a single Chinese word, *'liu* 'pomegranate', which he interpreted as a native folk etymology for a loan-word. The Indo-Europeanist Paul Tedesco paired off two Slavic adjectives of dubious descent, **pilbnъ* 'diligent' and *naglъ* 'sudden', which shared the one feature that their dubious origin could be most cogently identified through semantic analysis. Then again, the palaeo-Orientalist Albrecht Goetze (1951) scrutinized the pedigrees of, roughly, eight Hittite words (or word-variants), to wit: *wit(ant)*- 'year', *gim(ant)*- 'winter', *zena(nt)*- 'autumn', *hamešha(nt)*- 'spring', *išpant*- 'night', *šiwat*- 'day', *nekut*- 'nightfall', and *lukat*- 'morning', demonstrating that the terminology for 'year', 'season', and 'segment of the day' was inherited and coincided 'in all essential aspects with that found in the IE languages' (p. 476). What bracketed these words, predestining them for joint etymological analysis, was their common reference to the calendar. A second bond, not stated by Goetze, but transparently implied, was that, around 1950, he felt ready to pronounce on the eight germane problems of their lexical ancestry.

Juan Corominas, at the start of his career, alternately had recourse to either technique of grouping. In his 1947–8 pot-pourri, written chiefly for an American audience ('Problemas del diccionario etimológico', I–II), he targeted *alrededor* 'around', *bellaco* 'sly, wicked, knavish', *bostezar/acezar* 'to yawn', *escarmiento* 'penalty, caution', *garra* 'claw', *guisante* 'pea', etc. apparently for no other reason than the very advanced stage of his own investigation into their notoriously confusing vicissitudes. Elsewhere, in one of his previous 1941–2 pieces with which he had introduced himself to a South American readership, he alternated between the rival classificatory criteria of (a) assumed novelty, originality of the solution advocated (*allende* 'beyond'/*aquende* 'this side of', *caracol* 'snail', *hueco* 'hollow', *joroba* 'hump', etc.) and (b) a New World overtone in the problems selected for diagnosis (*orondo* 'hollow, puffed up, big-bellied', *embadurnar* 'to daub', *tripular* 'to man, equip, fit out'). Whatever the approach to selection in each individual instance, one comes away with the impression that Corominas, Goetze, Miller, Tedesco, and their peers were convinced of the legitimacy and perfectibility of advanced etymological analysis, rooted in thorough familiarity with the respective ancient cultures and with the earlier findings of reliable practitioners of historical grammar. Less visible is their expectation that their own discoveries can push forward our grasp of phonology and morphology. Thus, from Corominas' voluminous *œuvre* one cannot piece together his mental vision of the highly controversial growth of Old Spanish sibilants.

Here are some suggestions for an invigorating rejuvenation of etymology, viewed from a cross-linguistic perspective. First, students of some language families lean towards omitting from their purview any systematic analysis of the structure of primitives, a practice which I find objectionable. However, the fact that Spanish designations of physical defects (including speech defects and their mental implications) comprise, to the point of near-predictability, disyllabic paroxytones ending in *-o/-a*, is both grammatically and etymologically significant; cf. *calvo* 'bald', *ciego* 'blind', *cojo* 'lame', *corvo* 'bent', *flaco* 'emaciated', *lerdo* 'sluggish, heavy', *manco* 'one-handed', *mudo* 'dumb', *sordo* 'deaf', *tuerto* 'one-eyed', *zambo* 'knock-kneed' (besides the words for 'stupid': *bobo, lelo, memo, tonto, zonzo* or *sonso*). In contrast, Old and Modern French have given speakers complete freedom in this respect: monosyllabic *sourd* 'deaf' (also Old French *cieus* 'blind') have coexisted with trisyllabic *aveugle* 'blind' (clearly, a substitute word). Since some of these qualifiers represent etymological unknowns or puzzles, closer attention to the configuration of the primitives may greatly enliven the discussion.

Second, standard interjections as well as certain conversational formulas used on a par with, or in lieu of interjections (English *all right! right o(n)!;* German *na also!;* French *ma foi!;* Spanish *¡ya lo creo!* alongside *¡ojalá!;* Russian *nu vot!,* and the like) indisputably have been the stepchildren of linguistic research in general, and of etymological lucubration in particular. One feature of possible relevance to the student of word origins (who is likely to detect in this corner of the edifice quite a few unknowns) is the pitch contour of such words and frozen formulas. Yet, the last bit of useful information that one can hope to extract from existing guides to lexical usage is a record of the musical shape of such bits of material. Even in reference works that, as a rule, inform the user of the geographic spread of the given word and that provide drawings (or photographs) of, let us say, the species of butterfly under discussion, the melodic curve of German *Nanu! Zum Teufel!* or of Italian *davvero!* or of American English *oops!* will ordinarily be skipped. Acoustic effects should be granted as much attention as their optic (visual) counterparts.

Third, with certain well-known exceptions (for example, Berber, Basque, and Arabic words in Southern Spanish; Turkish words in circum-Aegean territories; Tartar words in Russian), etymological research is preponderantly pursued within a given family or subfamily. It took the large contingent of Romanists a shockingly long period of time to realize that the spread of Folk Latin as a whole, and of Northern Gallo-Romance in particular, cannot be seriously examined without an appropriate dosage of attention to English, Dutch, as well as the Rhenish and Danubian dialectal varieties of German. If such limitations are recognized as understandable but arbitrary, new inspiration can be drawn from a world-wide perspective. The origin of American English *okay* is an issue intricate enough; the reasons for its world-wide spread also invite attention, and some of the answers to that second question may prove enlightening even to those still engaged in the elucidation of the first problem.

Fourth, comparative etymological dictionaries prepared in the traditional vein (for example, those organized by Wilhelm Meyer-Lübke and, to some extent, by Walther von Wartburg) list alphabetically, as entries, the recorded, in addition to the reconstructed, ancestral bases that underlie the forms culled from the daughter languages, dialects included. This approach has merits and certainly need not be discontinued in the future. But, be it only to avoid monotonous repetition of a time-tested methodology, why should we not try to approach a complex situation the other way around? Why not extract, for a change, from some excellent dictionary of Latin, prepared by a team of seasoned classicists, an alphabetic list of such authentic words, peculiar to Antiquity and the early Middle Ages, as have not been handed down to the speakers (and scribes) of the daughter languages? Such a negative record (or, to put it differently, such a record of lexical losses) is apt to stimulate discussion, simply because any disappearance calls for a justification, including a statement of what remedies were appealed to in an effort to provide substitutes. One can scarcely hope for any more powerful stimulus for a fresh breeze of etymological discussion.

This list of readily available possibilities that come to mind almost at once can be considerably lengthened. The well-being of etymology depends, of course, also on other factors, and no firm prognosis of guaranteed success can as yet be offered. Under the conditions prevailing in the 'social contract' between etymological researchers and entrepreneurial publishers, however, all these models of selection and entries attuned to individual author's tastes and varying degrees of self-assurance cease to operate. As the printing and the distribution procedures (often by fascicles) are usually organized, the beleaguered author feels contractually obliged to pronounce on the backgrounds of all words beginning with, let us say, *a-* or *b-* long before he can dream of taking up the biographies of those introduced by *y-* or *z-*. To put it more drastically: a mere whim of the alphabetic order is allowed to predetermine the sequence of events, by lengthening or shortening the time reserved for sobering reflection. The author, in despair, may jot down, 'origin unknown' or, much worse, may thus label some case of remote possibility or even of a course of events wholly improbable: 'Presumably . . . ', 'in all likelihood', or some similar reassuring paraphrase. This state of affairs prompts many observers to argue that it is the monographic exploratory pieces rather than the dictionaries that qualify for genuine breakthroughs in etymology – granted the usefulness of dependable reference works, they are often indispensable.

But let us suppose for a moment that the aforementioned societal pressures (and, along with them, occasional retreats from such earlier commitments as had been beneficial) were nonexistent. Let us assume, just for the fun of such a presupposition, that scholars had been cut out to live and toil in an 'ideal' world. Would, under this set of imagined circumstances, the present-day status of etymology and the prospects for its immediate future rapidly improve? The answer need not be completely negative but, if given in an affirmative vein, must be very cautiously phrased, if it is to command respect.

Let us, by way of preliminaries, call to mind some characteristic relevant features of past periods. Etymological conjectures or plain guesses were indeed made in prehistory, in Antiquity, and also in the Middle Ages, and have continued to be practised as constituents of numerous so-called primitive cultures. The advent to influence of organized linguistic science offered eager etymologists a welcome chance to check the fruits of witty guesswork against certain (presumably overrated) norms of pointlessly rigid historical phonology. Next, an ineradicable residue of irritating exceptions forced another generation (or a different team) of explorers to look into the interplay of regular sound development with a wide variety of other forces, not a few of them somehow more 'human', hence more appealing to a certain category of investigators (for example, effects of humour, avoidance of homonymy or, conversely, leaning towards puns, phonosymbolism, and the like). The phenomenon of lexical borrowing had been very well known, and even understood, for centuries (Roman educators could effortlessly tell Hellenisms from lexical items of pristine Latin stock, Renaissance lexicographers were able to distil Italianisms from the cores of French and Spanish lexis, and so on); yet, the advent to prestige, ever since the end of the nineteenth century, of the linguistic atlases strengthened the advanced researchers' belief in the migration of lexical units by land or by sea as part of the broader process of diffusion, and so on. Viewing things in retrospect, one feels obliged to admit that in the past (including the fairly recent past, best recognizable to today's observers), it has invariably taken the rise of some new theory (however exaggerated if measured by later, more rigorous standards), or fashion, or some novel technique (however one-sided, if applied exclusively) to set in motion an innovative style of etymologizing.

It can be argued that what is most urgently needed at present is the preparation of more voluminous or more scrupulously supervised collections of raw data; and it is not at all difficult to demonstrate (as has indeed been successfully done more than once) that, in some dramatic instances, the new availability of some better-understood passage in an ancient manuscript or inscription, or of a cluster of seemingly marginal regionalisms, actually led to an instantaneous collapse of long-cherished etymological beliefs. By the same token, any new thesaurus, bursting with fresh information and conscientiously polished, remains a valuable tool in the hands of an experienced etymologist. But, for all its undeniable usefulness, whether it happens to be confined to a literary language or serves to capture a profusion of dialectal forms or else manages to combine these two seldom jointly tapped sources of information (as has been true, for example, of most volumes of Walther von Wartburg's celebrated *Französisches etymologisches Wörterbuch*), an etymological dictionary and a lexical thesaurus represent two entirely different genres of scholarly undertaking, whose complete merger is clearly inadvisable – for psychological, economic, and yet other reasons. What is urgently needed, by way of remedy, is a stimulating experiment with rejuvenation of method; and since linguistic theory is the order of the day, and general linguistics (in preference to 'particular linguistics', its older counterpart), for better or worse, exudes a special magnetisim, one sees no reason for studiously avoiding the discussion of possible bridge-building between the two disciplines. (A marginal likelihood of initial error must, obviously, be taken into account from the start; and a supply of elasticity for retreating from too hazardous gambits, and for renouncing over-optimistic expectations, is indispensable.)

At the risk, then, of courting reproaches for triviality, let us lay down the following set of conditions that are helpful in studying specimens of the simplest and most familiar situations. Let the language selected for conducting our etymological exercises be known as A; the word under investigation as a; the principal, if not sole, ancestor or purveyor of lexemes ('parent language') for that tongue as X; and the suspected source ('etymon') of a, as x. Let us further, by way of beginning, hypothesize that a and x sound (almost) alike. This (near-) identity can mean one of several disparate things. Conceivably, there were no sound changes in operation to interfere with the local transmission of x, a situation that we are free to signal with the more explicit transmission formula a^1; or there occurred no uninterrupted transmission by word of mouth, but x was allowed to perish, and then, at a distinctly later stage, deliberately borrowed from X on the tacit assumption that X continued to be read or recited (and, perhaps, to be written) while its spontaneously spoken forms had been allowed to advance by leaps and bounds ($=a^2$). Where the evidence available allows us no clear decisions as to whether a^1 or a^2 is involved, we can mark that stage of indeterminacy by

147

having recourse to the symbol a^3. Finally, language A had cognates, descended from the same source (X): B, C, D, . . . , some of them foreseeably more conservative than A. Conceivably, a, virtually unchanged, was preserved in B or in C, then loaned, in exceptional words, to A at a discernibly later stage, thus producing a^4.

Contrary to first impressions, however, all the situations so far surveyed are slightly abnormal. The ideal development includes foreseeable sound changes, in response to 'sound laws' (or, less conventionally speaking, 'sound correspondences') – such shifts, to put it differently, as carry with them no special messages. The product of a given ancestral form so developed deserves to be labelled a^5; but if special conditions attach to such an evolutionary curve, other tags may be preferable. If sound changes have coincided with some semantic innovation, we are free to speak of an a^6 variety of evolution; if the pattern holds solely in heavily stressed, lightly stressed, or entirely unstressed syllables, no commitment prevents us from classifying products thus conditioned by the symbol a^7, which invites further subdivision. Should the degree of heaviness of stress stand in alliance with semantic conditioning, a^8 would be an apposite formulaic description.

We have so far tacitly operated with the reassuring assumption that the territory assigned to a gradually emerging language is practically indivisible. But suppose the principle of basic territorial integrity and unitariness holds for the most part in a given case, except that East and West, with respect to certain stressed vowels, display slight divergences, an areally co-conditioned result of a form bequeathed by the ancestral language deserves some separate marking apt to catch the reader's attention, for example, as a^9. In certain complexly structured societies, one layer of the population (for example, men as against women, the old as against the young, the educated as against the illiterate) may tend to go its own ways in matters of decision-making bearing on features of speech; the analyst, to show that he has been forewarned, may confidently have recourse to the symbol a^{10}. Among certain groups of speakers and listeners, in selected cultures, considerations of decorum or reverence may make certain sounds, or at least sequences of sounds, highly undesirable and may invite either the complete avoidance of appealing words, or the substitution of neutral, less objectionable sounds, or sequences of sounds, for those deemed offensive: a^{11}. In some languages, the choice of the root vowel may carry a message of its own, by signalling, primarily among adjectives, some such meaning as colour, or a person's physical defect; to other languages such signalling (a^{12}) is wholly unknown. Observe that all such idiosyncrasies must not be confused with basic phonological peculiarities, as when one language allows its syllabic architecture to exert a direct influence on the growth and distribution of certain sounds, while another (perhaps its next-door neighbour) does not.

Such cross-language catalogues of potential conditioning factors, far more elaborate and sophisticated than the sketchy presentation of a few elementary examples here undertaken, have been experimentally toyed with before. Scholars have included in the fine-tuning of their schemes the presence, in certain quarters, of reduplicative formations; the vulnerability, of certain contingents of speakers, to homonymy, synonymy, and antonymy; the varying effects of exposure to phonosymbolism, and the like. But few, if any, attempts have so far been made to study in depth special constellations of conditioning factors on a genuinely cross-language scale. It could be very profitable for etymologists to have, within comfortably easy reach, monographs examining, in a wide variety of languages (both kindred and unrelated) the clashes between (a) changes of form fostered by polarization of meaning and (b) sound changes 'regular', 'pure and simple', i.e., semantically unmotivated. Unfortunately, polyglottal studies of this sort, which might help one immensely to assess the plausibility of a newly proposed etymological hypothesis, are readily available only in very exceptional instances.

There is, above all, a major difference, rich in all sorts of implications, between the etymological technique needed at the start of the entire operation and the skills required at more advanced stages of an etymological assignment. A person highly qualified to do the former job may not at all embody the perfect choice for the accomplishment of the latter task, and vice versa. Even teams of three workers are readily conceivable.

Suppose a new member of an already roughly established language family has all of a sudden been tentatively identified as a result of some, let us assume archaeological, chance discovery. In order that the impressionistically proposed identification becomes more solid, an etymologically inspired analyst will feel obliged to step in. He will be required to establish, as speedily as possible, the network of gross connections between the hypothetical older stage ('reconstructed or recorded ancestral language') and the suspected later stage ('the language newly stumbled upon'), mainly where the resemblances and differences observed smoothly fall into major patterns – with occasional side-glances at the previously identified members of the family. He will also be asked to weed out and reserve for the next round whatever seems to be refractory to such accelerated treatment. Ideally, the operator in charge should be a deft, experienced phonologist, grammarian, and student of lexis, but need not have accumulated special

149

expertise, tailored to local needs, through prior exposure to that same language family.

To pursue this report on an 'ideal' strategy, the next person in charge of the etymological decipherment of that same (presumably, refractory) addition to the language family at issue might be well-advised to come equipped with complementary talents and different chunks of information at his ready disposal, since he will be held responsible for handling the residue of the material aimed at: lexical items affected by taboo, lexical polarization, homonymy, expressivity, folk etymology, and the like; and, above all, unusual, even unique, combinations of such salient features. To understand the gambits made by each past generation of speakers of the given tongue, he must have acquainted himself with both linguistic and extralinguistic (broadly speaking, cultural) features of the society under investigation.

From the third investigator in this imagined procession of analysts it would be unfair to demand speed and measured efficiency. It would be more realistic to imagine him as a very slow and purposeful worker, eager to come to grips with the residue of difficulties, which are often entirely unforeseeable at earlier stages of the inquiry. He will have to be equipped with a superb mnemonic faculty. Having committed to memory the entire residue of difficulties, seeming contradictions, and irremediable lacunae in the corpus available and in adjoining provinces of knowledge, he will also have to train himself to be constantly on the look-out for very unlikely clues, obtained from fragmentary evidence, to a blurred and eroded turf. He will necessarily be expected to have developed a special flair for associating and reconciling utterly diverse bits of evidence.

It almost goes without saying that the pattern here toyed with of three categories of experts is purely arbitrary. With a spark of imagination, one can project many more such types that contain, under an exceptional, for the most part unavoidable, set of circumstances, a single truly brilliant etymologist who, by striking three or more diverse attitudes, as it were, can all by himself successfully perform what amounts to a number of fairly different assignments. Despite the availability, at rare intervals, of such exceptions, the mastermind in charge of the entire undertaking will, in most instances, want to pause before doling out assignments to chosen individuals, to make sure that the phase of research in need of immediate attention actually matches the candidate's temperamental and intellectual talents and idiosyncrasies. Where better-known or longer-studied languages (like those of the Romance or the Germanic family) are involved, it is usually the 'third type' of investigator that one can safely expect to produce the finest results. Under certain conditions, teamwork (with the appropriate complementarity of responsibilities) can be particularly rewarding. If the same individual is called upon to perform three (or more) duties, critics and continuers are apt to discover at a later juncture that his performance has been discernibly uneven.

A few concrete examples might conceivably lend a more welcome illustrative service in this context than continued discussion in a purely theoretical vein. Let us suppose that an etymologist had all along known that *iguarla* 'titbit' in Portuguese, adequately documented since the Middle Ages, was still lacking an acceptable etymon. (This kind of awareness or suspicion obviously produces a very advantageous climate for chance discoveries, on which the researcher, driven by his properly whetted appetite and guided by the forewarning, can almost literally pounce.) Let us suppose further that in thumbing through, by sheer coincidence, a collection of glosses traceable to Late Antiquity, he comes across a long-neglected entry, namely *iecuāria* 'meal prepared of (chopped?) liver', which appears to stem from Classical Latin *iecur* 'liver', a lexical item practically overlaid by **ficătum/*ficătum* and their variants (cf. Spanish *hígado*, French *foie*, etc.), as has been demonstrated in a number of masterly analyses ever since c. 1900. The lucky discoverer is overwhelmed by the temptation to argue that this is the long-sought last surviving vestige in Romance of the otherwise dislodged *iecur* family. But into how many obstacles is he apt to run in trying to consolidate his seemingly arbitrary speculation into a truly defensible opinion?

For a small minority of the shifts assumed to have taken place a quick consultation of any good historical grammar surely will do. The voicing of ancestral intervocalic /k/ to /g/, pronounced in certain contexts as /ɣ/, is a well-established fact, which can safely be taken for granted. The preservation of word-final -*a*, at least in script (it may as early as the Middle Ages have been pronounced [ɐ]), is a thoroughly credible assumption. The raising here of pretonic [ɛ] or [e] to [i] before /w/ of the following syllable – a product, in turn, of parental [ŭ] before stressed vowel – will raise no eyebrows. Virtually everything else, however, that the lucky conductor of the inquiry is before long apt to discover, seems problematic, not on account of its inherent implausibility, but as a consequence of the well-nigh ever-present existence of alternative /k/ solutions, i.e., of counterexamples, and also as a result of the lack or scarcity of suitable monographic investigations. Baffling questions arise at every turn. Here are a few of the relatively least complicated:

(a) The lack of any reflex of word-initial /j/ is astonishing, cf. Latin *iān(u)a* 'threshold' vs. Portuguese *jan-ela* 'window'. Since a lone trace

151

of *yegüería* has been detected in Old Spanish, could *iguaria* be an adaptation of *yegüería* to Atlantic Coast conditions?

(b) The suffix of *iecu-āria* is ordinarily rendered by *-eira* in Portuguese and by *-era* in Spanish. In this instance, however, a stress-shift has occurred, even though semantically Latin un-stressed *-ia* had little in common with Greek-Latin *-ía*, used chiefly to coin adjectival abstracts, ranks, and the like, rather than tags for choice food. Have any parallels been recorded?

(c) Could there have occurred any blend with some other word-family through a subtle interplay of formal and semantic resemblances? Could *aequāre* be suspected of interference, on condition that a pattern of partitioning the choice morsel into equal shares (pieces, chunks) could have been surreptitiously hinted at? Is the word-initial segment *ig-* somehow reminiscent of *(f)igu-eira* 'fig-tree', on the theory that extra-savoury animal livers could be obtained by letting pigs devour whole piles of figs? Might *yegüería* have been abandoned as a consequence of the threat of its infelicitous association with *yegua* 'mare'?

(d) Was the basic reason for the abandonment of *iecur* its heteroclitic declensional paradigm: *iecur, io-* or *ie-cineris*? Could a parallel be drawn with *cor, cordis* 'heart', an erratic declensional type which so weakened the status of the Old Spanish *cuer*, Portuguese *cór* as to have left the door wide open for the infiltration of the intrusive, innovative rival type Old Spanish/Old Portuguese *coraçón*?

(e) To avoid any repetition of intervocalic *r* (**iecurāria*), was the total loss of one of them practised as the sole available cure, or could some dissimilatory process have been seized upon with equal chances of success (for example, in Old Spanish if not so easily in Old Galician–Portuguese, the switch from *-r – r-* to, let us say, *-l – r-*)?

We shall delay drawing any sweeping conclusions from the consideration of just a single, manifestly intricate, case history, and turn our attention to other word biographies, which have more recently stood in the focus of attention. The etymological kernel of French *Noël* 'Christmas', our second example, is scarcely at issue for anyone who bothers to take into account Italian *Natale*, Portuguese *Nadal*, and, indirectly, Spanish *Na(ti)vidad*, which is basically semi-learned, yet secondarily syncopated; even Russian *Roždestvó* chimes in, as does the occasion of the holiday. So *(diē) nātāle*, extracted from *nātus* 'born' (contrastable, in turn, with *mortāle*, from *morte* 'death' and *mortu(u)* 'dead'), is a secure starting point, despite the limited co-existence of rival forms such as *Nael, Neel* in regional Old French. Still, the pretonic *o* in hiatus is an unexpected feature, which has disquieted generations of scholars. Now, without immediately pressing the issue, one may recall that Italian *nuotare* stands for 'swimming', erratically enough if one recalls its starting point in Antiquity, namely *năt-āre*, witness Spanish *nadar*. The point is that, at the Latin stage the two nuclei *năt-* 'born' and *năt-* 'swim' failed to stand in each other's way as long as distinctive vowel quantity counted, keeping near-homonyms apart, at least marginally. With this barrier to any hazard of merger or confusion before long eliminated, the responsibility for discrimination between vowels was assigned to a dissimilatory process, with **nŏt-* and *năt-* standing in mutual confrontation, except that **nŏt-*, in Italy, prevailed for 'swimming', much as *no-*, in medieval French, temporarily could stand for the same sport. Yet, the perilous proximity of *no(u)er* 'to tie (a knot)' and of such offshoots as *dénouer* 'to untie' < Old French *desnoer* ultimately counselled the adoption of *nag(i)er*, literally 'to navigate', for 'swimming'.

This is a grossly simplified account of what, at the outset, seemed a fairly plain sequence of events, except that the reality behind the schematic reconstruction was, in all likelihood, even more complicated. We have skipped any incidental mention of the change of Classical Latin *nūrus* 'daughter-in-law' into, first, *nūra* and, next, into reconstructible **nŭra*, **nŏra* as a precondition for the rise of Spanish *nuera*, echoing *suegra* 'mother-in-law'; also, we have refrained from elaborating on the biography of Spanish *nuez* 'walnut', which, unlike Italian *noce*, cannot have been directly bequeathed by Classical Latin *nŭce*, etc. To put it differently: the one, at first sight, minor, if not utterly trivial, irregularity of French *Noël*, a word otherwise entirely transparent, has stirred up hornet's nests of threatening difficulties. The turning point, we recall, was our discovery of a seemingly different knot in the history of Italian lexis, save for the fact that the two trouble spots, contrary to our initial expectation, stood in a relation of mutual complementarity.

Barring the analysts' awareness of some atypical sound change (for example, the emergence of an auxiliary vowel before word-initial *s impurum*), or their alertness to the special status of the word-openings Cons. + *l*, or their ability to identify an isolable prefix where none had been suspected, or else their flair for the simplification of word-initial consonant clusters like *hr-* or *wr-* as the price a Germanic word, or name, had to pay for its new admission to membership in a Romance language, Romanists have gradually come to expect a given word's initial consonant, followed by a vowel, to have already figured in its prototype. Hence their helplessness throughout the nineteenth century in those instances in which such an expectation simply has led nowhere.

Our third example here, Spanish and Portuguese *tomar* 'to take', is a case in point. It is tragicomic to observe even reputable comparatists (among them Hugo Schuchardt and Wilhelm Meyer-Lübke) coming up with abstruse, not to say absurd, conjectures, to the effect, for example, that *tomar* was an onomatopoeic (expressive) formation, or one of exotic background, and so on. They might at least have observed that *tomar* was not the sole word for 'taking' in the peninsular language; that it lacked cognates; and that it was accompanied by an astonishingly small retinue of derivational satellites.

It was an outsider, an Italian literary scholar endowed with a superb command of Latin, who, being free from the aforementioned prejudice, advanced the candidacy of *autumāre* 'to affirm, think, believe', a proposal greeted with mixed feelings by professional etymologists (the account of that reaction has been traced earlier in painstaking detail p. 77). What mattered most was not the overall felicity of that particular proposal (which, as a matter of fact, was not unquestionable), but the willingness of, at first, a single scholar, and, soon thereafter, of a small contingent of investigators, to cut loose from the obtrusive, obsessive tyranny of *t*- bases for *tomar*. Three quarters of a century later the problem (long deemed practically insoluble) may indeed have been cracked when the spokesman for another generation declared that the elusive base at issue was older Latin *aestumāre* 'to estimate, esteem' on its way to shifting to *aestimāre*, a stage better remembered at present. Beginning, at a certain point, to sound quaint, hence mildly ridiculous, at a time when *maxŭmu* 'greatest' and *optŭmu* 'best' were being converted, through regular sound development, into *maxĭmu* and *optĭmu*, respectively, *aestumāre* could be jokingly divided into *aes* 'money' and **tŭmāre* 'to grasp, seize, take', involving a special allusion (by the scoffers) to the hated Roman tax-collectors who were eager to make estimates of the value of taxable provincial estates.

The sole assumption here freely made is situational, simply because not all the jokes that were circulating found the right satirists or epigrammatists to perpetuate them for posterity. The wide use of *aes*, *aeris* 'copper, alloy, coin, money', not least in colloquial Hispano-Latin (cf. modern *alambre*, originally *arambre* 'wire'), vouches for the realism of the reconstruction, our third example.

Over a period of centuries, scholars, who were eager to confront the etymological problem underlying Spanish *rincón* '(inside) corner' (as in a room), perhaps without being entirely aware of that fact, made certain preliminary assumptions which then co-determined each of their further gambits. Of those presuppositions, some of them idle in retrospect, a few deserve to be called characteristic of our fourth case history. The following turned out to be particularly influential: (1) *rincón*, it was argued, represents an indivisible unit, involving a single root morpheme; (2) *rincón*, highly characteristic of Spanish, is confined, within the Romance domain, to the Iberian peninsula (the speakers of cognate languages have alternative lexical devices at their disposal to convey the same message); (3) variant forms of *rincón* (for example, *rencón*) may indeed have been randomly observed in older texts, or have been culled from samples of present-day dialect speech, but they constitute mere curiosities, hardly apt to provide clues to the ultimate source of the noun; (4) the fact that *rincón*, in sharp contrast to *esquina*, never refers to the outside corner, as seen, for example, at the intersection of two streets, was also either wholly overlooked or treated as a detail of minor relevance.

Within this sort of orientation, etymologists would come up with the wildest conjectures, which were mutually exclusive. These, on account of their irreconciliability, need not be specified here at any length.

The (relatively) most promising guess involved an Arabic word (or, more accurately speaking, a colloquial derivative therefrom), which alone would satisfy the demands of the interplay of sound correspondences. In the first third of the present century, this 'colourful' Orientalist thesis temporarily enjoyed a certain vogue.

By way of spadework for a critical evaluation of the motley material assembled, it is, first of all, necessary to grasp realistically the number and the structural design of the old and new variants of *rincón*. Features apt to be subject to variation include: (a) the presence or absence of a nasal before the /k/; and (b) the quality of the vowel presiding over the first syllable. The total range of emerging possibilities, unevenly distributed, gives this impression: *racón*, *recón*, *rancón*, *rencón*, *rincón*. There is no way of accurately hypothesizing the sequence of events, except that *rincón* unmistakably presupposes the prior existence of *rencón* (note the total absence from the scale of *ricón*), and that broader phonological experience with nasal inserts urges one to posit the anteriority of *racón* to *rancón*, and of *recón* to *rencón*.

This reshuffling of raw data, in turn, shatters two broad expectations. With *re-* serving as a very common prefix both at the Latin and at the Romance phases, the demand for the prototype's indivisibility, clearly, should be abandoned. Then again, the isolationist view that events must have steered a course in Spain incompatible with the sequence of events observable in other Romance territories invites radical liberalization.

155

If, then, one elects to start one's moves from *recón* as, presumably, the most archaic of the five variants at issue, one runs into no serious trouble in trying to dissect it into *re-* + *con*; and this elusive *-con* element, unavailable in isolation, begins to look beguilingly similar to French *coin* 'corner', which was pronounced /koñ/ in the Middle Ages and has, independently, been traced to Latin *cŭ-ne-u* 'wedge' compressed into *cŭ-neu*. The genuinely Spanish, native product of *cŭneu* has all along been known as *cuño* 'wedge' (with the by-form *cuña*, endowed with remarkable semantic potentialities of its own). Consequently, *-con* should be classed as an adaptation to local conditions, or a borrowing, of French *coin* as it was pronounced in the Middle Ages. To crown this hypothesis, the fourth in our arsenal of contentions, we are free to remind ourselves that French *coin* has, for centuries, been flanked by *recoin* 'nook, recess', which is present in the standard language as well as in certain groups of dialects, including those of the south-west coast of the Bay of Biscay, from where *recoin* could easily have penetrated into northern Spain, as a term of navigation and reconnoitring.

Does this reconstruction exclude the Arabic alternative? Not necessarily, but it subordinates it to the stronger thesis. Once firmly absorbed into Spanish, the palaeo-Gallicism *reco(i)n* could secondarily have allowed the Arabic word to contaminate it, presumably near the Peninsula's southern tip.

The epic quest for the ultimate root of Spanish and Portuguese *matar* 'to kill' – our fifth illustration – has needlessly become a notorious web of disappointments, in part avoidable, through difficulties, that could have been foreseen and thus eluded (e.g., inattention to certain very old branches, such as Spanish *amatar* 'to slay', *rematar* 'to finish off'). An additional factor, equally supererogatory, has been some influential researchers' romantic infatuation with the crowning performance of a *matador* at bull fights or with the elegant gambit of a *checkmate* in a courtly chess game. To a large extent, the positing of such connections was simply anachronistic, since *matar* was widely used centuries before the crystallization of any refined courtly culture in Western Europe. Yet, for a century and a half, the only alternative to Arabic *mât* 'dead' (as used, in reference to the Shah, by way of a formulaic exclamation uttered by the victorious chess-player), was, among serious etymologists, a Latin verb referring to ritualistic slaughtering (*mactāre* 'to offer, sacrifice, immolate') which, if assigned this role, would break an elementary and practically exceptionless sound correspondence: Latin *-act-* > Spanish *-ech-* /eč/, rather than /at/.

The second major point overlooked until a very recent date in virtually every quarter was the existence, in Italian, of the widely used verb *ammazzare* 'to kill, murder, slay, slaughter', which, on the semantic side, displays amazingly close resemblance to Spanish/Portuguese *matar* and, additionally, on the formal side, comes close to agreeing with Old Spanish *amatar*, except for the not so easily reconcilable contrast *t:zz*. It does help to remember that Italian *matto* means 'mad, crazy' and that the corresponding verb *ammattire*, appropriately enough, is equivalent to 'going mad', a state of affairs which, indeed, makes *ammazzare* 'to slay', vastly preferable to **ammattare*, the ideal counterpart of Old Spanish *amatar*; but such a comment does not explain away the basic difficulty: Did the Italophones have any choice and, if so, when?

Now, *ammazzare* happens to be genetically transparent. It is squarely based on *mazza* 'cudgel, club, hammer, stick, staff, mallet, mace' as well as on *mazzo* 'bundle, club, stick', a typical pair of words differentiated by gender and referring to tools (or weapons) of varying size, labels which scholars in unison have traced, for generations, to the ancestral lexical type **mattea* 'club', flanked – according to the reconstructionists – by **matteóla* and **matteúca*. All three bases are readily inferrable from numerous Romance languages, including – so Wilhelm Meyer-Lübke would assure his readers – Catalan, Romaunsch, Sardic, and Romanian, a remarkable network of representation. The relevant forms in Spanish encompass *maza* (original spelling: *maça*) 'mace, maul, hemp brake' and *mazo* 'mallet, maul, clapper', while in French *mass-ue* 'club, bludgeon' has made itself more conspicuous, and less ambiguous, than *masse* 'sledge hammer', with the substitution of the spelling -*ss*- for de-affricated -*ç*-.

The relation of Italian *ammazzare* to *mazza*, *mazzo* is nothing short of self-explanatory. But in Spanish the bridge – if there ever existed one – that may once have directly connected the nouns *maza*, *mazo* to a verb of the -*ar* conjugation is no longer visible. **Amazar* has been conspicuously absent from the record for a considerable length of time, and there is no positive proof that it was dislodged by *amatar*, from which *matar* ultimately cut loose, thus allowing for *rematar* and its offshoots (*remate*, etc.) to sprout.

Even if the sequence of events we have optimistically been toying with turns out to have been basically correct, there still remains, by way of unaccountable residue, the one (inflectional?) shift from a **-tiāre* to a **-tāre* infinitive.

The relation of -*tāre* to -*tiāre* (and, in its close vicinity, the one of -*sāre* to -*siāre*) in provincial Vulgar Latin is a singularly difficult issue, into which there exists a single inquiry, lamentably enough still left unpublished (Thomas J. Walsh's Berkeley dissertation). The verbs here hinted at must have been used by the Roman soldiery stationed in the various provinces, being in the legionaries' slang equivalent to 'killing with a bludgeon, finishing off, doing in'. While it is not unprecedented that there should have sprouted, from the same primitive, in one corner of the Republic or the Empire an *-āre* verb (better still, a parasynthetic *a-āre* verb) and, in some other corner, a *-iāre* or *a-iāre* verb, the details of the differentiation (including the controlling factors for the sharp split it eventually produced), typically, still elude us. We realize that Italian *abbassare* 'to lower, diminish, reduce' rests squarely on *bassus* (a Late Latin substitute for Classical Latin *altus*, when endowed with that meaning), and we credit the same starting point to French *baisser* alongside *bas*, to Spanish *bajar* (Old Spanish *baxar*) alongside *bajo* (*baxo*), and to Portuguese *(a)baixar* alongside *baixo*, all these based on *-iāre*. Could such a verb have derived from the comparative degree (*bass-ior*, *-ius*), as not a few adjectival verbs have, or appear to have, behaved in German? Contrast *erweitern*, *schmälern*, *verbreitern*, *verlängern* with *abkürzen*, *einebnen*, *einengen*, *vertiefen*, within the single category of dimensional qualities.

There still remains a host of side-issues for the future advocate of this conjecture to try to disentangle. Why, for example, has the single nominal offshoot of *matar* in Spanish been a derivative in *-ança* (modern *-anza*) 'slaughter, massacre' in consistent preference to, for instance, a radical-stressed postverbal or to a word geared to some rival suffix? Can the absence from Spanish lexis of any straight counterpart of Italian *matto* 'crazy' and the weak representation (despite *matiz* 'nuance') of the lexeme *mat-* 'pale' familiar from French be construed as direct consequences of the entrenchment, to the south of the Pyrenees, of the verb *matar*? Which is the most felicitous formula for reconciling the rapid spread of *matar* with the equally sudden decline and subsequent elimination of *occīdere*, literally 'to fell' (well preserved in Italian: *uccidere*, no less than in Old French: *occire*), not to mention the collapse of *interficere* and the re-interpretation of *necāre* (> Spanish *negarse*, French *se noyer* 'to drown')? Is it legitimate to draw any conclusions from the semantic shrinkage of *amatar* in dialectal Portuguese (Transmontano) 'to extinguish [a light]' as to the semantic history, in reverse direction, of French *tuer* < Latin *tū-tāre*, from *tūtus* 'safe'? Perhaps surprisingly, the well-known Arabic verb *ka:tala* 'to kill', *ká:tala* 'to murder' is not represented here; however, the startling Spanish construction *le han muerto* 'they have killed him' (lacking any counterpart in French) may have been suggested by an Arabic causative model. It is also fitting to mention here *asesinar*, demonstrably an Orientalism, to be sure, but one absorbed through special, unique channels.

In the past, etymological discussions have, upon occasion, been made gratuitously complicated and abounding in self-contradictions through almost wanton disregard of certain basic facts – in part linguistic, in part historical and environmental – which, as sober thinking teaches us, must have significantly co-determined the course of events. Spanish *combleza* 'concubine (of a married soldier)' is a case in point, and may here be presented as our sixth and concluding illustration.

The word itself, slightly obsolescent at present (in part because the status of such a woman is no longer being institutionalized under the current set of conditions), is actually, perhaps contrary to first impressions, by no means one of insuperable difficulty in terms of etymological probing. One should start out, of course, from the non-committal gathering of forms actually on record, preferably in texts that are both old and regionally coloured. *Combleza*, when exposed to such critical sifting of raw data, turns out to be a fairly recent, namely Golden Age, substitute for medieval *comblueça*, occasionally *combrueça*, which corresponded to *comborça* (or, less frequently, *combroça*) in Old Galician–Portuguese. These few authentic forms, if accurately pinpointed along the axes of space, time, and social setting, actually suffice to set the inquiry in motion. The initial segment *com-* at once gives the impression that we are dealing here with a Latin base, whether documented or merely reconstructible; and since the initial reference, under this set of circumstances, was plausibly made to the life-style and *mores* of the Roman legionaries stationed in far-off Hispania, at some time between the Second Punic War and the age of Pompey and Caesar, the Latinity involved could, transparently, be of archaic, although not necessarily preliterary, and hence not purely hypothetical, type. In that Latinity, which was peculiar to the Republican rather than the Imperial era, the verb *uortō, -ĕre* 'to turn' prevailed as the predecessor of Classical Latin *uertō, -ĕre*; and there existed (and was, in all likelihood, still productive) the suffix $-ia_1$ for the designation of females, as in *fīlia* 'daughter', *auia* 'grandmother' (alongside *auus* 'grandfather'), *atauia* 'greatgrandmother', and, in Folk Latin, *neptia* or, occasionally, *nepōtia* 'niece' (the direct forerunner of French *nièce* and, indirectly, of English *niece*) in eloquent preference to the standard form *neptis* and to such variants familiar, for example, from tomb inscriptions as *nepta* and *nepōta* as opposed to the $-ia_2$ of abstracts. *Conuortia*, so analysed, consequently might have meant 'a woman (or female) turning her attentions, or affection, to . . . '; Old Portuguese *comborça* would beautifully fit it in every phonologically relevant respect, and the assumption of a trivial instance of subsequent metathesis would suffice to allow us to postulate Old Spanish *combrueça* as a forerunner of better-remembered *comblueça* (cf. *templar* 'to moderate', via *temprar* from ancestral *temperāre*) and, eventually, of *combleza* arrived at through monophthongization of *ue*, as in the familiar derivational suffix *-dero* in lieu of older *-duero*. These concluding shifts no longer pose any serious problems.

In itself, the conjecture for which I have here taken up the cudgels (and which goes back to a heavily documented inquiry made available in 1985) represents nothing remarkable. It may acquire limited importance when placed alongside some choice alternative explanations excogitated over a period of, approximately, four centuries, by conjecturalists who, presumably, were very much in a hurry. (The relatively few scholars who, in the wake of L. A. de Cueto, were honest enough – when their turn to speak up approached – to confess their agnosticism or scepticism: a Castro, a Cuervo, a Meyer-Lübke, a Wagner, have in comparison earned our admiration.) The roster of experts who became embroiled in all sorts of invariably very far-fetched etymological hypotheses bearing on *combuerça/comborça* includes such names, in alphabetical order, as Juan Corominas, Sebastián de Covarrubias, Vicente García de Diego, W. Giese, F. del Rosal, J. da Silveira, and Leo Spitzer. A few of them came up with two or more proposals which were advanced consecutively and not always mutually compatibly. It cannot be stated that the later explanations were simpler or more persuasive than the initial excogitations; and the stridency of the tone increased steadily with the passing of time. Here are a few specimens of the ideas that have been toyed with from the late sixteenth century to the mid-1980s.

Among the most striking older conjectures one is tempted to mention one not devoid of a moralizing tone (*cum* or *con* + *pellice*, from *pellex*), castigating the relationship as adulterous. More colourful was the suggestion of the locale where such an affair, typically, takes place: a sort of outdoors or fresh-air bed: 'cama que se arma sobre çarços', with special reference, by implication, to *combreza*, an arbitrarily selected variant which empowered the etymologist at issue to cast a bridge to older Spanish *brezo* or *brizo*, a cognate, one learns, of French *berceau* (*de treille*). Though apparently made aware of the erstwhile existence of *combreça*, in all likelihood through readings of older texts, the etymologist, in his own discussion, had recourse to *combleza*, and for no good reason, let his imagination stray to the dialectal, rustic use of the noun *briço* and the verb *briçar*, irreconcilable in both form and meaning

('concamerario'?): 'En algunas partes de las montañas hazen a los niños
unas cunas colgadas en el ayre con sogas . . . '.

Phytonymic curiosity about *brezo* and *brizo*, in addition to *broza*, began
to develop in the late nineteenth century among otherwise respectable
scholars, who allowed their fancy to move away from the lovers' behaviour
in the direction of the bed allegedly suspended between the branches of a
tree or half-hidden by the greenery of the meadow (three experts succumbed to this temptation).

A few late nineteenth-century Hispanists, apparently aghast at this sort of
unbridled fantasizing, now began to admit their ignorance of the ultimate
provenance of the elusive word, and preferred to collect stubbornly its rarer
variants, culling them chiefly from older, less easily accessible, sources.
Combl(u)eça/comborça began to loom important in the context of ongoing
inquiries into the sources of the Old Spanish sibilants.

Authors of etymological dictionaries faced the special problem of finding
somewhere a niche for a word of highly controversial extraction. One of
them, over the years, wavered between **bersium* and **bertium/bretium*
'cradle, box' as appropriate entries, but, ironically or paradoxically, used
this device to state his disbelief in the given derivation (without seeing fit to
offer any superior solution).

The human urge to engage in guesswork being well-nigh irresistible, a
former student of the prudent sceptic chose, of all channels of communication a book review to launch a new conjecture upon stumbling over Old
Spanish *comblueça* 'pellex' and *comblueço* 'rivalis'. For a change, he chose
as his starting point a hypothetical verb, to wit, **convoltiāre*, based on
convol(ū)tus, the past participle of *convolvere*. Obviously, he was less
fascinated by the configuration of the bed than by the lubricity of the lustful
lovers' movements; the fact that the oldest variants displayed an *r* rather
than an *l* seemed relatively unimportant in such an exciting context.

Has the bed, elaborately nuptial or merely makeshift, now at long last
been banished from the etymologists' laboratory? Not so, contrary to one's
expectations. It makes its reappearance towards the middle of the twentieth
century, to be sure, clad in a more pretentious garb. The starting point
(pre-Roman, conceivably Celtic) is now being spelled **combortia/
*combrottia, and is connectible with **bertium/**bretium* on the assumption
of Palaeo-Indo-European apophony. *Berço*, *comborça*, and French *berceau*
can, through this sleight-of-hand, allegedly be traced back to a single
starting point. We have meanwhile reached the mid-1950s, and to lend
company to our bold reconstructionist, a Portuguese scholar, who is not
injudicious on other occasions, sets out to posit **cumbolottea* as the

foundation of *comborça*. A few years later, however, he abruptly changes his mind, choosing on that occasion in favour of *concumbŭla*, and the derogatory suffix *-ŏtteu*. The segment *cumb-* was, obviously, evocative of the Latin verb for 'lying (outstretched), leaning upon', cf. English *recumbent* and, less transparently on the semantic side, *incumbent*. The major advantage of his new interpretation, its proponent argued passionately, was the fact that it dispensed with any need to have recourse to a Celtic base.

This is not the end of the story. Sufficient material, however, has been marshalled to demonstrate how a relatively simple problem can be complicated, indeed distorted beyond easy recognition, through the rash introduction of all sorts of basically gratuitous assumptions.

Traditionally, etymology has been tied up very closely with phonology; yet, the regularity, to the point of predictability, of sound changes – the familiar battlefield of Neogrammarianism – can neither be championed nor, for that matter, impugned without, it would seem, constant references to issues in lexical identity. Without challenging this tradition, one can legitimately point out certain instances of a very close connection of attempted etymological identification with successful attacks on inflectional (i.e., at bottom, morphological) problems.

One case in point is offered by the biography of Portuguese *perder* 'to lose', which abounds in all sorts of twists totally alien to its Spanish counterpart *perder*. Suffice it to mention the disquieting fact that in the north-western corner of the Iberian peninsula regional and obsolete forms for the 1st person singular present indicative in *-co*, *-ço*, and *-go*, rather than expected *-do*, have been ferreted out, with the entire paradigm of the present subjunctive, as usual, chiming in. The starting point for the zigzags was doubtless the fact that *perdō, -ĕre* was not a typical Latin compound verb, and that its fit into the *dō, dăre* family, right at the start, was erratic. As the leading French Latinists Alfred Ernout and Antoine Meillet, unaware of the service they were obliquely lending Romance scholarship, remarked sixty years ago, *perdō*'s compositional design, before long, was blurred. New compounds sprang up, their genesis being observable through the texts: *dēperdō* alongside *disperdō*; the latter especially was not infrequently confused with *dispergō*, which belongs to *spargō, -ĕre* 'to scatter'.

In most daughter languages and dialects the oscillation was eventually brought under control. But in the Portuguese–Galician-Asturian zone, on the one hand, and, on the other, in southern Italy, the vibrations of the local descendants of *perdere* have continued for centuries. The individual attractions of synonyms, near-homonyms, and polar antonyms to which the regional outcomes of *perdere* fell prey were, little by little, identified by the pioneer Lusophiles Jules Cornu, Carolina Michaëlis de Vasconcelos, the Marquis of Valmar, H. R. Lang, J. Leite de Vasconcelos, and others. But the general reason for the centuries-long restless comportment of the local reflexes of *perdere* in certain territories did not immediately become visible to them. Neither did they at once grasp the basic difference between (a) the split of the Tuscan preterite into *perdei, perdetti,* and *persi* and (b) the division of the corresponding past participle into *perduto* and *perso,* all five forms by no means abnormal, and such thoroughly erratic relationships as *perco/perca* (which has survived to the present), or *pergo/perga,* or else *perço/perça:perdere,* truly unique, and traceable to the Iberian peninsula.

Old-style philological precision-work has in the meantime clarified various details: *perço* /pɛrs-/ preceded *perco* /pɛrk-/ in Old Portuguese proper; *pergo* /pɛrg-/ was characteristic of Old Galician notarial style and, independently, calls to mind certain findings in South Italy vouched for by the authority of Gerhard Rohlfs.

The problems that have emerged as pivotal at a fairly late stage of investigation, i.e., after the basic issues in normal correspondences – such as those relevant to historical grammar – have been duly brought under control, are, to confine ourselves to mere random samples, those peculiar to diachronic lexicology. Here are a few illustrations:

> Contamination, predominantly, starts not at the centres, but at the peripheries of far-flung, complexly structured word-families (*perdere* vs. *spargere*); the explorer's romantic infatuation with sports, military exploits, colourful local customs, spasms of love-life can be as damaging to the analytical cause he has espoused as is stern morality (*matar, combleza*), sober concern with documented archaicity as against addiction to musing about hypothetical prehistoric layers bids fair to yield sound results (*uortĕre* vs. *uertĕre, aestumāre* vs. *aestimāre*); such processes, elusive on account of their sporadicity, as vowel dissimilation (which involves a tendency rather than a set of 'laws'), invite very careful inspection, since their neglect in the past accounts for many impasses (witness the cases of Italian *nuotare* and French *Noël,* viewed against the background of *a-á > o-á*); as regards the consequences of the loss of vowel length, i.e., the eventual collision of near-homonyms, etymologists have only scratched the surface (*nāt-/năt-*); apparently justified appeals to metathesis lack cogency, as long as that area remains neglected (*combuerça < combrueça*); chronological and other implica-

tions of the rise of nasal inserts remain to be provided (*racón* vs. *rancón*); semantic peculiarities cannot be overlooked with impunity (*rincón* vs. *esquina*); practically unavoidable simplification of initial consonant clusters (for example, in Romance adaptations of Germanic *hr-*, *wr-*) are a sharp reminder that base and product need not have started with the same consonant (*tomar*); saltatory change of stem vowel may signal semantic affinity and social hegemony, as when *nūra* is subordinated to *sŏc(e)ra*; the switch to a sex-suggestive vowel is visible in *nūrus* > **nūra*; syllabic syncope is observable even in learned words (*Navidad*); the role of an accent shift has only in rare instances been carefully defined (*iecuāria* > *iguaría*, *yegüería*). Other sources of doubt are: the wisdom – still left undefined – of reckoning with the interference by some other word (*iecur aequāre?*); humorous exploitations of some ongoing sound change (*aes-tŭmāre*); hazards courted in positing an effect of onomatopoeia or expressive orchestration (*tomar*); are variant forms mere trifles, or possible clues to the sequence of effects? (*rencón*, *rancón*); indivisible unit as an alternative to operating with a combination of derivational morpheme + root (*rincón*); dearth vs. ready availability of special social channels (French *assassiner*, Spanish *asesinar*); semantic expansion vs. shrinkage (French *tuer* vs. Portuguese *amatar*); soldiers' slang, regionally differentiated (**mattāre* vs. **mattiāre*); consequences of inattention to a given word-family's very ancient branches (*a-*, *re-matar*); delayed discovery of long-overlooked congeners (French *re-coin*, Spanish *re-*, *ren-cón*); conjectures convergent (*autumāre* → *aestumāre*) or irreconcilably divergent (older statements on *rincón*).

This is, to be sure, a very loose collection of scattered ideas ('Einfälle') – ideas not even tentatively organized into a coherent whole. Some of them bear on salient features of the material brought together, others emanate from the interpretative schema proposed; yet others remark on the varying attitudes that consecutive generations of investigators have tended to strike in coming to grips with problems of that sort.

Whether a fuller and more deftly arranged corpus of such loose individual observations can ever be pared down to a single, tightly worded theory, or method, or technique of etymologizing remains highly problematic. Showing what kind of doubts the model word biographies succinctly presented above tend to raise (their number could effortlessly have been doubled or tripled) is all that has been provisionally aimed at. These questions, for all their chequered appearance, differ sharply from those (equally legitimate) that had previously been raised by over-confident architects of historical grammar and, at later stages of planned research, by dialect geographers (or diffusionists), by students of deliberate lexical borrowing, and especially by advocates of the '*Wörter und Sachen*' approach who were often oblivious of qualifiers, quantifiers, verbs, pronouns, prepositions, and conjunctions.

Conclusion

Almost exactly a century ago etymological research reached its all-time peak of appeal and recognition, at several levels of intellectual life. The legitimacy and even desirability of etymological inquiries went unchallenged in practically all advanced countries, as did the inclusion of etymology in the ensemble of historico-linguistic disciplines. Ambitious scholars made a point of their ability to engage in etymologizing, while editors of respected learned journals, usually characterized as 'philological', were only too eager to reserve a prominent section of each number for brief, pungent discussions of this kind. Earlier pronouncements of the 'pre-scientific' era were mentioned, at best, in more or less casual manner and, not infrequently, in an ironic or condescending tone.

Such a favourable situation does not at all obtain at present, but strangely enough, the current state of affairs in the 'linguistic' domain is self-contradictory, with participants and policy-makers (as if to complicate things still more) seldom stooping to ventilating such inconsistencies. A dispassionate observer quickly becomes aware of a certain confusion of values, but may search in vain for any enlightening analyses of what makes etymology 'unscientific' (subjectivity of pronouncements? insufficiently objective tone? the general air of archaicity?).

There obtains, to begin with, a hazardous discrepancy between the degrees of attention our societies tend to reserve for dictionary-style compilations of comments on word-origins as against monographic investigations into them. Where world languages are involved (especially such as are still living), one notices that the laconically brief identification of the background of each entry unquestionably has become a desideratum; in fact, it serves as one of the criteria that helps a lay user distinguish between a good and an excellent dictionary. Of course, the mandatory succinctness

167

of each comment allows the editor to set off the dubious provenance of certain words solely by parenthetic qualifiers such as 'perhaps' or 'probably', or else to confess 'of dubious provenance', unless simply a question mark in parentheses is used. The lay reader's naïve curiosity may thus be momentarily aroused, but is seldom if ever satisfied, i.e., channelled into a series of systematic assessments of probability.

On an unavoidably more limited scale, our book markets also – at least marginally – tolerate certain etymological dictionaries designed for specialists and non-specialists alike, i.e., comprehensibly worded rather than formulaically phrased. For languages such as English, French, German, Spanish, or Italian, such select dictionaries – typically compressed into a single volume – are launched every twenty or thirty years. Then, for ancient tongues, or for languages newly discovered or for social and regional dialects restricted in actual use, there predictably develops an, at least, temporary demand, but only among true professionals (Hittite being an example in point). In such instances, the budgetary support of a government agency or of a learned society can be taken for granted, provided the quality of the research involved justifies such subsidy.

Over against this, all told, not unencouraging landscape stands the grim picture of today's society's almost total indifference to monographic explorations in this field, unless they are somehow disguised (starting with the titles: 'word origins', 'Herkunftswörterbuch', and the like). The very term 'etymology' has virtually disappeared from announcements of journal notes and articles, or from series of academy memoirs. For a young scholar, it is at present inadvisable, at least for career purposes in the teaching field, that he or she be known as aiming to qualify mainly as an etymologist, the way his next-door neighbours may safely declare their eagerness to pass off as phoneticians, phonologists, semanticists, pragmaticists, syntactitians, and the like.

Now it is, indisputably, desirable that one should not cultivate etymology in strict isolation. Its study can be very fruitfully combined with inquiries into models of regular sound change, phonosymbolism, morphology (with particular emphasis on derivation and compounding), and so on; even a certain partnership with the fashionable probing of newly coined words might be highly commendable. But society is in error if it, directly or indirectly, encourages, or even provokes, the publication of reference books, which, practically by definition, should contain no entirely new facts or ideas on the side of word origins, but instead, provide only novel approaches to relationships established elsewhere, while sorely neglecting the diffusion of purely exploratory writings.

Over the last forty years or so, there have appeared, in fairly quick succession, introductions to the methodology (theoretical presuppositions, techniques, familiarity with auxiliary tools such as dictionaries and atlases, and so on) of etymology, as practised today in many quarters. Most – unfortunately not all – of these initiations have come from seasoned practitioners of the discipline, call it an art or a science, and to that extent they have been welcome indeed. But, while the methods of etymological inspection have indisputably undergone a change as a whole, the history or record of cutting a path through every language's etymological jungle is also apt to change radically with the pressure of time, regardless of the calendar date. To clarify this point, it is useful to operate with successive 'stages' of a typical ongoing operation. A gross division of the entire task of etymologizing a given lexis into Stage A and Stage B may here be advisable, despite the crude simplification involved in this proposal.

At Stage A, the advance proceeds at a fairly predictable rate, assuming the ready availability of guides to the chosen language (X) as well as to the impressionistically (or thoroughly) identified ancestral languages (Y_1, Y_2, Y_3, . . .) as well as of tongues of the past and the present with which X is independently known to have been in contact, friendly or hostile, at consecutive periods.

The two preconditions additionally required for the application of this scenario are: (a) the analyst's pre-existent familiarity with the sets of normal sound correspondences between successive phases of the growth, as well as with the standard ranges of inflectional, derivational, and compositional patterns; and (b) his or her earlier exposure to the varying latitudes of semantic shifts. The rate of progress, I repeat, under these conditions is roughly predictable, and the punctual appearance of fascicle after fascicle of an announced reference work can safely be guaranteed. Where the ancestral configuration of the language at issue cannot be textually ascertained, it can often be reconstructed through systematic comparison with its ancestors.

As a rule, the above-stated simplistic techniques peculiar to Stage A leave a shockingly high percentage of etymological 'riddles' unsolved. This residue (B), whether it comprises one quarter, one third, or one half of the whole, is illustrative of individual developments, i.e., of word biographies that exhibit the more or less sporadic intervention, to varying extents, of forces that refuse to fall into any rigid schemata: lexical diffusion and contamination; phonosymbolic appeal (or 'expressivity'); temporary avoidance of a given word under pressure from social taboo; interplays of assimilatory or dissimilatory tendencies; the crystallization or dilapidation of vocalic scales; also the impacts of folk belief, mythology, material civilization, and playfulness, and the like. At intervals, five or more such interferential factors must be identified before the investigator dares to come up with a new interpretation. Since not a few requisite discoveries tend to be made incidentally (if they turn out to be at all possible), a scholar who espouses this philosophy cannot make firm commitments to his publishers as to the deadline for the promised delivery of the manuscript. Given the high degree of controversiality of this kind of material, not to say the typicality of relevant clashes of opinion, every new proposal is normally accompanied by a scrupulous 'historique du problème', a requirement which further slows down the process of completion.

Readers will meanwhile have recognized the resemblance of Stage A to the neogrammatical style of stringent analysis, while Style B may call up memories of the virulent reaction to it. But the whole point of the present statement is not to repeat what has long been known, namely the facts that the neogrammarian movement reached its peak around the year 1890, while most of its tenets were abandoned or relaxed half a century later. If etymological probing in reference to a newly identified language were to start around 1990, there would, in all likelihood, still emerge, perhaps unannounced, a Stage A, presumably with different terminological accoutrements, to be succeeded, in due time, by the advent to influence of Stage B, however cleverly disguised.

Our society, by favouring the etymologically tinged dictionary, yet simultaneously discouraging the necessarily lengthy monographs (as essayed for the first time, *qua* innovative genre, by Hugo Schuchardt) thus renders a potential disservice to the steady advance of etymology.

This mild rebuke does not mean that the scholars themselves have been consistently blameless. The incessant launching of meagrely controlled etymological conjectures in regard to languages already well investigated may amount to a source of urbane entertainment for weakly motivated readers, but will not fail to irritate fellow-workers. Another infelicity of which some of us have of late been guilty is the confusion of the formal establishment of a corpus, whether inscriptional or culled from the testimony of living languages and dialects, with an etymological dictionary, which can and should be compact and may well concentrate on essentials rather than devoting hundreds, even thousands of pages in consecutive volumes to lexical units perfectly transparent from the start, as are most Hellenisms and Latinisms in modern languages.

The threshing-out of such organizational disagreements can be quite as stimulating and free from acrimony as experimental returns to the dwindling residues of etymological unknowns.

But what is the wisdom of the moderns' occasional return to pre-1800 pronouncements, especially if those verdicts, measured by present-day standards, have turned out to be faulty? It seems permissible to furnish two answers to that question: first, one can expect to improve one's own methodology by taking into account, at intervals, the aberrations of pioneers; second, the incidental bits of factual information that those pace-setters, perhaps by virtue of their naïveté, were sometimes in the habit of providing can turn out to be priceless.

REFERENCES

Note: The spelling of titles has been modernized where circumstances so
warranted (especially in regard to German and Portuguese material).

Abel, Karl (1869). *Über Sprache als Ausdruck nationaler Denkweise. Ein Vortrag.*
Berlin: n. pub.

(1872). *Über den Begriff der Liebe in einigen alten und neuen Sprachen.* Berlin:
Habel.

(1881). *Über den Ursprung der Sprache.* 2nd edn. Berlin: Liepmannssohn.

(1882). *Linguistic essays.* English and Foreign Philosophical Library, 30.
Boston: Houghton Mifflin.

(1884). *Über den Gegensinn der Urworte.* Leipzig: Friedrich.

(1886). *Einleitung in ein aegyptisch–semitisch–indoeuropäisches Wurzelwörter-*
buch. Leipzig: Friedrich.

(1890). *Ägyptisch–indoeuropäische Sprachverwandtschaft.* Leipzig: Friedrich.
Rev. 2nd edn. Berlin: Luckhardt, 1903.

(1905–6). *Über Gegensinn und Gegenlaut in den klassischen, germanischen und*
slavischen Sprachen. 2 vols. Frankfurt: Diesterweg.

Academiae Quinque Germanicae (1900–). *Thesaurus Linguae Latinae*, 1–.
Leipzig: Teubner.

Aebischer, Paul (1924a). *Sur l'origine et la formation des noms de famille dans le*
canton de Fribourg. Bibl. dell'*Archivum Romanicum*, 2:6. Geneva: Olschki.

(1924b). *L'anthroponymie wallonne d'après quelques anciens cartulaires.* Repr.
from *Bulletin du Dictionnaire wallon.* Liège: H. Vaillant-Carmanne.

(1948). *Estudios de toponimia y lexicografía románicas.* Barcelona: Escuela de
Filología.

(1978). *Études de stratigraphie linguistique.* Romanica Helvetica, 87. Berne:
Francke.

& Olivier, E. (1938). *L'herbier de Moudon. Un recueil de recettes*
médicales . . . , notes sur la botanique médicale du Moyen Age. Aarau:
Sauerländer.

References

Alcalá, Pedro de (n.d.: 1504?). *Arte para ligeramente saber la lengua aráviga*. Granada. Repr. New York: Hispanic Society of America, 1928; rev. 2nd edn, Granada, 1505.

Aldrete, Bernardo (José) (1606). *Del origen y principio del la lengua castellana o romance que oi se usa en España*. Rome: Carlo Willietto.

Algeo, John & Adele, *et al.* (1989, 1990, 1991). Among the new words, *American Speech*, 64, 65–73, 150–61, 244–51, 334–43; 70–9, 136–47, 238–48, 367–76; 66, 71–81.

American Heritage dictionary of the English language, The (1969, etc.). ed. William Morris. Boston: Houghton Mifflin. College edn, 1976.

American Speech (1925–). Ed. at Duke University; University of Alabama Press (for the American Dialect Society). New York: Columbia University Press.

Anderson, James J., & Creore, Jo Ann (1972–3). *Readings in Romance linguistics*. The Hague: Mouton.

Ascoli, Graziadio Isaia (1865). *Zigeunerisches; besonders auch als Nachtrag zu dem Pottschen Werke: 'Die Zigeuner in Europa und Asien'*. Halle: Heynemann; London: Williams & Norgate; Turin and Florence: Loescher.

Atlantic Monthly, The (1857–). Boston: The Atlantic Monthly Co.

Baist, Gottfried (1881, 1882). Etymologisches [32 Romance etymologies]. *Zeitschrift für romanische Philologie*, 5, 233–48; [14 Romance etymologies], 6, 116–19.

— (1888). Die spanische Sprache. In *Grundriß der romanischen Philologie*, ed. G. Gröber, Vol. I, 689–714. Strasbourg: Trübner. Rev. 2nd edn (1904–6), 878–915.

— (1904). Etymologien [13 problems of Romance etymology]. *Zeitschrift für romanische Philologie*, 28, 105–13.

Baldinger, Kurt (1982). Johannes Hubschmid zum 65. Geburtstag. In *Festschrift für Johannes Hubschmid zum 65. Geburtstag*. Berne and Munich: Francke, 11–34.

Bammesberger, Alfred, ed. (1983). *Das etymologische Wörterbuch. Fragen der Konzeption und Gestaltung*, Eichstätter Beitrage, vol. VIII. Regensburg, Friedrich Pustet.

Barbier, Paul (1925–38). Miscellanea Lexicographica, 1–18. Etymological and lexicographical notes on the French language . . . , in *Proceedings of the Leeds Philosophical Society: Literary and Historical Section*, 1–4.

— (1947, 1948, 1951, 1953, 1954, 1955). Nouvelles études de lexicologie française. *Romance Philology*, 1:1, 11–22; 1:4, 287–96; 4:2–3, 257–67; 6:2–3, 186–90; 7:4, 342–6; 9:1, 6–11.

Barnhart, Robert K. (ed.) (1988). *The Barnhart dictionary of etymology*. n.p.: Wilson.

Bartoli, Matteo G. (1910). Alle fonti dei neolatino, in *Miscellanea di studi in onore di Attilio Hortis*. Trieste: Caprin, 889–918.

— (1925). *Introduzione alla neolinguistica: principi, scopi, metodi*. Bibl. dell'

Archivum Romanicum, 2:12. Geneva: Olschki.

(1939–40). I riflessi di *afflāre* e *conflāre* nell'Italia meridionale. *Atti della R. Accademia delle scienze di Torino*, 75, 202–45.

(1945). *Saggi di linguistica spaziale*. Turin: Bona.

& Bertoni, Giulio (1928). *Breviario di neolinguistica*. Modena: Società Tipografica Modenese.

& Vidossi, Giuseppe (1943). *Lineamenti di linguistica spaziale*. Milan: Le lingue estere.

Battisti, Carlo & Alessio, Giovanni (1950–57). *Dizionario etimologico italiano*. 5 vols. Florence: Barbèra.

Belloni, Pietro & Nilsson-Ehle, Hans (1957). *Voci romanesche: aggiunte e commenti al vocabolario romanesco Chiappini–Rolandi*. Lund: Gleerup.

Benfey, Theodor (1869). *Geschichte der Sprachwissenschaft und orientalischen Philologie in Deutschland seit dem Anfange des 19. Jahrhunderts* . . . . Geschichte der Wissenschaften in Deutschland, Neuere Zeit, 8. Munich: Cotta.

Benveniste, Émile (1928). Sogdien *βrγˋr*. *Bulletin de la Société de Linguistique de Paris*, 28, 7–8.

Berneker, Erich (1896). *Die preußische Sprache. Texte, Grammatik, etymologisches Wörterbuch*. Strasbourg: Trübner.

(1908–14). *Slavisches etymologisches Wörterbuch*. 2 vols. Heidelberg: Winter; 2nd edn, 1924.

Bertoldi, Vittorio (1923). *Un ribelle nel regno dei fiori. I nomi romanzi del 'Colchicum autunnale L.' attraverso il tempo e lo spazio*. Bibl. dell' *Archivum Romanicum*, 2:4. Geneva: Olschki.

Bezzenberger, Adalbert (1876). *Die Bildung der altpreussischen Personennamen; ein Versuch einer Deutung*. Königsberg: Rosbach.

(ed.) (1877–1906). *Beiträge zur Kunde der indogermanischen Sprachen*. 30 vols. Göttingen: Peppmüller.

Bindseil, Heinrich Ernst (1876). *Wurzel-, Wort-, Namen- und Sachregister* = vol. 6 of rev. edn of Pott, *Etymologische Forschungen* . . . .

Bloch, Oscar & von Wartburg, Walther (1932). *Dictionnaire étymologique de la langue française*. Preface by A. Meillet. 2 vols. Paris: Presses Universitaires de France. 2nd end, rev. by W. von Wartburg, 1950; rev. 4th edn, 1964; rev. 5th edn, 1968.

Bloch, R. Howard (1983). *Etymologies and genealogies. A literary anthropology of the French Middle Ages*. Chicago and London: University of Chicago Press.

Blondheim, David S. (1929, 1937). *Les gloses françaises dans les commentaires talmudiques de Raschi*. 2 vols. Vol. I (with Arsène Darmesteter): Paris: Champion. Vol. II: Baltimore: Johns Hopkins Studies in Romance.

Bloomfield, Leonard (1914). *An introduction to the study of language*. New York: Holt.

(1912). Etymologisches. *Beiträge zur Geschichte der deutschen Sprache und Literatur. Paul & Braunes Beiträge*, 37. 245–61.

References

(1933). *Language*. New York: Henry Holt.

(1965). *Language history*, from *Language* (1933 edn), ed. Harry Hoijer. New York: Holt, Rinehart, & Winston.

Bolza, Giovanni Battista (1852). *Vocabolario genetico etimologico della lingua italiana*. Vienna: I. R. Stamperia di Corte e di Stato.

Bonaparte, Prince Louis-Lucien (1880–81). On neuter Neo-Latin substantives. *Transactions of the Philological Society*, 45–64.

Bonfante, Giuliano (1947). The Neolinguistic position. *Language*, 23, 344–75.

Bopp, Franz (1816). *Über das Conjugationssystem der Sanskritsprache in Vergleichung mit jenem der griechischen, lateinischen, persischen und germanischen Sprache*. Frankfurt am Main: Andreäische Buchhandlung.

(1820). Analytical comparison of the Sanskrit, Greek, Latin, and Teutonic languages, shewing the original identity of their grammatical structure. In *Annals of Oriental Literature*, 1, 1–65. Repr. in *Internationale Zeitschrift für allgemeine Sprachwissenschaft*, 4, 1889, 14–60; also ed. E. F. K. Koerner, Amsterdam: Benjamins, 1974.

(1824). *Ausführliches Lehrgebäude der Sanskritasprache*. Berlin: Dümmler. Rev. 2nd edn, 1827.

(1829) *Grammatica critica linguae sanscritae*. Berlin: Dümmler. Rev. 2nd edn, 1832; *Kritische Grammatik . . . in kürzerer Fassung*, Berlin: Nicolai, 1834; 2nd edn, 1845; rev. 3rd edn, 1863; 4th edn, 1868.

(1833–42). *Vergleichende Grammatik des Sanskrit, Zend, Griechischen, Lateinischen, Litauischen, [Altslawischen], Gothischen und Deutschen*. 4 vols. Berlin: Dümmler. Rev. 2nd edn, with addition of Armenian, 3 vols., 1857–61. *A comparative grammar of the Sanskrit . . . and Slavonic languages*, tr. Edward B. Eastwick *et al.*, London: Madden & Malcom, 1845–53; 2nd edn, 3 vols., London: Murray, 1850–60; 3rd edn, 1862; 4th edn, 1885. *Grammaire comparée des langues indo-européennes . . .* , tr. M. Bréal, 4 vols., Paris: Imprimerie Impériale, 1866–74; 2nd edn, 5 vols., Paris: Imprimerie Nationale, 1874–8; 3rd edn, 1884–9.

(1835). *Über die Zahlwörter im Sanskrit, Griechischen, Lateinischen, Lithauischen, Gothischen und Altslavischen*. Abhandlungen der Koeniglich-preussischen Akademie der Wissenschaften, Historisch-philologische Klasse, 1833, 163–9. Berlin.

(1836). *Vokalismus; oder, Sprachvergleichende Kritiken über J. Grimms Deutsche Grammatik und [E. G.] Graffs Althochdeutschen Sprachschatz mit Begründung einer neuen Theorie des Ablauts*. Berlin: Nicolai.

(1828, 1830, 1847). *Glossarium Sanscritum in quo omnes radices et vocabula usitatissima explicantur et cum vocabulis Graecis, Latinis, Germanicis, Lithuanicis, Slavicis, Celticis comparantur*. Berlin: Dümmler. Rev. 3rd edn (*Glossarium comparativum . . .*), Berlin: Dümmler (Harrwitz & Gossman), 1867.

(1972). *Kleine Schriften zur vergleichenden Sprachwissenschaft. Gesammelte*

Berliner Akademie-abhandlungen 1824–1854. Leipzig: Zentralantiquariat der Deutschen Demokratischen Republik.

Brachet, Auguste (1868). *Dictionnaire des doublets, ou doubles formes de la langue française.* Paris: Franck. *Supplément,* 1871.

(c.1868). *Grammaire historique de la langue française,* Preface by É. Littré, 2nd edn, Paris: Hetzel. 41st edn, after 1900. *A historical grammar of the French tongue,* tr. G. W. Kitchin, Oxford: Clarendon Press, 1868, 1872, 1874, 1878, 1884, 1888; rewritten and enlarged by Paget Toynbee, 1896, 1898.

(1868, 1871). Supplément au *Dictionnaire des doublets. Mémoires de la Société de Linguistique de Paris,* 1, 358–71, and Paris: Franck, 1871.

(1870?). *Dictionnaire étymologique de la langue française.* Preface by Émile Egger. 2nd edn Paris. *An etymological dictionary of the French language,* tr. G. W. Kitchin, Oxford: Clarendon Press, 1873.

Bréal, Michel (1863a). *De Persicis nominibus apud scriptores Graecos.* Diss. Paris. Paris: Durand.

(1863b). *Hercule et Cacus, étude de mythologie comparée.* Paris: Durand.

(1868). Les doublets latins. *Mémoires de la Société de Linguistique de Paris,* 1, 358–71.

(1877). *Mélanges de mythologie et de linguistique.* Paris: Hachette. 2nd edn, 1882.

(1900). *Essai de sémantique (science des significations).* Paris: Hachette. *Semantics. Studies in the science of meanings.* New York: Holt, 1900; London: Heinemann, 1900.

& Bailly, Anatole (1885). *Dictionnaire étymologique latin; les mots latins groupés d'après le sens et l'étymologie.* Paris: Hachette. 2nd edn, 1886; 3rd edn, 1891 (=Leçons de mots, cours supérieur); 4th edn, 1898; 10th edn, 1922.

Browne, Walter R. (1880–1a). On the distribution of English place-names. *Transactions of the Philological Society,* 86–98.

(1880–1b) Distribution of Place-Names in the Scottish Lowlands. *Transactions of the Philological Society,* 322–34.

Brüch, Josef (1923–4). Zu Walther von Wartburgs *Französischen etymologischen Wörterbuch. Zeitschrift für romanische Philologie,* 43, 513–77.

(1924). Review of Walther von Wartburg, *Französisches etymologisches Wörterbuch.* In *Die neueren Sprachen,* 32, 424–36.

(1925). Etymologisches: afr. *ancenge,* afr. *mahaignier* und Sippe, frz. *gruyer,* frz. *rechigner. Zeitschrift für französische Sprache und Literatur,* 48, 103–20.

(1925). Etymologisches: 1. Aprov. *mazan;* 2. Die aprov. Verbalsubstantiva auf *-t;* 3. Frz. *moyen, moyeu, aide;* 4. Frz. *noise;* 5. Afr. *larris;* 6. Frz. *entamer. Zeitschrift für romanische Philologie,* 45, 70–83.

(1926, 1927, 1929). Bemerkungen zum *Etymologisches Wörterbuch* E. Gamillschegs. *Zeitschrift für französische Sprache und Literatur,* 49, 290–318; 50, 299–355; 52, 393–483.

References

(1931, 1932). Zu Gamillschegs etymologischen Wörterbuch. *Zeitschrift für romanische Philologie*, 51, 461–526; 679–702; 52, 321–50.

Brunot, Ferdinand (1887). *Précis de grammaire historique de la langue française, avec une introduction sur les origines et le développement de cette langue.* Paris: Masson. 2nd end, 1889; 3rd edn, 1894; 4th edn, 1899; new edn, rev. by C. Bruneau, 1937; rev. 3rd edn, 1949.

& Bruneau, Charles (eds.) (1905–79). *Histoire de la langue française des origines à 1900.* 15 vols. in 20 tomes. Paris: Colin.

Buck, Carl Darling (1933, 1969). *Comparative grammar of Greek and Latin.* Chicago: University of Chicago Press.

(1949). *A dictionary of selected synonyms in the principal Indo-European languages. A contribution to the history of ideas.* Chicago: University of Chicago Press.

Burchfield, Ronald W. (ed.) (1987). *Oxford studies in lexicography.* Oxford: Clarendon Press.

Burrow, Thomas & Emeneau, Murray B. (1961). *A Dravidian etymological dictionary.* Oxford: Clarendon Press.

& Emeneau, Murray B. (1962). *Dravidian borrowings from Indo-Aryan.* University of California Publications in Linguistics, 26. Berkeley: University of California Press.

& Emeneau, Murray B. (1968). *A Dravidian etymological dictionary. Supplement.* Oxford: Clarendon Press.

Cabrera, Ramón (1837). *Diccionario de etimologías de la lengua castellana . . .* ed. Juan Pedro Ayegui. 2 vols. Madrid: Imprenta de M. Calero.

Caix, Napoleone (1878). *Studi di etimologia italiana e romanza. Osservazioni ed aggiunte al Vocabolario etimologico delle lingue romanze di F. Diez.* Florence: Sansoni.

Candrea-Hecht, J.-A. (1902). *Les éléments latins dans la langue roumaine; le consonantisme.* Paris: Bouillon.

& Densuşianu, O. (1907). *Dicţionarul etimologic al limbii romîne. Elementele latine (A–P).* Bucharest: Socec.

Canello, Ugo A. (1878). Gli allòtropi italiani. *Archivio glottologico italiano*, 3, 285–419.

Cassidy, Frederic G., (ed.) (1985). *Dictionary of American regional English* [= *DARE*], I: Introduction and *A–C*. Cambridge, Mass. and London: Harvard University Press.

Castro, Américo (1918, 1919). Adiciones hispánicas al Diccionario etimológico de W. Meyer-Lübke. *Revista de filología española*, 5, 21–42; 6, 337–42.

(ed.) (1936). *Glosarios latino–españoles de la Edad Media.* Suppl. 22 to *Revista de filología española*. Madrid: Centro de Estudios Históricos.

Chambon, Jean-Pierre & Lüdi, Georges (eds.) (1991). *Actes du Colloque international organisé à l'occasion du centenaire de la naissance de Walther von Wartburg*. Tübingen: Niemeyer.

Chiappini, Filippo (1933). *Vocabolario romanesco. Edizione postuma delle schede a cura di Bruno Migliorini*. Rome: Leonardo da Vinci (Istituto di Studi Romani). 2nd edn, 1945; 3rd edn, 1967.

Cihac, Alexandru de (1870–79). *Dictionnaire d'étymologie daco-romane*, I: *Éléments latins* . . . ; II: *Éléments slaves, magyars, turcs, grecs-moderne et albanais*. Frankfurt: St. Goar.

Clark, Mary E., & Joseph, Brian D. (1988). The etymology of *bum*: mere child's play, *Journal of English Linguistics*, 21:1, 24–8.

Clifford, Paula M. (1973). *Inversion of the subject in French narrative prose from 1500 to the present day*. Oxford: Blackwell.

Coelho, Francisco Adolfo (1890?). *Dicionário manual etimológico da língua portuguesa*, contendo a significação e prosódia. 2nd printing. Lisbon: Plantier.

(1892). *Os ciganos de Portugal; com um estudo sobre o calão*. Memória destinada à X. Sessão do Congresso internacional dos orientalistas. Lisbon: Imprensa Nacional.

Cohen, Marcel (1928). Mots d'origine présumée océanienne dans le monde méditerranéen. Compléments au sujet du 'contenant à entrelacs', *Bulletin de la Société de Linguistique de Paris*, 28, 48–62.

(1929). Quelques voyages de mots (sémitique et domaines voisins), *Bulletin de la Société de Linguistique de Paris*, 29, 132–7.

Cornu, Jules (1884). Mélanges espagnols: remarques sur les voyelles toniques; observations étymologiques; le possessif en ancien espagnol. *Romania*, 10, 185–314.

Corominas, Juan (1931). *Vocabulario aranés*. Diss. Madrid. Barcelona: Imprenta de la Casa de Caridad.

(1936). Mots catalans d'origen aràbic. *Butlletí de dialectologia catalana*, 24, 1–81.

(1941–2). Rasgos semánticos nacionales. *Anales del Instituto de Lingüística [de Cuyo]*, 1, 1–29.

(1942–4). Nuevas etimologías españolas (= Estudios etimológicos). *Anales del Instituto de Lingüística [de Cuyo]*, 1, 119–53; 2, 1–43.

(1941–2). Aportaciones [hispanoamericanas] a cuestiones pendientes, *Anales del Instituto de Lingüística [de Cuyo]*, 1, 154–65.

(1941–2). Problemas por resolver. *Anales del Instituto de Lingüística [de Cuyo]*, 1, 166–81.

(1942–4). Espigueo de latín vulgar. *Anales del Instituto de Lingüística [de Cuyo]*, 2, 128–54.

(1944). Indianorománica; estudios de lexicología hispanoamericana. *Revista de filología hispánica*, 6, 1–35, 139–75, 209–54.

(1947–8). Problemas del diccionario etimológico. *Romance Philology*, 1:1–2, 23–38, 79–104.

(1954–7). *Diccionario crítico etimológico de la lengua castellana*. 4 vols. Madrid:

References

Gredos, and Berne: Francke. Repr. 1970.

(1961). *Breve diccionario etimológico de la lengua castellana.* Biblioteca románica hispánica, 5:2. Madrid: Gredos. Rev. 2nd edn, 1967; rev. 3rd edn, 1973.

& Pascual, José A. (1980–). *Diccionario crítico etimológico castellano e hispánico.* 6 vols. Madrid: Gredos.

& Gulsoy, Joseph & Cahner, Max (1980–91). *Diccionari etimológic complementari de la llengua catalana.* 9 vols. Barcelona: Curial Edicions Catalanas/Caixa de Pensions 'La Caixa'.

Cortelazzo, Manlio & Zolli, Paolo (1979–88). *Dizionario etimologico della lingua italiana.* 5 vols. Bologna: Zanichelli.

Covarrubias (H)orozco, Sebastián de (1611). *Tesoro de la lengua castellana o española.* Madrid: Luis Sánchez. Rev. 2nd edn, Madrid: Melchor Sánchez, 1673–4, ed. Martín de Riquer, Barcelona: Horta, 1943.

Cuervo, Rufino José (1886–93). *Diccionario de construcción y régimen de la lengua castellana.* 2 vols. (*A–D*). Paris: Roger & Chernoviz, 1886–93. Repr. and Vol. III added: Bogotá: Instituto Caro y Cuervo, 1953–61.

Curtius, Ernst Robert (1948). *Europäische Literatur und lateinisches Mittelalter.* Bern: Francke. Rev. 2nd edn, 1954; 3rd edn, 1961. *European literature and the Latin Middle Ages,* tr. Willard R. Trask, New York: Pantheon Books, 1953.

Curtius, Georg (1858–62). *Grundzüge der griechischen Etymologie.* 2 vols. Leipzig: Teubner. Rev. 2nd edn, 1866; rev. 3rd edn, 1869; 4th edn (durch Vergleichungen aus den keltischen Sprachen von Ernst Windisch erweitert), 1873; rev. 5th edn, 1879. *Principles of Greek etymology,* 4th edn, tr. A. S. Wilkins & E. B. England, 2 vols., London: Murray, 1875; 5th edn, 1896.

Darmesteter, Arsène (1874). *Traité de la formation des mots composés dans la langue française comparée aux autres langues romanes et au latin.* Paris: Franck. 2nd edn, rev. by Gaston Paris, 1894.

(1877). *De la création de mots nouveaux dans la langue française, et des lois qui la régissent.* Paris: Vieweg.

(1887). *La vie des mots étudiée dans leurs significations.* Paris: Delagrave. Rev. 2nd edn, 1887; 3rd edn, 1889; 4th edn, 1893; 5th edn, 1899, etc.; 19th edn, 1937. *The life of words as the symbols of ideas,* London: Kegan Paul, Trench, 1886.

(1891–7). *Cours de grammaire historique,* ed. E. Muret & L. Sudre. 4 vols. Paris: Delagrave. Rev. 2nd edn, 1895–1905; repr. 1930–4. *A historical French grammar,* tr. A. Hartog, London and New York: Macmillan, 1899.

& Hatzfeld, Adolphe, & Thomas, Antoine (1895–1900). *Dictionnaire général de la langue française, du commencement du XVIIe siècle jusqu'à nos jours.* 2 vols. Paris: Delagrave. 6th edn, 1920.

& Blondheim, David S. (1929–37). *Les gloses françaises dans les commentaires talmudiques de Raschi.* 2 vols. Paris: Champion.

Dauzat, Albert (1925–8). *Les noms de personnes, origine et évolution.*
Prénoms–noms de famille–surnoms–pseudonymes. Paris: Delagrave. 2nd &
3rd edns, 1925; 4th edn, 1939.

(1926–8). *Les noms de lieux, origine et évolution. Villes et villages–pays–cours
d'eau–montagnes–lieux-dits.* Paris: Delagrave.

(1938). *Dictionnaire étymologique de la langue française.* Paris: Larousse. Rev.
10th edn (avec un supplément lexicologique et un supplément
chronologique), 1949.

(1951). *Dictionnaire étymologique des noms de famille et prénoms de France.*
Paris: Larousse. 3rd edn, rev. Marie-Thérèse Morlet, 1960.

& Rostaing, Charles (1963). *Dictionnaire étymologique des noms de lieux en
France.* Paris: Larousse.

& Dubois, Jean, & Mitterand, Henri (1964, 1982). *Nouveau dictionnaire
étymologique et historique.* Paris: Larousse.

Devic, L. Marcel (1876). *Dictionnaire étymologique des mots français d'origine
orientale (arabe, persan, turc, hebreu, malais).* Paris: Hachette. 2nd edn,
1892. [Attached to *Supplément* of E. Littré's *Dictionnaire de la langue
française*, 1877.]

Devoto, Giacomo (1966). *Avviamento alla etimologia italiana; dizionario
etimologico.* Florence: Le Monnier; rev. 2nd edn, 1968.

& Oli, Gian Carlo (eds.) (1967). *Vocabolario illustrato della lingua italiana.* 2
vols. Milan: Selezione dal Reader's Digest. [Selectively etymological]

Diez, Friedrich (1836–44). *Grammatik der romanischen Sprachen.* 3 vols. Bonn:
Weber, 1836–44. Rev. 2nd edn, 1856–60; rev. 3rd edn, 1870–2; posth. 4th
edn, Bonn: Weber-Flittner, 1876–7; 5th edn, checked by F. Apfelstedt & E.
Seelmann, 1882; Supplement: *Romanische Wortschöpfung* (1874–5).
Complete or partial translations: *Introduction à la grammaire des langues
romanes*, tr. G. Paris, Paris: Franck, 1963; *Grammar of the Romance
languages: elements and jurisdiction of the Romance languages*, tr. C. B.
Cayley, London and Edinburgh; Williams & Norgate, 1863; *Grammaire des
langues romanes*, tr. A. Brachet, A. Morel-Fatio & G. Paris, Paris: Franck,
Vieweg, 1874–6.

(1858). *Etymologisches Wörterbuch der romanischen Sprachen.* Bonn: Marcus.
2nd edn, 1861; rev. 3rd edn, 2 vols., 1869–70; posth. 4th edn, with a
Supplement by A. Scheler, 1878; 5th edn, with a revised Supplement by A.
Scheler, 1887.

(1859). *Kritischer Anhang zum Etymologischen Wörterbuch der romanischen
Sprachen.* Bonn: Marcus.

Dozy, R. P. A. (1845). *Dictionnaire détaillé des noms des vêtements chez les
Arabes.* Amsterdam: Jean Müller.

(1867). *Oosterlingen. Verklarende lijst der Nederlandsche woorden, die uit het
Arabisch, Hebreeuwsch, Chaldeeuwsch, Perzisch en Turksch afkomstig zijn.*
The Hague: Nijhoff.

References

Duden, Konrad (1893). *Etymologie der neuhochdeutschen Sprache, mit einem ausführlichen etymologischen Wörterverzeichnis* . . . . München: Beck.

Eguílaz y Yanguas, Leopoldo de (1886). *Glosario etimológico de las palabras españolas (castellanas, catalanas, gallegas, . . .) de origen oriental (árabe, hebreo, malayo, persa y turco).* Granada: Imprenta de la Lealtad.

Eilers, Wilhelm (1938). *Der Name Demawend.* Hildesheim, Zurich and New York: Olms.

Emeneau, Murray B., & Burrow, T. (1984). *A Dravidian etymological dictionary.* Oxford: Clarendon Press, 1961. Rev. 2nd edn.

Engelmann, W. H. (1869). *Glossaire des mots espagnols et portugais dérivés de l'arabe.* Leiden: Brill, 1861. Rev. 2nd edn, in collaboration with R. P. A. Dozy.

Ernout, Alfred (1909). *Les éléments dialectaux du vocabulaire latin.* La Société de Linguistique, Collection, 3. Paris: Champion.

— (1929). Le groupe *cernō–crēscō*. *Bulletin de la Société de Linguistique de Paris,* 29:3, 82–102.

— (1946–65). *Philologica.* 3 vols. Études et commentaires, 1, 26, 59. Paris: Klincksieck.

— (1954). *Aspects du vocabulaire latin.* Paris: Klincksieck.

— & Meillet, Antoine (1932). *Dictionnaire étymologique de la langue latine. Histoire des mots.* Paris: Klincksieck. 2nd edn, rev. by Ernout 1939; rev. 3rd edn, 2 vols., 1951; rev. 4th edn, 1959. 3rd printing, rev. by Jacques André, 1979.

Farinelli, Arturo (1925). *'Marrano': storia di un vituperio.* Bibl. dell' *Archivum Romanicum,* 2:10. Geneva: Olschki.

Feist, Sigmund (1888). *Grundriß der gotischen Etymologie.* Sammlung indogermanischer Wörterbücher, 2. Strasbourg: Trübner.

— (1909). *Etymologisches Wörterbuch der gotischen Sprache, mit Einschluß des sog[enannten] Krimgotischen.* Halle: Niemeyer. Rev. 2nd edn [. . . *und sonstiger gotischer Sprachreste*], 1923. Rev. 3rd edn [. . . *und sonstiger zerstreuter Überreste*]. Leiden: Brill, 1939. 4th edn, rev. by Winfred P. Lehmann, 1986.

— (1939). *Vergleichendes Wörterbuch der gotischen Sprache mit Einschluss des Krimgotischen und sonstiger zerstreuter überreste des Gotichen.* 3. neubearbeitete und vermehrte Auflage. Leiden: Brill.

Fick, August (1868). *Wörterbuch der indogermanischen Ursprache.* Göttingen: Vandenhoeck & Ruprecht.

— (1870–71). *Vergleichendes Wörterbuch der indogermanischen Sprachen. Ein sprachgeschichtlicher Versuch.* 2 vols. Göttingen: Vandenhoeck & Ruprecht. Rev. 3rd edn, 4 vols., 1874–6; 4th edn, rev. by A. Bezzenberger, H. Falk, A. Fick, W. Stokes, and A. Torp, 3 vols., 1890–1909.

— (1874). *Die griechischen Personennamen nach ihrer Bildung erklärt, mit den Namensystemen verwandter Sprachen verglichen und systematisch geordnet.*

Göttingen: Vandenhoeck & Ruprecht. 2dn edn, rev. by Fritz Bechtel, 1894.

(1876). Die namenartigen Bildungen der griechischen Sprache. In G. Curtius (ed.), *Studien zur griechischen und lateinischen Grammatik*, Leipzig: Hinzel, 165–98.

(1905). *Vorgriechischen Ortsnamen als Quelle für die Vorgeschichte Griechenlands verwertet.* Göttingen: Vandenhoeck & Ruprecht.

(1909). *Hatiden und Danubier in Griechenland. Weitere Forschungen zu den Vorgriechischen Ortsnamen.* Göttingen: Vandenhoeck & Ruprecht.

Fillmore, Charles J. (1974). Rev. of Leech, Geoffrey N., *Towards a semantic description of English* (London: Longman, 1969). In *Journal of Linguistics*, 10, 281–302.

Flechia, Giovanni (1876, 1878). Postille etimologiche. *Archivio glottologico italiano* 2, 1–58, 313–84; 3, 121–76. [Critical comments on Giovanni Galvani, *Saggio di un glossario modenese* . . . Modena, 1868.]

Förstemann, Ernst (1852). Über deutsche Volksetymologie, *Zeitschrift für vergleichende Sprachforschung*, 1, 1–27.

(1956–72). *Altdeutsches Namenbuch*, 2 vols. (I. *Personennamen*, II. *Ortsnamen*). Nordhausen: Förstemann. Rev. edn, Bonn: Hanstein, 1900–16; repr., Munich: Fink, 1966–7 (2 vols. in 3). [Rev. edns. use, for Vol. II, the subtitle: *Orts- und sonstige geographische Namen* and include the period 1100–1200.]

Foerster, Wendelin, & Breuer, Hermann (1914). *Kristian von Troyes. Wörterbuch zu seinen sämtlichen Werken* . . . Romanische Bibliothek, 21. Halle: Niemeyer. 2nd edn, revised by H. Breuer, 1933.

Folena, Gianfranco (1956). Bibliografia degli scritti di Bruno Migliorini. In Migliorini, *Saggi linguistici*, xi–xxvii.

Ford, Jeremiah D. M. (1911). *Old Spanish readings, selected on the basis of critically edited texts, with introduction, notes, and vocabulary.* International Modern Language Series. Rev. 2nd edn, Boston: Ginn; repr., 1939. [The original eds. of 1906 lacked the Glossary.]

Foulet, Lucien (1955). *Glossary of the First Continuation* [of the Old French *Perceval* Romance, by Chrétien de Troyes]. Philadelphia: American Philosophical Society. [See Vol. 3:2 of *The Continuations of the Old French Perceval of Chrétien de Troyes*, edited by William Roach. Philadelphia: University of Pennsylvania Press, 1949–.]

Foy, Willy (1897, 1900). Vedische Beiträge. *Zeitschrift für vergleichende Sprachforschung*, 34, 224–83; 36, 123–43.

Français Moderne, Le (1933–). Founding ed. Albert Dauzat. Paris: d'Artrey.

Frings, Theodor (1913). *Studien zur Dialektgeographie des Niederrheins zwischen Düsseldorf und Aachen.* Diss. Marburg, 1910. Deutsche Dialektgeographie, 5. Marburg: Elwert.

(1916). *Die rheinische Akzentuierung. Vorstudie zu einer Grammatik der rheinischen Mundarten.* Deutsche Dialektgeographie, 14. Marburg: Elwert.

183

References

(1918). *Uber die neuere vlämische Literatur. Zwei Vorträge.* Marburg: Elwert.

(1924). *Rheinische Sprachgeschichte, Überblick.* Essen: Baedeker. [Originally in Aubin, H. *et al.* (1922). *Geschichte des Rheinlandes von der ältesten Zeit bis zur Gegenwart.* Essen: Baedeker (Published for the Gesellschaft für rheinische Geschichtskunde).]

(1932a). *Sprache und Siedlung im mitteldeutschen Osten.* Leipzig: Hirzel.

(1932b). *Germania Romana.* Teuthonista, Suppl. 4. Halle: Niemeyer. 2nd edn, rev. by Gertraud Müller, Mitteldeutsche Studien, 19. Halle: Niemeyer, 1966.

(1949). *Minnesinger und Troubadours.* Berlin: Akademie-Verlag.

(1936). *Die Grundlage des meißenischen Deutsch. Ein Beitrag zur Entstehungsgeschichte der deutschen Hochsprache.* Halle: Niemeyer.

(1938). *Europäische Heldendichtung.* Groningen: Wolters.

(1947). *Brautwerbung.* Leipzig: Hirzel.

(1948). *Grundlegung einer Geschichte der deutschen Sprache.* Halle: Niemeyer. 2nd edn, 1950.

(1949). *Antike und Christentum an der Wiege der deutschen Sprache.* Berlin: Akademie-Verlag.

& Karg-Gasterstädt, Elisabeth (1933). *Eduard Sievers.* Verh. Sächs. Akad. Leipzig, 85:1. Leipzig: Hirzel.

& Karg-Gasterstädt, Elisabeth (1952–). *Althochdeutsches Wörterbuch.* Berlin: Akademie-Verlag.

& Müller, Gertraud (1963). *Germania Romana und Romania Germanica zwischen Mittelmeer, Rhein und Elbe. Zur Geschichte romanisch–germanischer Wörter im Bereich SALIX Weide*, Sitz.-ber. Akad. Leipzig, 108:5.

& Schieb, Gabriele (1947–52). *Heinrich von Veldeke.* 4 vols. Halle: Niemeyer.

& Schieb, Gabriele (1949). *Drei Veldeke-Studien. Das Veldeke–problem, der Eneideepilog, die beiden Stauferpartien.* Berlin: Akademie-Verlag.

& Schieb, Gabriele (eds.) (1964–5). *Henric van Veldeken, Eneide.* Berlin: Akademie-Verlag.

& Vandenheuvel, Jozef (1921). *Die südniederländischen Mundarten. Texte, Untersuchungen, Karte, I.* Deutsche Dialektgeographie, 16. Marburg: Elwert.

& Wartburg, Walther von (1937, 1938). Französisch und Fränkisch: I. Deutsch *Hees*, französich *haise*, deutsch *Heister*, französisch *hêtre. Zeitschrift für romanische Philologie*, 57, 193–210. [Cf. reply, *Zeitschrift für romanische Philologie*, 58, 542–9, to E. Gamillschegs criticism.]

Funk, Charles Earle (1940). Preface to Reider T. Sherwin, *The Viking and the red man: the Old Norse origin of the Algonquin language*, New York and London: Funk & Wagnalls.

(1948). *A hog on ice and other curious expressions.* New York: Harper.

(1950). *Thereby hangs a tale. Stories of curious word origins.* New York: Harper.

(1958). *Horsefeathers and other curious words.* New York: Harper.

Gabelentz, Georg von der (1888). [August Friedrich] Pott. In *Allgemeine deutsche Biographie*, 26, 478–85. Repr. in *Portraits of linguists; a biographical source book for the history of Western linguistics, 1746–1963*, ed. Thomas A. Sebeok, 251–61, Bloomington and London: Indiana University Press, 1966.

Galvani, Giovanni (1868). *Saggio di un glossario modenese, ossia, studii del conte Giovanni Galvani intorno le probabili origini di alquanti idiotismi della città di Modena e del suo contado.* Modena, Tipografia dell'Immacolata Concezione.

Gamillscheg, Ernst (1919–20, 1921–2). Französische Etymologien. ([Anicroche – fringuer.]) *Zeitschrift für romanische Philologie*, 40, 129–90, 513–42; 41, 503–37, 631–647.

(1926–8). *Etymologisches Wörterbuch der französischen Sprache, mit einem Wort- und Sachverzeichnis von Heinrich Kuen.* Heidelberg: Winter. Rev. 2nd edn, 1966–9.

(1928). *Die Sprachgeographie und ihre Ergebnisse für die allgemeine Sprachwissenschaft.* Bielefeld and Leipzig: Velhagen & Klasing.

& Spitzer, Leo (1919). *Die Bezeichnungen der Klette im Galloromanischen.* Sprachgeographische Arbeiten, 1. Halle: Niemeyer.

García de Diego, Vicente (1914). *Elementos de gramática histórica castellana.* Burgos: no pub.

(1923). *Contribución al diccionario hispánico etimológico.* Suppl. 2 to *Revista de filología española.* Madrid: Junta por la ampliación de estudios históricos; repr. 1943.

(1926). *Problemas etimológicos. Discurso leído ante la Real Academia Española, en el acto de su recepción, por . . . y contestación, de Ramón Menéndez Pidal.* Ávila: no pub.

(1951). *Gramatica histórica española.* Manuales universitarios, 8. Madrid: Gredos.

(1957). *Diccionario etimológico español e hispánico.* Madrid: S.A.E.T.A.; 2nd edn, ed. Carmen García de Diego. Madrid: Espasa-Calpe, 1985.

(1964). *Etimologias españolas.* Madrid: Aguilar.

(1968). *Diccionario de voces naturales.* Madrid: Aguilar.

Gardiner, Alan H. (1932). *The theory of speech and language.* Oxford: Clarendon Press. Rev. 2nd edn, 1951.

(1940). *The theory of proper names, a controversial essay.* London and New York: Oxford University Press. H. Milford; 2nd edn, 1954.

(1947). *Ancient Egyptian Onomastica.* 2 vols. Oxford University Press.

Gilliéron, Jules (1912). *Étude de géographie linguistique. L'aire CLĀVELLUS d'après l'Atlas linguistique de la France.* Résumé de conférences. Neuveville: Beerstecher.

(1917). *Généalogie des mots qui ont désigné l'abeille.* Paris: Champion.

(1918). *Généalogie des mots qui désignent l'abeille, d'après l'ALF.* Bibl. de l'École des Hautes Études, 225. Paris: Champion.

(1919). *La faillite de l'étymologie phonétique.* Résumé de conférences.

References

Neuveville: Beerstecher.

(1915). *Pathologie et thérapeutique verbales*. Résumé de conférences.
Neuveville: Beerstecher; also, Collection de la Soc. de Linguistique de Paris,
11. Paris: Champion, 1921.

(1922). *Les étymologies des étymologistes et celles du peuple*. Paris: Champion.

(1923). *Thaumaturgie linguistique*. Collection de la Soc. de Linguistique de
Paris, 13. Paris: Champion.

& Edmont, Edmond (1902–20). *Atlas linguistique de la France*. 17 portfolios.
Paris: Champion, 1912. Preceded by pamphlet: *Notice servant à l'intelligence
des cartes* (1902); followed by *Table* (1912), *Corse* (1914–15), and
Supplément, 1 (1920), all published by Champion.

& Mongin, J. (1905). *'Scier' dans la Gaule romane du Sud et de l'Est*. Paris:
Champion.

& Roques, Mario (1912). *Études de géographie linguistique d'après l'Atlas
linguistique de la France*. Paris: Champion.

Goetze, Albrecht (1951). On the Hittite words for 'Year' and the Seasons, and
for 'Night' and 'Day'. *Language*, 27, 467–76.

Graff, E. G. (1834–46). *Althochdeutscher Sprachschatz, oder, Wörterbuch der
althochdeutschen Sprache . . . etymologisch und grammatisch bearbeitet*. 7
vols. (incl. Index). Berlin: Nicolai.

Grandgagnage, Charles (1845–80). *Dictionnaire étymologique de la langue
wallonne*. 2 vols. (2nd part of Vol. II revised by A. Scheler). Liège: Oudart.

Grebe, Paul (1960). *Fremdwörterbuch* (= *Der große Duden*, V). Mannheim:
Bibliographisches Institut.

(1963). *Etymologie. Herkunftswörterbuch der deutschen Sprache*. (= *Der große
Duden*, VII). Mannheim: Bibliographisches Institut.

Grimm, Jakob (1822–37). *Deutsche Grammatik*. 4 vols. Göttingen: Dieterich. 2nd
edn, ed. Wilhelm Scherer, Gustav Roethe, & Eduard Schröder, 1870–98.

& Wilhelm (1854–1960). *Deutsches Wörterbuch*. 16 vols. Leipzig: Hirzel;
Quellenverzeichnis, 1966–71.

Gröber, Gustav (1884–9). Vulgärlateinische Substrate romanischer Wörter (with a
Supplement). *Archiv für lateinische Lexikographie und Grammatik . . .* , 1–6,
in instalments.

Guiraud, Pierre (1956). *L'argot*. Que sais-je?, 700. Paris: Presses universitaires de
France.

(1961). *Les locutions françaises*. Que sais-je?, 903. Paris: Presses universitaires
de France.

(1964). *L'étymologie*. Que sais-je?, 1122. Paris: Presses universitaires de
France.

(1965). *Les mots étrangers*. Que sais-je?, 1166. Paris: Presses universitaires de
France.

(1967). *Structures étymologiques du lexique français*. Paris: Larousse. Rev. 2nd
edn by Alain Rey, 1986.

(1968a). *Le jargon de Villon, ou le gai savoir de la Coquille*. Paris: Gallimard.

(1968b). *Patois et dialectes français*. Que sais-je?, 1285. Paris: Presses universitaires de France.

(1968c). *Les mots savants*. Que sais-je?, 1325. Paris: Presses universitaires de France.

(1978). *Dictionnaire érotique. Le langage de la sexualité. I. Dictionnaire historique, stylistique, rhétorique de la littérature érotique, précédé d'une introduction sur les structures étymologiques du vocabulaire érotique. II. Sémiologie de la sexualité; essai de glosso-analyse*. Paris: Payot.

(1982). *Dictionnaire des étymologies obscures*. Paris: Payot.

(1985). Encore des étymologies 'obscures': l'*h* aspiré. In *Hommage à Pierre Guiraud*, ed. C. P. Bouton, É. Brunet, L.-J. Calvet. Paris: Les Belles Lettres, 11–20.

Hall, Robert A. (Jr) (1941). *Bibliography of Italian linguistics*. Baltimore: Linguistic Society of America.

(1942). Bibliography of Sardinian Linguistics. *Italica*, 19, 133–57.

(1946). Bàrtoli's Neolinguistica, *Language*, 22, 273–83.

(1958). *Bibliografia della linguistica italiana*. Rev. 2nd edn, 3 vols. Florence: Sansoni. *Supplemento decennale*, 1969; 1980; 1988.

Hamp, Eric P. (1990). See bibliography of his writings in Matoris, A. T. E. and Melia, Daniel E. (eds.) *Celtic Language, Celtic Culture: a Festschrift for Eric P. Hamp*, Van Nuys, Calif.: Ford & Bailie, 345–415.

Hanssen, Friedrich (1910). *Spanische Grammatik auf historischer Grundlage*. Halle: Niemeyer.

(1913). *Gramática histórica de la lengua castellana*. Halle: Niemeyer.

Harris, Martin (1974). Review of Anderson & Creore, *Readings in Romance linguistics*, (The Hague: Mouton, 1972). In *Journal of Linguistics*, 10, 356–8.

Henríquez Ureña, Pedro (1938). *Para la historia de los indigenismos*. Biblioteca de dialectología hispanoamericana, 3. Buenos Aires: Universidad.

Hesseling, Dirk Christian (1903). *Les mots maritimes empruntés par le grec aux langues romanes*. Amsterdam: Müller.

Hiersche, Rolf (1986). *Deutsches etymologisches Wörterbuch*, fasc. I–II (*a – anheischig*). Germanische Bibliothek, Neue Folge. Heidelberg: Winter.

Hildebrandt, Reiner, & Knoop, Ulrich (eds.) (1986). *Brüder-Grimm-Symposion zur historischen Wortschöpfung. Beiträge zu der Marburger Tagung vom Juni 1985*. Berlin and New York: de Gruyter.

Hillen, Wolfgang (1973). *Sainéans und Gilliérons Methode und die romanische Etymologie*. Romanistische Versuche und Vorarbeiten, 45. Bonn: Romanisches Seminar der Universität Bonn.

Höfler, Max (1899). *Deutsches Krankheitsnamen-Buch*. Munich: Piloty & Loehle.

Hofstra, Tette (1985). *Ostseefinnisch und Germanisch: frühe Lehnbeziehungen im nördlichen Ostseeraum im Lichte der Forschung seit 1961*. Groningen: Rijksuniversiteit Groningen.

References

Hubschmid, Johannes (1943). Bezeichnungen für 'Kaninchen' – 'Höhle' – 'Steinplatte'. In *Sache, Ort und Wort. Festschrift für Jakob Jud*, Romanica Helvetica, 20. Geneva: Droz, 246–80.

(1949). *Praeromanica: Studien zum vorromanischen Wortschatz der Romania, mit besonderer Berücksichtigung der frankoprovenzalischen und provenzalischen Mundarten der Westalpen*. Diss. Zurich. Romanica Helvetica, 30. Berne: Francke.

(1950). Vorindogermanische und jüngere Wortschichten in den romanischen. Mundarten der Ostalpen. *Zeitschrift für romanische Philologie*, 66, 1–94.

(1951) *Alpenwörter romanischen und vorromanischen Ursprungs*. Bern: Francke.

(1953). *Sardische Studien. Das mediterrane Substrat des Sardischen, seine Beziehungen zum Berberischen und Baskischen sowie zum eurafrikanischen und hispano–kaukasischen Substrat der romanischen Sprachen*. Romanica Helvetica, 41. Berne: Francke.

(1954). *Pyrenäenwörter vorromanischen Ursprungs und das vorromanische Substrat der Alpen*. Acta Salmanticensia, 7:2. Salamanca: Universidad.

(1955). *Schläuche und Fässer. Wort- und Sachgeschichtliche Untersuchungen mit besonderer Berücksichtigung des romanischen Sprachgutes in und außerhalb der Romania sowie der türkisch–europäischen und türkisch–kaukasisch–persischen Lehnbeziehungen*. Romanica Helvetica, 54. Berne: Francke.

(1960a). Substratprobleme: eine neue iberoromanisch–alpinlombardische Wortgleichung vorindogermanischen Ursprungs und die vorindogermanischen Suffixe *-áno* und *-s(s)-*. *Vox Romanica*, 19:1–2, 124–79.

(1960b). *Mediterrane Substrate, mit besonderer Berücksichtigung des Baskischen und der west–östlichen Sprachbeziehungen*. Romanica Helvetica, 70. Berne: Francke.

(1963–5). *Thesaurus Praeromanicus. Grundlagen für ein weitverbreitetes mediterranes Substrat, dargestellt an romanischen, baskischen und vorindogermanischen p-Suffixen. II. Problem der baskischen Lautlehre und baskisch–vorromanische Etymologien*. Berne: Francke.

(1982). Schriftenverzeichnis. In Winkelmann, Otto and Braisch, Maria (eds.), *Festschrift für Johannes Hubschmid zum 65. Geburtstag. Beiträge zur allgemeinen, indogermanischen und romanischen Sprachwissenschaft*. Berne & Munich: Francke, 993–1017.

Hübschmann, H. (1900). Zur persischen Lautlehre. *Zeitschrift für vergleichende Sprachforschung*, 36, 179–201.

Humboldt, Wilhelm von (1836–9). *Über die Kawi-Sprache auf der Insel Java, nebst einer Einleitung über die Verschiedenheit des menschlichen Sprachbaues* . . . . Berlin: Abhandlungen der Königlichen Akademie der Wissenschaften, 1832, 3 vols. Rev. 2nd edn of Introduction (*mit erläuternden Anmerkungen und Exkursen . . . Einleitung . . . Nachträgen* by A. F. Pott). 2 vols. Berlin: Calvary, 1880. Repeatedly reprinted.

Iordan, Iorgu (1932). *Introducere în studiul limbilor romanice. Evoluția și starea actuală a lingvisticii romanice*. Iași: Editura Institutului de Filologie romînă.
⸻ (1937). *An introduction to Romance linguistics, its schools and scholars*, tr. and rev. John Orr. London: Methuen. 2nd edn, with a Supplement 'Thirty years on', by Rebecca Posner. Oxford: Blackwell; Berkeley and Los Angeles, University of California Press, 1970.
Isidorus (episcopus Hispalensis) (1911). *Etymologiarum sive Originum libri XX*, ed. W. M. Lindsay. Oxford: Clarendon Press.
Jaberg, Karl (1908). *Sprachgeographie. Beitrag zum Verständnis des 'Atlas linguistique de la France'*. Aarau: Sauerländer.
⸻ (1922). Dreschmethoden und Dreschgeräte in Romanisch Bünden. *Bündnerisches Monatsblatt*, No. 2, 33–58.
⸻ (1925). Die Bezeichnungsgeschichte des Begriffes 'anfangen'. *Revue de linguistique romane*, 1, 118–45.
⸻ (1935). Wie der Hundedachs zum Dachs und der Dachs zum Iltis wird. *Festschrift für Ernst Tappolet*, Basle: Benno Schwabe, 111–21.
⸻ (1936). *Aspects géographiques du langage. Conférences faites au Collège de France (décembre 1933)*. Société de publications romanes et françaises, 18. Paris: Droz.
⸻ (1946). Zu den französischen Benennungen der Schaukel; Lautverstärkung. *Vox Romanica*, 8 (1946), 1–33.
⸻ (1946). Géographie linguistique et expressivisme phonétique: les noms de la balançoire en portugais. *Revista portuguesa de filologia*, 1, 1–44.
⸻ (1951). Krankheitsnamen. Metaphorik und Dämonie. *Heimat und Humanität. Festschrift für Karl Meuli zum 60. Geburtstag = Schweizerisches Archiv für Volkskunde*, 47, 77–113.
⸻ (1954). Die Schleuder; zur expressiven Wortgestaltung. *Sprachgeschichte und Wortbedeutung. Festschrift A. Debrunner*. Bern: Francke.
⸻ (1965). Bibliographie der Veröffentlichungen von K. Jaberg (comp. S. Heinimann). In *Sprachwissenschaftliche Forschungen und Erlebnisse. Neue Folge*. Romanica Helvetica, 75, XV–XXII. Berne: Francke.
⸻ & Jud, Jakob (1928–40). *Sprach- und Sachatlas Italiens und der Südschweiz* [AIS]. 8 Vols. Zofingen: Ringier.
⸻ & Jud, Jakob (1960). *Sprach- und Sachatlas Italiens und der Südschweiz. Index*. Berne: Stämpfli.
Journal of English Linguistics (1967–). Bellingham, WA: R. A. Peters, Western Washington State College.
Journal of Linguistics (1965–). Current ed.: Nigel Vincent, University of Manchester. Published for the Linguistics Association of Great Britain: Cambridge University Press.
Jud, Jakob (1905). Die Zehnerzahlen in den romanischen Sprachen. In *Aus romanischen Sprachen und Literaturen. Festschrift Heinrich Morf zur Feier seiner fünfundzwanzigjährigen Lehrtätigkeit von seinen Schülern dargebracht.*

References

Halle: Niemeyer, 233–70.

(1907). Recherches sur la genèse et la diffusion des accusatifs en -*ain* et en -*on*, 1. Diss. Zurich. Halle: Karras.

(1908a). *Poutre*: eine sprachgeographische Untersuchung (Habilitationsschrift Zurich), *Archiv für das Studium der neueren Sprachen*, 120, 72–95.

(1908b, 1910). Fr[anzösisch] *aune* 'Erle'. *Archiv für das Studium der neueren Sprachen*, 120, 76–95; 124, 83–108.

(1908c). Oberitalienisch *barba* 'Onkel'. *Archiv für das Studium der neueren Sprachen*, 121, 96–102.

(1908d). Review of I. A. Candrea & O. Densuşianu, *Dicţionarul etimologic limbei romîne. Elementele latine*. In *Archiv für des Studium der neueren Sprachen*, 120, 458–64.

(1908e). Review of J. Gilliéron & J. Mongin, '*Scier*' *dans la Gaule romane au sud et à l'est*. In *Literaturblatt für germanische und romanische Philologie*, 29, 332–6.

(1908f). Review of P. E. Guarnerio, *Carta de Logu de Arborea. L'antico campidanese dei secoli XI–XIII*. In *Romania*, 37, 459–65.

(1908g). Review of Max L. Wagner, *Lautlehre der südsardischen Mundarten*. In *Romania*, 37, 459–65.

(1911–12). Neue Wege und Ziele der romanischen Wortforschung. *Wissen und Leben*, 9, 270–7, 320–8.

(1925). A propósito del español *tomar*. In *Homenaje ofrecido a Menéndez Pidal*, II. Madrid: Hernando, 21–7.

(1946). Zur Geschichte der romanischen Reliktwörter in den Alpenmundarten der deutschen Schweiz. *Vox Romanica*, 8, 34–109.

(1946). Bemerkungen zum Aufsatz Zur Frage der vorrömischen Bestandteile der alpinlombardischen und rätoromanischen Mundarten . . . . *Vox Romanica*, 8, 216–9.

(1947). Altfranzösisch *estuet*; bündnerromanisch *stuver, stuvair*. *Vox Romanica*, 9, 29–56.

(1950). It[alien] *menzogna*, français *mensonge*, esp[agnol] *mentira*. *Vox Romanica*, 11, 101–24.

(1973). Bibliographie. In Huber, Konrad & Ineichen, Gustav (eds.), *Romanische Sprachgeschichte und Sprachgeographie. Ausgewählte Aufsätze*, Zurich and Freiburg im Breisgau: Atlantis.

Kahane, Henry & Renée (1948–9). The augmentative feminine in the Romance languages. *Romance Philology*, 2:2–3, 135–75.

(1961). Romano-Aegyptica. *Romance Philology*, 14:4, 287–94.

(1965, 1968). Graeco-Romance etymologies. *Romance Philology*, 19:2, 261–7; 21:4, 502–10.

(1979–80). *Graeca et Romanica. Scripta Selecta*, 3 vols. Amsterdam: Hakkert.

& Tietze, Andreas (1958). *The lingua franca in the Levant. Turkish nautical terms of Italian and Greek origin*. Urbana: University of Illinois Press.

Kahane, Renée (1938). Italienische Marinewörter im Neugriechischen . . . . *Archivum Romanicum*, 22, 510–82.

Klaeber, Friedrich (ed.) (1922). *Beowulf and the fight at Finnsburg*. Boston: Heath. 3rd edn, 1950.

Klein, Ernest (1966–7). *Comprehensive etymological dictionary of the English language*. 2 vols. Amsterdam, London and New York: Elsevier.

Kluge, Friedrich (1883). *Etymologisches Wörterbuch der deutschen Sprache*. Strasbourg: Trübner. Rev. 4th edn, 1889; rev. 5th edn, 1894; rev. 6th edn, 1899; rev. 7th edn, 1910; rev. 8th edn, 1915; rev. 9th edn, Berlin and Leipzig: de Gruyter, 1921; rev. 10th edn, 1924; 11th edn, rev. Wolfgang Krause & Alfred Götze, 1934; 13th edn, 1943; 15th edn, rev. A. Götze & H. Krahe, 1951; 17th edn, rev. A. Schirmer & W. Mitzka, 1957; 18th edn, rev. W. Mitzka, 1960; 19th edn, 1963; 20th edn, 1967; 21st edn, 1975. *An etymological dictionary of the German language*, tr. J. F. Davis. London: Bell, 1891.

(1895). *Deutsche Studentensprache*. Strasbourg: Trübner.

(1911). *Seemannsprache. Wortgeschichtliches Handbuch deutscher Schifferausdrücke älterer und neuerer Zeit* . . . . Halle: Niemeyer.

& Lutz, Frederick (1898). *English etymology. A select glossary serving as an introduction to the history of the English language*. Boston: Heath.

Körting, Gustav (1891). *Lateinisch–romanisches Wörterbuch*. Paderborn: Schöningh, 1891; rev. 2nd edn, 1901; rev. 3rd edn, 1907 (new subtitle: *Etymologisches Wörterbuch der romanischen Hauptsprachen*).

Kretschmer, Paul (1900). Etymologisches, nos. 5–7. *Zeitschrift für vergleichende Sprachforschung*, 36, 264–70.

Kronasser, Heinz, & Neu, Erich (1962–6). *Etymologie der hethitischen Sprache*. Vol. I. Wiesbaden: Harrassowitz. Vol. II = Bd. 2. *Ausführliche Indices zu Band 1*. Zusammengestellt von Erich Neu. Wiesbaden: Harrassowitz, 1987.

Kuhn, Adalbert (ed.) (1852–). *Zeitschrift für vergleichende Sprachforschung auf dem Gebiete der indogermanischen Sprachen*. Berlin. (Title varies.)

Lapesa, Rafael (1942). *Historia de la lengua española*. Madrid: Escelicer. Rev. 2nd edn, 1951; rev. 3rd edn, 1955; rev. 4th edn, 1959; rev. 6th edn, 1965; rev. 7th edn, 1968; rev. 8th edn, 1980.

Lehmann, Winfred P. (1986). *A Gothic etymological dictionary, based on the third edition of Vergleichendes Wörterbuch der gotischen Sprache by Sigmund Feist*. Leiden: Brill.

Leihener, Erich (1908). *Croneberger Wörterbuch (mit wortgeschichtlicher, grammatischer und dialektgeographischer Einleitung)*. Deutsche Dialektgeographie, 2. Marburg: Elwert.

Lejeune, Michel (1929). Grec: πρῶτος. *Bulletin de la Société de Linguistique de Paris*, 29, 117–21.

Lerch, Eugen (1927–8). Kulturhistorisches im französischen Wortschatz, aus Anlaß von Gamillschegs *Etymologisches Wörterbuch*. *Jahrbuch für Philologie*,

References

3, 189–202, 251–72.

Levi, Enrico (1914). *Vocabolario etimologico della lingua italiana.* Livorno: Giusti.

Lida de Malkiel, María Rosa (1951). *Arpadas lenguas.* In *Estudios dedicados a Menéndez Pidal,* Vol. II. Madrid: Consejo Superior de Investigaciones Científicas, 227–52.

Lingua Nostra (1939–) (founded by Giacomo Devoto & Bruno Migliorini). Florence:Sansoni.

Littré, Émile (1863–72). *Dictionnaire de la langue française, contenant la nomenclature . . . la grammaire . . . la signification des mots . . . la partie historique . . . l'étymologie,* 4 vols. Paris: Hachette; *Supplément,* 1877. 2nd edn, 1875–89; 'Édition intégrale', 7 vols., Paris: Gallimard–Hachette, 1959–61.

(1863). *Histoire de la langue française. Etudes sur les origines, l'étymologie, la grammaire, les dialectes, la versification et les lettres au moyen âge.* 2 vols. 4th edn, 1867; 5th edn, Paris: Didier, 1869; 6th edn, 1873; 8th edn, 1878, 1882; 9th edn, 1886.

(1880). *Études et glanures, pour faire suite à l'Histoire de la langue française.* Paris: Didier.

(1888). *Comment les mots changent de sens,* ed. Michel Bréal. Paris: Delagrave.

(1897). *Comment j'ai fait mon dictionnaire de la langue française.* Foreword by Michel Bréal. Paris: Delagrave.

Lloyd, Albert L., & Springer, Otto (1988). *Etymologisches Wörterbuch des Althochdeutschen,* Vol. I. Göttingen and Zurich: Vandenhoeck & Ruprecht.

Lokotsch, Karl (1927). *Etymologisches Wörterbuch der europäischen (germanischen, romanischen und slavischen) Wörter orientalischen Ursprungs.* Heidelberg: Winter.

Luft, Wilhelm (1900). Gotische Wortdeutungen. *Zeitschrift für vergleichende Sprachforschung,* 36, 143–9.

Mahn, Karl August Friedrich (1854–64). *Etymologische Untersuchungen auf dem Gebiete der romanischen Sprachen.* Specs. 1–24. Berlin: Dümmler.

(1856–64). *Etymologische Untersuchungen über geographische Namen.* 8 vols. Berlin: Dümmler.

Malkiel, Yakov (1944). The etymology of Portuguese *iguaria.* *Language,* 20, 108–30.

(1947). Three Hispanic word studies: Latin *macula* in Ibero–Romance; Old Portuguese *trigar*: Hispanic *lo(u)çano.* *University of California Publications in Linguistics,* I:7, 227–96.

(1952–3). *Vera(s)* and *mentira(s)*; a study in lexical polarization. *Romance Philology,* 6:2–3, 121–72.

(1973). One short-lived genre of etymological research. *Romance Philology,* 26:4, 747–9.

(1977). The analysis of lexical doublets; the Romanists' earliest contribution to general linguistics. In Feldman, David M. (ed.) *Homenaje a Robert A. Hall, Jr: Ensayos lingüísticos y filológicos* . . . , Madrid: Playor, 191–6.

(1979). Problems in the diachronic differentiation of near-homophones. *Language*, 55, 1–36.

(1983). Trois examples nouveaux de la polarisation lexicale en roman, I. *Romania*, 104: 415, 289–315. [includes *perder*].

(1984). *Crumēna*, a Latin lexical isolate, and its survival in Hispano–Romance (Sp. *colmena*, dial. *cormena* Beehive). *Glotta*, 62, 106–23.

(1985). Para el marco histórico de *comborça/comberça* concubina. In *Homenaje a Álvaro Galmés de Fuentes*, Vol. I. Madrid: Gredos, 191–211.

(1986). Sapir as a student of linguistic diachrony. In W. Cowan, M. K. Foster & K. Koerner, (eds.). *New perspectives in language, culture and personality* . . . Amsterdam: Benjamins, 315–40.

(1987). The early romance vicissitudes of Latin OPUS EST. Jakob Jud's reconstruction reconsidered. *Classica et Mediaevalia*, 38, 189–202.

(1989). Old French *nöer* (var. *näer*) 'to swim' and its congeners. In *Continuations: Essays on Medieval French literature and language in memory of John L. Grigsby*. Birmingham, Ala.: Summa, 297–310.

(1990). Las avatars de l'explication étymologique de (esp. port.) *tomar*. *Revue de linguistique romane*, 54, 33–57.

(1990). Las vicisitudes etimológicas de *rincón*. *Revista de filología española*, 70, 5–44.

(forthcoming). Dubious, pseudo-, hybrid, and mock-orientalisms in Romance. To appear in Kaye, Alan S. (ed.) *Semitic studies in honor of Wolf Leslau on the occasion of his 85th birthday*, Wiesbaden: Harrassowitz. [Includes *matar*.]

Manno, Giuseppe (1855). *Della fortuna delle parole libri due*. Florence: Le Monnier; 8th edn, Turin: Unione tipografico-editrice, 1868. Rev. edn by B. Migliorini, Roma: Tumminelli, 1947.

Martineau, Russell (1880–81). On the Romontsch or Rhaetian language in the Grisons and Tirol. *Transactions of the Philological Society*, 402–60.

Matisoff, James A. *Sino-Tibetan etymological dictionary and Thesaurus*. Berkeley: University of California Press (project started 1987 and ongoing).

Matzel, Klaus (1989). Review of Vol. 1 (*A–Bi*) of Albert L. Lloyd & Otto Springer, *Etymologisches Wörterbuch des Althochdeutschen*, I (*-a – bezzisto*). In *Kratylos*, 34, 128–41.

Mayáns y Siscar, Gregorio (ed.) (1737). *Origenes de la lengua española, compuestos por varios autores*. 2 vols. Madrid: de Zúñiga.

Mayrhofer, Manfred (1953–80). *Kurzgefaßtes etymologisches Wörterbuch des Altindischen*. Indogermanische Bibliothek, Reihe 2. 32 fasc. Heidelberg: Winter.

(1986–). *Etymologisches Wörterbuch des Altindoarischen*. Heidelberg: Winter.

& Schmitt, Rüdiger (eds.) (1986). *Iranisches Personennamenbuch. IV: Nomina Propria Iranica in Nummis: Materialgrundlagen zu den iranischen*

References

Personennamen auf antiken Münzen by Michael Alram. Vienna: Österreichische Akademie der Wissenschaften.

Meid, Wolfgang (1987). *Studien zum indogermanischen Wortschatz*. Innsbrucker Beiträge zur Sprachwissenschaft, 52. Innsbruck: Institut für Sprachwissenschaft der Universität Innsbruck.

Meier, Harri (1984). *Notas críticas al 'DECH' de Corominas/Pascual*, Suppl. 24 to *Verba*. Santiago de Compostela: Universidade.

Meillet, Antoine (1896). *Notes d'étymologie grecque*. Paris: Laroche.

— (1902–5). *Etudes sur l'étymologie et le vocabulaire du vieux slave*. Bibliothèque de l'École Pratique des Hautes Études, 139. Paris: E. Bouillon. Repr. Paris: Champion, 1961.

— (1903). *Esquisse d'une grammaire comparée de l'arménien classique*. Vienna: Imprimerie des Pères Mékhitharistes. Rev. 2nd edn, 1936.

— (1913). *Aperçu d'une histoire de la langue grecque*. Paris: Hachette.

— (1928). *Esquisse d'une histoire de la langue latine*. Paris: Hachette.

— (1928). Observations sur quelques mot latins. *Bulletin de la Société de Linguistique de Paris*, 28, 40–47.

— (1929). Les noms des nombres ordinaux en indo-européen. *Bulletin de la Société de Linguistique de Paris*, 29, 29–37.

— & Benveniste, Émile (1931). *Grammaire du vieux-perse*. Rev. 2nd edn, Collection linguistique, 34. Paris: Champion.

— & Vendryes, Joseph (1927). *Traité de grammaire comparée des langues classiques*. 2nd printing. Paris: Champion. Rev. 4th edn, 1968.

Meister, Richard (1900). Der lakonische Name *Oíbălos*. *Zeitschrift für vergleichende Sprachforschung*, 36, 458–9.

Menéndez Pidal, Ramón (1900). Etimologías españolas. *Romania*, 29, 334–79.

— (1904). *Manual (elemental) de gramática histórica española*. Madrid: Suárez. Rev. 6th edn, Madrid: Espasa-Calpe, 1941.

— (ed.) (1908–11). *'Cantar de Mio Cid'. Texto, gramática y vocabulario*. 3 vols. Madrid: Bailly-Baillière et Hijos. 2nd edn, Madrid: Espasa-Calpe, 1944–6. [= *Obras completas*, Vols. III–V.]

— (1914). *Elena y María (Disputa del clérigo y del caballero)*: poesía leonesa inédita del siglo XIII. *Revista de filología española*, 1, 52–96.

— (1920). Notas para el léxico románico. *Revista de filología española*, 7, 1–36. [Review of W. Meyer-Lübke *Romanisches etymologisches Wörterbuch*.]

— (1952). *Toponimia prerromânica española*. Biblioteca románica hispánica, 2:9. Madrid: Gredos.

— (1954). A propósito de *-LL-* y *-L-* latinas. Colonización suditálica en España. *Boletín de la R. Academia Española*, 34, 161–216.

Meringer, Rudolf (1891). Studien zur germanischen Volkskunde. Das Bauernhaus und dessen Einrichtung. *Mitteilungen der Anthropologischen Gesellschaft in Wien*, 21, 101–52.

— (1892). Das deutsche Bauernhaus. *Studien zur germanischen Volkskunde. Nachtrag zu Bd. XXI, 101 foll. Mitteilungen der Anthropologischen*

Gesellschaft in Wein, 22, 101–6.

(1897). *Indogermanische Sprachwissenschaft.* Sammlung Göschen, 59. Leipzig: Göschen. Rev. 2nd edn, 1899; rev. 3rd edn, 1908. *Lingüística indoeuropea*, tr. P. U. González de la Calle. Madrid: Suárez, 1925.

(1898). Etymologien zum geflochtenen Haus. *Abhandlungen zur germanischen Philologie. Festgabe für R. Heinzel.* Halle: Niemeyer, 173–88.

(1901). *Die Stellung des bosnischen Hauses und Etymologien zum Hausrat.* Sitz-ber. Ak. Wien, 144:6.

(1908). *Aus dem Leben der Sprache. Versprechen, Kindersprache, Nachahmungstrieb.* Berlin: Behr.

(1909). Die Werkzeuge der *pinsere*-Reihe und ihre Namen. (*Keule, Stampfe, Hammer, Anke*). *Wörter und Sachen*, 1, 3–28 [with 35 illustrations].

(1909). Sprachlich-sachliche Probleme [1–10]. *Wörter und Sachen*, 1, 164–210 [with 40 illustrations].

& Mayer, Karl (1895). *Versprechen und Verlesen. Eine psychologisch–linguistische Studie.* Stuttgart: Göschen.

& al. (eds.) (1909–). *Wörter und Sachen.* Heidelberg: Winter.

Meunier, [Louis] Francis (1872). *Etudes de grammaire comparée. Les composés syntactiques en grec, en latin, en français et subsidiairement en zend et en indien.* Paris: Durant & Lauriel.

Meyer, Leo (1857). *Bemerkungen zur ältesten Geschichte der griechischen Mythologie.* Göttingen: Vandenhoeck & Ruprecht.

(1869). *Lessico delle radici indo–italo–greche*, tr. Domenico Pezzi. Turin: Loescher. [A part of Pezzi's tr. of Meyer's *Vergleichende Grammatik der griechischen und lateinischen Sprache.*]

(1901–2). *Handbuch der griechischen Etymologie.* 4 vols. Leipzig: Hirzel.

Meyer-Lübke, Wilhelm (1886). Romanische Etymologien. *Zeitschrift für romanische Philologie*, 10, 171–4.

(1887). Etymologisches. *Zeitschrift für romanische Philologie*, 11, 205–7.

(1888). Die lateinische Sprache in den romanischen Ländern. In Gröber, G. (ed.), *Grundriß der romanischen Philologie*, Vol. I. Strasbourg: Trübner, 351–82. Rev. 2dn edn, 1904–6, Vol. I, 451–97.

(1890–1902). *Grammatik der romanischen Sprachen. Lautlehre; Formenlehre; Satzlehre; Registerband.* Leipzig: Fues & Reisland.

(1901). *Einführung in das Studium der romanischen Sprachwissenschaft.* Heidelberg: Winter. Rev. 2nd edn, 1909; rev. 3rd edn, 1920.

(1909a). Romanisch BAST-, *Wörter und Sachen*, 1, 28–39.

(1909b). Zur Geschichte der Dreschgeräte. *Wörter und Sachen*, 1, 211–44.

(1911–20). *Romanisches etymologisches Wörterbuch.* Heidelberg: Winter. 2nd edn (= repr. of 1st), New York: Stechert, 1924; rev. 3rd edn, 1930–35.

(1921). *Historische Grammatik der französischen Sprache*, Vol. II: *Wortbildungslehre.* Heidelberg: Winter. 2nd edn, rev. by Joseph M. Piel, 1954.

Michaëlis de Vasconcelos, Carolina (1874). Etymologisches. *Jahrbuch für*

References

romanische und englische Literatur (New Series), 1, 202–7, 202–27.

(1876). *Studien zur romanischen Wortschöpfung.* Leipzig: Brockhaus.

(1883). *Spanische Etymologien. Zeitschrift für romanische Philologie*, 7, 102–15.

(1886). Studien zur hispanischen Wortdeutung. In Ascoli, G. I. *et al.* (eds.), *In memoria di N. Caix e U. A. Canello. Miscellanea di filologia e linguistica.* Florence: Le Monnier, 113–66.

(1887–9). Etimologias portuguesas. *Revista Lusitana*, 1, 117–32, 298–305.

(1893–4). Fragmentos etimológicos. *Revista Lusitana*, 3, 29–90.

(1908). Contribuições para o futuro dicionário etimológico das línguas hispánicas. *Revista Lusitana*, 11, 1–62.

(1910–11). Mestre Giraldo e o seu tratado de albeitaria e cetraria; . . . Contribuições para o futuro dicionário etimológico das línguas românicas peninsulares. *Revista Lusitana*, 13:3–4, 149–432.

(1914). *A saudade portuguesa. Divagações filológicas e literar-históricas em volta de Inês de Castro* . . . . Oporto: Renascença Portuguesa. Rev. 2nd edn, 1922.

Migliorini, Bruno (1927). *Dal nome proprio al nome comune. Studi semantici sul mutamento dei nomi propri di persona in nomi comuni negl'idiomi romanzi.* Biblioteca dell' *Archivum Romanicum*, 2:13. Geneva: Olschki. Rev. 2nd edn, 1968, with a 'Supplemento' also included in *Atti e memorie dell'Accademia Toscana di Scienze e Lettere La Colombaria*, 33.111–88.

(1938). *Lingua contemporanea.* Biblioteca del Leonardo, 5. Florence: Sansoni. Rev. 3rd edn, Biblioteca di *Lingua Nostra*, 4. Florence: Sansoni, 1943. Republished in Migliorini (1990), 3–118.

(1941). *Saggi sulla lingua del Novecento.* Biblioteca di *Lingua Nostra*, 1. Florence: Sansoni. 2nd edn, 1942; repr., with an introductory essay by Ghino Ghinassi, in Migliorini (1990), 119–293.

(1948). *Lingua e cultura.* Nuova biblioteca italiana, 32. Rome: Tumminelli.

(1960). *Storia della lingua italiana.* Florence: Sansoni. 2nd end, 1960; 3rd edn, 1961; rev. edn, 1968.

(1963). Parole nuove. *Appendice di dodicimila voci al Dizionario moderno* di Alfredo Panzini. Milan: Hoepli.

(1966). *The Italian language.* Tr., abridged and recast by T. Gwynfor Griffith. The Great Languages. London: Faber & Faber.

(1968). *Profili di parole.* Bibliotechina del saggiatore, 27. Florence: Le Monnier.

(1990). *La lingua italiana del Novecento.* A cura di Massimo L. Fanfani, con un saggio introduttivo di Ghino Ghinassi. Florence: Le Lettere.

& Duro, Aldo (1950). *Prontuario etimologico della lingua italiana.* Turin: Paravia. 2nd edn, 1953; 3rd edn, 1958; 4th edn, 1964.

Miller, Roy Andrew (1951). The etymology of Chinese *'liu* 'pomegranate'. *Language*, 27, 154–8.

Moderna Språk (1906–). Göteborg: Modern Language Teachers' Association of Sweden.

Monlau, Pedro Felipe (1856). *Diccionario etimológico de la lengua castellana (ensayo), precedido de unos rudimentos de etimología*. Madrid: M. de Rivadeneyra. 2nd edn, Madrid: Aribau, 1881. New edn, with a Preface by Avelino Herrero Mayor, Buenos Aires: El Ateneo, 1941, 1944, 1946.

Moreu Rey, Enric (1978–9). A propos du vocabulaire érotique. *Anuario de Filología*, 4, 503–22.

Much, Rudolf (1909). Holz und Mensch. *Wörter und Sachen*, 1, 39–48.

Müller, Bodo (1987). *Diccionario del español medieval* (= DEM), fasc. I–II: *a–abollado*. Heidelberg: Winter.

(1987). Das Lateinische und das Latein der etymologischen Wörterbücher der romanischen Sprachen. *Latein und Romanisch: Romanistisches Kolloquium*, ed. Wolfgang Dahmen *et al.*, Tübingen: Narr, 311–22.

Murko, Matija (1909). Slov. *sužénj* 'Sklave', *muka* 'Marter'. *Wörter und Sachen*, 1, 109–11.

Nebrija, Elio Antonio de (1909). *Gramática castellana*. Salamanca, 1492; ed. E. Walberg. Halle: Niemeyer; ed. I. González-Llubera, London and New York: Oxford University Press, 1926; ed. P. Galindo Romeo & L. M. Muñoz, Madrid: n.pub., 1946.

Neueren Sprachen, Die (1893–1943, 1952–). Frankfurt; preceded by *Phonetische Studien* (1887–93).

Noydens, Benito Remigio (1673–4). *Parte primera [-segunda] del Tesoro de la lengua castellana o española, compuesto por . . . Don Sebastián de Covarruvias Orozco . . . añadido por . . . Benito Remigio Noydens*. Madrid: G. de León.

Olivieri, Dante (1953). *Dizionario etimologico italiano, concordato coi dialetti, le lingue straniere e la toponomastica*. Milan: Ceschina. Rev. 2nd edn, 1961.

Onions, Charles Talbut, Friedrichsen, G. W. S., & Burchfield, R. W. (1966). *The Oxford dictionary of English etymology*. Oxford: Clarendon Press.

Orr, John (1955). *Words and sounds in English and French*. Oxford: Blackwell.

(1962a). *Old French and modern English idiom*. Oxford: Blackwell.

(1962b). *Three studies on homonymics*. Edinburgh: Edinburgh University Press.

(1963). *Essais d'étymologie et de philologie françaises*. Bibliothèque française et romane, A, 4. Paris: Klincksieck.

Osthoff, Hermann (1878). *Das Verbum in der Nominalkomposition im Deutschen, Griechieschen, Slavischen und Romanischen*. Jena: Costenoble.

(1884). *Zur Geschichte des Perfekts im Indogermanischen, mit besonderer Rücksicht auf Griechisch und Lateinisch*. Strasbourg and London: Trübner.

(1901). *Etymologische Parerga*, 1. Leipzig. Hirzel.

& Brugmann, Karl (1878–1910). *Morphologische Untersuchungen auf dem Gebiete der indogermanischen Sprachen . . . .* 6 vols. in 4. Leipzig: Hirzel.

Panzini, Alfredo (1905). *Dizionario moderno. Supplemento ai dizionari italiani . . . Storia, etimologia e filosofia delle parole*. Milan: Hoepli. Rev. 2nd edn, 1908; rev. 3rd edn, 1918; rev. 4th edn, 1923; rev. 5th edn, 1927; rev. 6th edn, 1931; rev. 7th edn, 1935.

(1942). *Dizionario moderno delle parole che non si trovano nei dizionari comuni*. Rev. 8th edn. Rev. 9th edn, 1950; rev. 10th edn, 1963.

Paris, Gaston (1901). *Ficatum* en roman. In *Miscellanea linguistica in onore di G. I. Ascoli*. Turin: Loescher, 41–63.

Pattison, David Graham (1975). *Early Spanish suffixes. A functional study of the principal nominal suffixes of Spanish up to 1300*. Oxford: Blackwell.

Paul, Hermann (1879). Zur Geschichte des germanischen Vokalismus. *Beiträge zur Geschichte der deutschen Sprache und Literatur*, 6, 1–261.

(1880). *Prinzipien der Sprachgeschichte*. Halle: Niemeyer. Rev. 2nd edn, 1886; rev 3rd edn, 1898; rev. 4th edn, 1909; rev. 5th edn, 1920. *Principles of the history of language*, tr. H. A. Strong. London: Sonnenschein, 1891.

(1897). *Deutsches Wörterbuch*. Halle: Niemeyer. Rev. 2nd edn, 1908; 3rd edn, 1921; 4th edn, rev. by Karl Euling, 1933–5; 5th edn, rev. by Werner Betz, Tübingen, 1957–66; 7th edn, rev. by Alfred Schirmer, 1960.

(1916–20). *Deutsche Grammatik*. 5 vols. Halle: Niemeyer. 5th edn, 1958–9.

Peile, John (1869). *An introduction to Greek and Latin etymology*. London and Cambridge: Macmillan. Rev. 2nd edn, 1872; rev. 3rd edn, 1875.

Pfister, Max (1977). Review of O. Bloch & W. von Wartburg, *Dictionnaire étymologique de la langue française*, rev. 5th edn (1968). In *Zeitschrift für romanische Philologie*, 87, 106–27.

(1980). *Einführung in die romanische Etymologie*. Darmstadt: Wissenschaftliche Buchgesellschaft.

(1984, 1987). *Lessico etimologico italiano (=LEI)*, vol. I: *ab–alburnus*; vol. II: *albus–apertura*. Wiesbaden: Reichert.

Pharies, David A. (1980). Gottfried Baist (1953–1920) as etymologist. *Zeitschrift für romanische Philologie*, 96, 92–107.

Pianigiani, Ottorino (1907). *Vocabolario etimologico della lingua italiana*. Preface by F. L. Pullè. 2 vols., Rome: Società editrice Dante Alighieri di Albrighi Segati ec. 2nd edn, Milan: Casa editrice Sonzogno . . . 1937.

(1926). *Aggiunte, correzioni e variazioni* al *Vocabolario etimologico della lingua italiana*. Florence: Ariani.

Pietrangeli, Angelina (1962). Analytical bibliography of the writings of H. & R. Kahane. *Romance Philology*, 15:3, 207–20.

Pisani, Vittore (1947). *L'etimologia. Storia, questioni, metodo*. Milan: Renon. Rev. 2nd edn, Brescia: Paideia, 1967.

(1975). *Die Etymologie: Geschichte, Fragen, Methode*, tr. Irene Rimer. Munich: Fink.

Pogatscher, Franz (1909). Wörter- und Sachverzeichnis. *Wörter und Sachen*, 1, 259–62.

Posner, Rebecca, & Green, John N. (eds.) (1980–2). *Trends in Romance linguistics and philology*. 4 vols. The Hague: Mouton.

Postage, J. P. (1880–81). Dare 'to give' and *-dere* 'to put'. *Transactions of the*

Philological Society, 99–105.

Pott, August Friedrich (1883–6). *Etymologische Forschungen auf dem Gebiete der indogermanischen Sprachen, mit besonderem Bezug auf die Lautumwandlung im Sanskrit,* . . . . 2 vols. Lemgo: Meyersche Hofbuchhandlung. Rev. 2nd edn (. . . *Berücksichtigung ihrer Hauptformen* . . .), 6 vols., Lemgo and Detmold: Meyer, 1859–76.

(1844–5). *Die Zigeuner in Europa. Ethnographisch-linguistische Untersuchung, vornehmlich ihrer Herkunft und Sprache, nach gedruckten und ungedruckten Quellen.* 2 vols. Halle: Heynemann. Repr. Leipzig, 1964.

(1847). *Die binäre und vigesimale Zählmethode bei Völkern aller Weltteile, nebst ausführlichen Bemerkungen über die Zahlwörter indogermanischen Stammes und einem Anhange über Fingernamen.* Halle: Schwetschke.

(1853). *Die Personennamen, insbesondere die Familiennamen und ihre Entstehungsarten, auch unter Berücksichtigung der Ortsnamen. Eine sprachliche Untersuchung.* Leipzig: Brockhaus. Rev. 2nd edn, with *Register*, 1859. Repr. Wiesbaden: Sändig, 1968.

(1856). *Die Ungleichheit menschlicher Rassen, hauptsächlich vom sprachwissenschaftlichen Standpunkte* . . . *Ein ethnologischer Versuch.* Lemgo and Detmold: Meyer.

(1859). *Studien zur griechischen Mythologie*; repr. from *Jahrbücher für klassische Philologie*, 3. Leipzig: Teubner.

(1863a). *Etymologische Legenden bei den Alten. Philologus*: Suppl. Vol. Göttingen.

(1863b). *Anti-Kaulen; oder, Mythische Vorstellungen vom Ursprunge der Völker und Sprachen, nebst Beurteilung der zwei sprachwissenschaftlichen Abhandlungen Heinrich von Ewalds.* Lemgo: Meyer.

(1868). *Die Sprachverschiedenheit in Europa. An den Zahlwörtern nachgewiesen sowie die quinäre und vigesimale Zählmethode.* Halle: Waisenhaus. Repr., Amsterdam: Rodopi, 1971.

(1875). *Über vaskische Familiennamen. Zur Erinnerung an den glücklichen Schluß des durch Otto Böhtlingk und Rudolph Roth* . . . *1875 beendeten Sanskrit-Wörterbuches dargebracht.* Detmold: Meyer.

(1880). *Wilhelm von Humboldt und die Sprachwissenschaft.* Berlin: Calvary.

(1887). *Zur Litteratur der Sprachkunde Europas.* Internationale Zeitschrift für allgemeine Sprachwissenschaft, Supplement 1. Leipzig: Barth.

Preobraženskij, Aleksandr G. (1910–16). *Ètimologičeskij slovar' russkogo jazyka.* Fasc. I–XII. Moscow: Lissner & Sobko.

Puhvel, Jaan (1984). *Hittite etymological dictionary*, I: Words beginning with *A*; II: Words beginning with *E* and *I*. Berlin: Mouton.

Puşcariu, Sextil (1905). *Etymologisches Wörterbuch der rumänischen Sprache, I: Lateinisches Element, mit Berücksichtigung aller romanischen Sprachen.* Heidelberg: Winter.

(1909). TENUARE im Rumänischen. *Wörter und Sachen*, 1, 111–14.

References

Quadri, Bruno (1952). *Aufgaben und Methoden der onomasiologischen Forschung. Eine entwicklungsgeschichtliche Darstellung.* Diss. Zurich. Romanica Helvetica, 37. Berne: Francke.

Rajna, Pio (1919). Discussioni etimologiche: *tomar. Revista de Filología Española* 6, 1–13.

Ramisch, Jacob (1908). *Studien zur niederrheinischen Dialektgeographie.* Diss. Marburg, 1906. Deutsche Dialektgeographie, 1. Marburg: Elwert.

Random House dictionary of the English language, The (1966). New York: Random House. 2nd edn, 1987.

Rask, Rasmus Christian (1932–7). *Ausgewählte Abhandlungen . . .* , ed. L. Hjelmslev. Preface by H. Pedersen. 3 vols. Copenhagen: Levin & Munksgaard.

Read, William A. (1927). *Louisiana place-names of Indian origin.* Louisiana State University Bulletin, New Series, 19:2. Baton Rouge.

Regula, Moritz (1928). Beiträge zur Technik des Etymologisierens. Aus Anlaß des neuen etymologischen Wörterbuchs der französischen Sprache von E. Gamillscheg. *Archivum Romanicum*, 12, 265–87.

Rheinfelder, Hans (1928). *Das Wort 'persōna'. Geschichte seiner Bedeutungen, mit besonderer Berücksichtigung des französischen und italienischen Mittelalters*, Suppl. 77 to *Zeitschrift für romanische Philologie.* Halle: Niemeyer.

Richardson, Henry B. (1930). *An etymological vocabulary to the Libro de buen amor of Juan Ruiz, Arcipreste de Hita.* Yale Romanic Studies, 2. New Haven: Yale University Press; London: Milford, Oxford University Press.

Richter, Oswald (1900). Griech[isch] *despótēs. Zeitschrift für vergleichende Sprachforschung*, 36, 111–13.

Rieu, Charles (1880–81). Remarks on some phonetic laws in Persian. *Transactions of the Philological Society*, 1–22.

Rohlfs, Gerhard (1949–54). *Historische Grammatik der italienischen Sprache und ihrer Mundarten.* 3 vols. Berne: Francke.

Sachs, Georg (ed.) (1936). *El libro de los caballos. Tratado de albeitería del siglo XIII, con introducción y vocabulario. Revista de Filología Española*, Suppl. 23. Madrid: Centro de Estudios Históricos.

Sainéan, Lazare (1905–7). *La création métaphorique en français et en roman. Images tirées du monde des animaux domestiques.* 2 vols. *Zeitschrift für romanische Philologie*, Suppl. 1 and 10. Halle: Niemeyer.

(1907). *L'argot ancien (1455–1850), ses éléments constitutifs, ses rapports avec les langues secrètes et l'argot moderne . . . .* Paris: Champion.

(1912). *Les sources de l'argot ancien.* 2 vols. Paris: Champion.

(1920). *Le langage parisien au XIXe siècle. Facteurs sociaux/contingents linguistiques/Faits sémantiques/Influences littéraires.* Paris: de Boccard.

(1922–28). *Le langage de Rabelais.* 2 vols. Paris: de Boccard.

(1925–30). *Les sources indigènes de l'étymologie française.* 2 vols. Paris: de Boccard.

(1935). *Autour des sources indigènes. Études d'étymologie française et romane.*
Biblioteca dell' *Archivum Romanicum*, 2:20. Florence: Olschki.

Salvioni, Carlo (1909). Filis[ur] *batschlauna* 'pigna'. *Wörter und Sachen*, 1, 114–5.

Sánchez, Tomás Antonio, (ed.) (1779–90). *Colección de poesías castellanas
anteriores al siglo XV . . . .* 4 vols. Madrid: de Sancha.

Sapir, Edward (1921). *Language, an introduction to the study of speech.* New
York: Harcourt Brace, & World.

(1949). *Selected writings in language, culture, and personality*, ed. David G.
Mandelbaum. Berkeley: University of California Press.

Saussure, Ferdinand de (1916). *Cours de linguistique générale*, ed. C. Bally, A.
Rïedlinger, A. Sechehaye. Lausanne: Payot. 2nd edn, Paris: Payot, 1922; 3rd
edn, 1931; 4th edn, 1949; 5th edn, 1955. Critical edn by Rudolf Engler, 3
vols., Wiesbaden: Harrassowitz, 1967–8. *Corso di linguistica generale*, tr. &
ed., Tullio De Mauro, Bari: Laterza, 1972; *Grundfragen der allgemeinen
Sprachwissenschaft*, tr. H. Lommel, ed. Peter von Polenz. 2nd edn, Berlin:
de Gruyter, 1967.

Scheler, Auguste (1845). *Mémoire sur la conjugaison française considérée sous le
rapport étymologique.* Brussels: Mémoires de l'Académie Royale.

(1861). *Glossaire érotique de la langue française depuis son origine jusqu'à nos
jours . . . .* Brussels: n. pub., 1861. [Pseud. Louis de Landes.]

(1862). *Dictionnaire d'étymologie française d'après les résultats de la science
moderne.* Brussels: Schnée. Rev. 2nd edn, Brussels: Muquardt, 1873; rev. 3rd
edn, Brussels: Falk, 1888. [= *DEF.*]

(1865–). *Kurzgefaßtes etymologisches Wörterbuch der französischen Sprache.
Auszug aus des Verfassers Dictionnaire d'etymologie française.* Brussels:
Schnée.

Schirmer, Alfred (1926). *Deutsche Wortkunde. Eine Kulturgeschichte des
deutschen Wortschatzes.* Sammlung Göschen, 929. Berlin & Leipzig: de
Gruyter. 5th edn, 1965, rev. by Walther Mitzka; 6th edn, 1969.

Schleicher, August (1856–7). *Handbuch der litauischen Sprache. I. Grammatik; II
Lesebuch und Glossar.* Prague: Calve.

(ed. & tr.) (1857). *Litauische Märchen, Sprichworte, Rätsel und Lieder.*
Weimar: Böhlau.

(1858). *Volkstümliches aus Sonneberg im Meininger Oberlande.* Weimar:
Böhlau. 2nd edn, Sonneberg: Albrecht, 1894.

(1861–2). *Compendium der vergleichenden Grammatik der indogermanischen
Sprachen.* 2 vols. Weimar: Böhlau. Rev. 2nd edn, 1866; 3rd edn, 1871; 4th
edn, 1876. *A compendium of the comparative grammar of the
Indo-European . . .*, tr. H. Bendall, London: Trübner, 1874–7. *Compendio
di grammatica comparativa . . .*, tr. Domenico Pezzi, Turin: Loescher, 1869.

(1862). *Tomy imën čislitel'nyx (količestvennyx i porjadočnyx) v
litvo-slavjanskom i nemeckom jazykax.* St Petersburg: Akademija Nauk,
Zapiski, 10.

References

(1863). *Die Darwinsche Theorie und die Sprachwissenschaft. Offenes Sendschreiben an* . . . *Ernst Haeckel.* Weimar: Böhlau. 2nd and 3rd edns, 1873.

(ed.) (1865). *Christian Donaleitis [1714–80] litauische Dichtungen, mit Glossar.* St Petersburg: Kaiserliche Akademie der Wissenschaften.

& Ebel, H., Leskien, A., Schmidt, J. (eds.) (1869). *Indogermanische Chrestomathie. Schriftproben und Lesestücke.* Weimar: Böhlau.

Schuchardt, Hugo (1866–8). *Der Vokalismus des Vulgärlateins.* 3 vols. Leipzig: Teubner.

(1870). *Über einige Fälle bedingten Lautwandels im Churwälschen.* Habilitationsschrift Leipzig. Gotha: Thienemann.

(1874). Phonétique comparée. *Romania*, 3, 1–30.

(1885). *Über die Lautgesetze; gegen die Junggrammatiker.* Berlin: Oppenheim.

(1898, 1899). *Romanische Etymologien*, 1–2. Sitz.-ber. Akad. Wiss. Wien 138:1, 141:3.

(1900). *Über die Klassifikation der romanischen Mundarten.* Probevorlesung, gehalten zu Leipzig am 30. April 1870. Graz: n. pub. (printed by Styria).

(1901). Sichel und Säge, Sichel und Dolch. *Globus*, 80, 181–7, 204–9.

(1902). Etymologische Probleme und Prinzipien. *Zeitschrift für romanische Philologie*, 26, 384–427.

(1903–4). *Trouver*, I–III. *Zeitschrift für romanische Philologie*, 27, 97–105; 28, 36–55.

(1903a). Lat[einisch] *īlex*; lat[einisch] *cisterna. Zeitschrift für romanische Philologie*, 27, 105–10.

(1903b). Franz[ösisch] *sage. Zeitschrift für romanische Philologie*, 27, 110–2.

(1904). Ital[ienisch] *corbezuolo*, span[isch] *madroño*, . . . 'Zürgelbaum'. *Zeitschrift für romanische Philologie*, 28, 192–5.

(1906). *Baskisch und romanisch. Zu De Azkues baskischem Wörterbuch*, I. Suppl. 6 to *Zeitschrift für romanische Philologie.* Halle: Niemeyer.

(1918). *Die romanischen Lehnwörter im Berberischen.* Sitz.-ber. Akad. Wiss. Wien, 188:4.

(1922). *Hugo Schuchardt Brevier, ein Vademekum der allgemeinen Sprachwissenschaft* . . . , ed. Leo Spitzer. Halle: Niemeyer. Rev. 2nd edn, 1928.

(1925a). *Der Individualismus in der Sprachforschung.* Sitz.-ber. Akad. Wiss. Wien, 204:2.

(1925b). *Das Baskische und die Sprachwissenschaft.* Sitz.-ber. Akad. Wiss. Wien, 202:4.

Schulz, Hans, & Basler, Otto (1913–). *Deutsches Fremdwörterbuch.* 2 vols. Strasbourg: Trübner; later Berlin: de Gruyter.

Sebeok, Thomas A. (1966). *Portraits of linguists. A biographical source book for the history of Western linguistics 1746–1963.* Bloomington: Indiana University Press.

Seebold, Elmar (1981). *Etymologie. Eine Einführung am Beispiel der deutschen Sprache*. Munich: Beck.

Shipley, Joseph T. (1945). *Dictionary of word origins*. New York: Philosophical Library. 2nd edn, New York: Greenwood Press, 1969.

(1984). *The origins of English words. A discursive dictionary of Indo-European roots*. Baltimore and London: Johns Hopkins University Press.

Skeat, Walter W. (1876). *A list of English words, the etymology of which is illustrated by comparison with Icelandic* . . . . Oxford: Clarendon Press. [Bound with R. Cleasby & G. Vigfasson, *An Icelandic–English dictionary* . . . , Oxford: Clarendon Press, 1874.]

(1880–81). A rough list of English words found in Anglo-French, especially during the thirteenth and fourteenth centuries: with numerous references. *Transactions of the Philological Society*, Appendix V, 91–186.

(1882). *An etymological dictionary of the English language*. Oxford: Clarendon Press; New York: Macmillan. Rev. 2nd edn, 1884, 1888, 1893; 4th edn, 1909–10, repr. 1946, 1958, etc.

(1887). *Principles of English etymology (1. The native element, 2. The foreign element)*. Oxford: Clarendon Press. 2nd edn, in 2 vols, 1891–2.

(1901). *Notes on English etymology: chiefly reprinted from the Transactions of the Philological Society*. Oxford: Clarendon Press.

(1914). *A glossary of Tudor and Stuart words, especially from the dramatists, collected by Walter W. Skeat . . . Ed., with additions, by A. L. Mayhew*. Oxford: Clarendon Press.

Spiro, Socrates (1904). *Note on the Italian words in the modern spoken Arabic of Egypt*. Cairo: Al Mokattam Print.

Spitzer, Leo (1921). *Lexikalisches aus dem Katalanischen und den übrigen iberoromanischen Sprachen*. Biblioteca dell' *Archivum Romanicum*. 2:1. Geneva: Olschki.

(1923–4). Persönliches und Prinzipielles zu Gamillschegs Aufsatz hier . . . . *Zeitschrift für romanische Philologie*, 43, 759–66.

(1926). Ein neues *Französisches etymologisches Wörterbuch. Zeitschrift für romanische Philologie*, 46, 563–617.

(1928). Zur Methodik der etymologischen Forschung. *Zeitschrift für romanische Philologie*, 48, 77–113.

(1938). Review of Américo Castro (ed.), *Glosarios latino–españoles de la Edad Media*, in *Modern Language Notes*, 53, 122–46.

(1956, 1957, 1959). A new Spanish etymological dictionary (review of Juan Corominas, *Diccionario crítico etimológico de la lengua castellana*). *Modern Language Notes*, 71, 271–83, 373–86; 72, 579–91; 74, 127–49.

Steiger, Arnald (1932). *Contribución a la fonética del hispano–árabe y de los arabismos en el ibero–románico y el siciliano. Revista de Filología Española*, Suppl. 17. Madrid: Centro de Estudios Históricos.

Steinthal, Heymann (1856). *Gesammelte sprachwissenschaftliche Abhandlungen*.

References

Berlin: Dümmler.

(1880). *Sprachwissenschaftliche Abhandlungen und Rezensionen. Gesammelte kleine Schriften*. Berlin: Dümmler.

Stevens, Captain John (1706). *A new Spanish and English dictionary. Collected from the best Spanish authors; containing several thousand words . . . with their etymology . . . .* London: Sawbridge.

(1726). *A new dictionary, Spanish and English, and English and Spanish*. London: Darby.

Stewart, George R. (1945). *Names on the land: A historical account of place-naming in the United States*. New York: Random House. Rev. and enl. edn, Boston: Houghton Mifflin, 1958.

Stokes, Whitley (1900). Hibernica. Nos. 18–23. *Zeitschrift für vergleichende Sprachforschung*, 36, 273–6.

Sturtevant, Edgar H. (1931). Hittite ctymologies. *Language*, 7, 1–13.

(1947). *Introduction to linguistic science*. New Haven: Yale University Press.

Sweet, Henry (1880–81). Recent investigations on the Indo-Germanic vowel-system. *Transactions of the Philological Society*, 155–62.

(1880–1). Sound-notation. *Transactions of the Philological Society*, 177–235.

(1913). *Collected papers by Henry Sweet*. Arranged by H. C. Wyld. Oxford: Clarendon Press.

(1971). *The indispensable foundation. A selection from the writings of Henry Sweet*. Ed. Eugenie J. A. Henderson. London: Oxford University Press.

Tagliavini, Carlo (1940). Osservazioni sugli elementi italiani in turco. *Istituto Superiore Orientale di Napoli: Annali*. New Series, 1, 191–204.

(1955–7). *Un nome al giorno. Origine e storia di nomi di persona italiani*. 2 vols. Turin: Edizioni Radio Italiana.

Tappolet, Ernst (1895). *Die romanischen Verwandtschaftsnamen, mit besonderer Berücksichtigung der französischen und italienischen Mundarten. Ein Beitrag zur vergleichenden Lexikologie*. Strasbourg: Trübner.

Techmer, Friedrich (ed.) (1884–90). *Internationale Zeitschrift für allgemeine Sprachwissenschaft . . . .* Vols. I–V. Leipzig: Barth; New York: Westermann.

Tedesco, Paul (1951). Slavic *pilbnb* and *naglb*: two etymologies based on meaning. *Language*, 27, 18–33.

Tekavčić, Pavao (1972). *Grammatica storica dell'italiano*. 3 vols. Bologna: il Mulino.

Terlingen, J. H. (1943). *Los italianismos en español desde la formación del idioma hasta principios del siglo XVII*. Diss. Utrecht. Amsterdam: Noord-hollandsche uitgevers maatschappij.

Thomas, Antoine (1897). *Essais de philologie française*. Paris: Bouillon.

(1902). *Mélanges d'étymologie française*. Paris: Alcan. Rev. 2nd edn, Paris: Champion, 1927.

(1904). *Nouveaux essais de philologie française*. Paris: Bouillon.

(1908, 1909, 1910). Notes étymologiques et lexicographiques. *Romania*, 37,

110–39; 38, 353–405; 39, 184–267.

(1911). Etymologies provençales et françaises. *Romania*, 41, 58–89.

(1913). Etymologies françaises et provençales. *Romania*, 42, 370–429.

Thumb, Albert (1900). Etymologien [nos. 1–10]. *Zeitschrift für vergleichende Sprachforschung*, 36, 179–201.

Tilander, Gunnar (1932). *Glanures lexicographiques*. Lund: Gleerup.

(1953). *Essais d'étymologie cynégétique*. Cynegetica, 1. Lund: Almqvist.

Tobler, Adolf, & Lommatzsch, Erhard (1915–). *Adolf Toblers Altfranzösisches Wörterbuch*. Berlin: Weidmann; Wiesbaden: Steiner.

Transactions of the Philological Society. (1854–). London: Bell.

Valkhoff, Marius (1931). *Les mots français d'origine néerlandaise*. Diss. Amsterdam. Amersfoort: Valkhoff, 1931.

Vasmer, Max (1944). *Die griechischen Lehnwörter im Serbokroatischen*. Abh. der Preuss. Akad. Wiss. 3. Berlin.

(1950–58). *Russisches etymologisches Wörterbuch*. 3 vols. Indogermanische Bibliothek, Second Series, Heidelberg: Winter. Tr. C. N. Trubačëv. *Ètimologičeskij slovar' russkogo jazyka*. Moscow: Progress, 1964–73.

(1960–69). *Wörterbuch der russischen Gewässernamen*. Wiesbaden: Osteuropa-Institut an der Freien Universität Berlin.

& Bräuer, Herbert (1962–4). *Russisches geographisches Wörterbuch*, ed. Ingrid Coper. Wiesbaden: Harrassowitz.

Vendryes, Joseph (1921). *Le langage: introduction linguistique à l'histoire*. Paris: La Renaissance du livre; Paris: Michel, 1950 (L'Évolution de l'humanité, 1:3). *Language. A linguistic introduction to history*. Translated by Paul Radin. London: K. Paul, Trench, Trübner; New York: Knopf, 1925.

Vidos, B. E. (1939). *Storia delle parole marinaresche italiane passate in francese*. Bibl. dell'*Archivum Romanicum*, 2:24. Geneva and Florence: Olschki.

Wagner, Max Leopold (1941). *Historische Lautlehre des Sardischen. Zeitschrift für romanische Philologie*, Suppl. 93. Halle: Niemeyer.

(1952). *Historische Wortbildungslehre des Sardischen*. Romanica Helvetica, 39. Berne: Francke.

(1957–64). *Dizionario etimologico sardo*. 3 vols. Sammlung romanischer Elementar- und Handbücher, 3:6. Indexes by G. Urciolo. Heidelberg: Winter.

Walde, Alois (1905–6). *Lateinisches etymologisches Wörterbuch*. Heidelberg: Winter, 1905–6. Rev. 2nd edn, 1910; 3rd edn, in 2 vols, 1938–54, rev. by J. B. Hofman; 4th edn, in 3 vols, 1954–65. Index volume (Registerband) by Elsbeth Berger.

Wartburg, Walther von (1912). *Die Ausdrücke für die Fehler des Gesichtsorgans in den romanischen Sprachen und Dialekten*. Diss. Zurich. Hamburg: Sekretariat der Société internationale de dialectologie romane.

(1918). *Zur Benennung des Schafes in den romanischen Sprachen. Ein Beitrag zur Frage der provinziellen Differenzierung des späteren Lateins*. Berlin: Abh.

Preuss. Akad. Wiss., Philos.-hist. Klasse, Jahrg. 1918, nr. 10.

(1928). *Französisches etymologisches Wörterbuch. Eine Darstellung des galloromanischen Sprachschatzes.* Numerous volumes; several places and publishers.

(1934). *Bibliographie des dictionnaires patois.* Soc. de publications romanes et françaises, 8. Paris: Droz. Supplément, ed. H.-E. Keller & J. Renson. Soc. de publications romanes et françaises, 52; Geneva/Lille, 1955. Rev. 2nd edn, in collaboration with H.-E. Keller & R. Geuljans.

& Keller, Hans Erich, & Geuljans, Robert (1969). *Bibliographie des dictionnaires.*

(1943). *Einführung in Problematik und Methodik der Sprachwissenschaft.* Halle: Niemeyer. Rev. 2nd edn (in collaboration with Stephen Ullmann), Tübingen: Niemeyer, 1962; 3rd edn (checked by Gustav Ineichen), 1970.

(1952). Die griechische Kolonisation in Südgallien und ihre sprachlichen Zeugen im Westromanischen. *Zeitschrift für romanische Philologie*, 68 (1952), 1–48; offprint, Tübingen: Niemeyer, 1953. [Revised version in Wartburg (1956)].

(1956). *Von Sprache und Mensch: gesammelte Aufsätze.* Berne: Francke, 1956. [Contains a bibliography of publications, compiled by Kurt Baldinger and Alfred Thierbach, and a revised version of Wartburg (1952).]

(1969). . . . *patois galloromans (1550–1967).* New edn completely revised and updated. Publ. romanes et françaises, 103. Geneva: Droz.

Watkins, Calvert (ed.) (1985). *The American Heritage dictionary of Indo–European roots*, rev. edn, Boston: Houghton Mifflin.

Weekley, Ernest (1907–10). Etymologies, chiefly Anglo-French. *Transactions of the Philological Society*, 288–331.

(1911). *The romance of words.* New York: Dover; London: Murray, 1912. Rev. 2nd edn, 1913; 3rd edn, 1917; 4th edn, New York: Dutton, 1922; 5th edn, 1925.

(1914). *The romance of names.* Rev. 2nd edn, London: Murray; New York: Dutton, 1914. Rev. 3rd edn, 1922.

(1916). *Surnames.* New York: Dutton, 1916. 2nd edn, 1917 (repr. 1927); 3rd edn, 1936.

(1921). *An etymological dictionary of modern English.* London: Murray, 1921. Repr., with a biographical memoir, 2 vols., New York: Dover 1967.

(1924). *A concise etymological dictionary of modern English*, New York: Dutton, 1924, 1952.

(1926). *Words, ancient and modern.* New York: Dutton; London: Murray, 1946.

(1927). *More words, ancient and modern.* London: Murray; New York: Dutton.

(1930). *Adjectives – and other words.* London: Murray; New York: Dutton.

(1932). *Words and names.* London: Murray.

(1935). *Something about words.* London: Murray, 1935; New York: Dutton.

(1939). *JACK AND JILL. A study in our Christian names.* London: Murray;

New York: Dutton, 1940. 2nd edn, 1948.

Whitney, William D. (1867). *Language and the study of language. Twelve lectures on the principles of linguistic science.* New York: Scribner. 2nd edn, 1868; 3rd & 4th edns, 1869; 5th edn, 1870; 6th edn, 1895.

(1873–4a). Review John Peile, *An introduction to Greek and Latin etymology* (rev. 2nd edn). In *Transactions of the Philological Society*, 299–327.

(1873–4b). *Oriental and linguistic studies.* 2 vols. New York: Scribner, Armstrong & Co. 2nd edn, 1893.

(1875). *The life and growth of language. An outline of linguistic science.* London: King; New York: Appleton. *Leben und Wachstum der Sprache*, tr. August Leskien. Leipzig: Brockhaus, 1876.

(1876). *Language and its study, with special reference to the Indo-European family of languages.* Seven lectures, ed. R. Morris. London: Trübner. 2nd edn, 1890. [Extracted from *Language and the study of language.*]

(1877).A botanico-philological problem. *Transactions of the American Philological Association for 1876*, 73–86. Repr. in *Selected writings*, 336–49.

(1879). *A Sanskrit grammar, including both the Classical language and the older dialects of Veda and Brahmana.* Leipzig: Breitkopf & Härtel. 2nd edn, Leipzig & Boston: Ginn, 1889; 3rd edn, 1896; 4th edn, 1921; London: Oxford University Press, 1923; Cambridge, Mass.: Harvard University Press, 1931, 1941, 1950, 1955. *Indische Grammatik . . .* , tr. Heinrich Zimmer. Leipzig: Breitkopft & Härtel, 1879.

(1885). *The roots, verb forms, and primary derivatives of the Sanskrit language. A supplement to his [W.D.W.'s] Sanskrit grammar.* Bibliothek indogermanischer Grammatiken, 2, Suppl. 2. Leipzig: Breitkopf & Härtel; Boston, 1887.

(1892). *Max Müller and the science of language. A criticism.* New York: Appleton.

(1971). *Whitney on language. Selected writings*, ed. Michael Silverstein. Introduction by Roman Jakobson. Cambridge, Mass.: Massachusetts Institute of Technology Press.

& Edgren, August Hjalmar (1879). *A compendious German and English dictionary with notations of correspondences and brief etymologies.* London: Macmillan, 1887, 1891, 1901; New York: Holt, 1905, 1915.

Wörter und Sachen; Kulturhistorische Zeitschrift für Sprach- und Sachforschung (1909–). Ed. R. Meringer, W. Meyer-Lübke, J. J. Mikkola, R. Much, M. Murko. Heidelberg: Winter.

Wood, Francis A. (1902). *Color-names and their congeners; a semasiological investigation.* Halle: Niemeyer.

(1931). Some Latin etymologies. *Language*, 7, 136–8.

(1932). Some Germanic etymologies. *Language*, 8, 213–14.

Wrenn, C. L. (ed.) (1953). *Beowulf, with the Finnesburg Fragment.* London: Harrap. Rev. 2nd edn, 1958.

Zaccaria, Enrico (1927). *L'elemento iberico nella lingua italiana.* Bologna:

References

Cappelli.

Zambaldi, Francesco (1889). *Vocabolario etimologico italiano*. Città di Castello: Lapi. 2nd edn (. . . *con appendice dei nomi di persona*), Città di Castello. Lapi, 1913.

Zamboni, Alberto (1976). *L'etimologia*. Biblioteca linguistica, 2. Bologna: Zanichelli.

Zauner, Adolf (1902). *Die romanischen Namen der Körperteile. Eine onomasiologische Studie*. Habilitationsschrift Wien. Erlangen: Junge. [Also published as article in: *Romanische Forschungen*, 14 (1903), 339–530.]

Zeitschrift der deutschen morgenländischen Gesellschaft (1847–1919). Leipzig.

Zeitschrift für vergleichende Sprachforschung auf dem Gebiete der indogermanischen Sprachen (1852–). Berlin. [See also under Kuhn, Adalbert.]

Zimmer, H. (1900). Keltische Studien, 17. *Zeitschrift für vergleichende Sprachforschung*, 36, 418–58.

Zink, Gaston (1987). *L'ancien français, XIe-XIIIe siècle*. Que sais-je?. Paris: Presses Universitaires de France. 2nd edn, 1990.

INDEXES

Index of names

Abel, K., 24
Aebischer, P., 82–4
Alcalá, P. de, 6
Aldrete, B., 5, 14
Alessio, G., 107, 139
Alfonso X, king of Castille and León, 3
Algeo, A., 122
Algeo, J., 122
Anderson, J. M., 37, 108
Anglade, J., 65
Anttila, R., 37
Arlotto, A., 37
Ascoli, G. I., 14
Avitus, Alcimus, 65

Bailly, A., 28, 36
Baist, G., 34, 51
Baldinger, K., 52, 92
Barbier, P., 50
Barnhart, R. K., 109, 112
Bartoli, M., 84–5
Battisti, C., 107, 139
Bédier, J., 138
Behrens, W., 52
Benfey, T., 21
Benveniste, É., 38, 95, 96, 98, 125
Berneker, E., 56
Bertoldi, V., 39, 92
Bindseil, H. E., 12
Bloch, O., 29, 105
Bloch, R. H., 3
Blondheim, D. S., 30, 100
Bloomfield, L., 38, 42, 101, 109
Bloomfield, M., 41
Boas, F., 41
Bolza, G. B., 32
Bonaparte, Prince Louis-Lucien, 45

Bonfante, G., 84–5
Bopp, F., 9–10, 110, 140
Bouton, C. P., 123
Brachet, A., 11, 27–8, 48
Bréal, M., 10, 27, 28, 34, 35–6, 98
Breuer, H., 47, 138
Browne, W. R., 45
Brüch, J., 81, 127
Brugmann, K., 98
Bruneau, C., 128
Brunel, E., 123
Brunot, F., 128
Buck, C. D., 140
Bühler, C., 33
Burchfield, R. W., 108
Burrow, T., 101, 108
Bynon, T., 37

Cabrera, R., 14, 32
Caix, N., 106
Calvet, L.-J., 123
Candrea-Hecht, J. A., 46, 86
Canello, U. A., 28, 48
Carter, C. M., 120–2
Castro, A., 52, 114, 115
Cayley, C. B., 12
Chambon, J.-P., 106
Chiappelli, F., 129
Chiappini, F., 128
Cihac, A. de, 46
Clark, M. E., 122
Clifford, P. M., 107
Coelho, F. A., 14
Cohen, M., 95–6
Cornu, J., 47, 163
Corominas, J., 50, 102, 115, 116, 140–2, 143, 160

209

Indexes

Zamboni, A., 39, 106
Zauner, A., 13, 59
Zimmer, H., 54
Zink, G., 123
Zinsli, P., 95
Zolli, P., 107
Zupitza, E., 53

Index of concepts

adoptions, culturally conditioned
    deliberate, 22
Aegean territories, 144
affixation, 131 *see also* prefixation;
    suffixation
African, South and Central, 13
Albanian, 53, 54
Alpine words, 118
Alpino-Lombard, 92
American English, 121–2, 144
analogy, 97
    versus sound laws, 22, 23
Anatolian, 110, 118
    Ancient, 100
Anglo-French, 32, 45
anthologies, with appended etymological
    bric-à-brac, 47
anthropology, and etymology, 60
anthroponymy, 13, 28, 35, 42, 83, 113
antique etymologies, 3
antonymy, 149
Arabic, 6, 11, 46, 144
    Egyptian, Italianisms in, 90
Aragonese, 115
Aramaic, 46
archaeology, links with etymology, 26
archaisms, 97
areal characterization
    of Indo-Iranian, 97
    of Latin and Celtic, 97
areal distribution, 84–5
Argentinian Spanish, 140
Armenian, 10
    Old, 54, 98
articles
    on etymology, 44
    development of, 51–7
    historique du problème approach, 55–7,
        170
Aryan (Proto-Indo-European), 31, 32, 45
Auseinandersetzung technique, 65–6
Austria, 34
Avestan, 10, 12

Balkan-Romance, 64, 84
Basque, 13, 25, 35, 67, 106, 118, 144

Belgium, 26
Berber, 25, 118, 144
borrowings, 6, 22, 31, 133 *see also* lexical
    diffusion
Breton, 91, 106
British Isles *see* United Kingdom

Canada, British, 100
Caribbean languages, 100
cartographic approach, 58, 59, 74
case histories, etymological, 14–15, 19
Catalan, 102, 141
    Arabisms in, 90
    Old, 141
Celtic, 6, 10, 12, 19, 91, 97, 118
celtomania, 6
Central Europe, 41–2, 95, 99–100, 112–13, 133
charters, 83
Chinese, 142
chromonyms, 126
Churwälsch (Grisons' dialect, Western
    Rhaeto-Romance), 64
classical education, 117–18
coinage, 28
colloquial 'mistakes', 119
comparative linguistics, 3, 34
compounding, 28, 131
    tautological and advocative, 126
concordance of dialect forms, 80–2
contamination, 163, 169
conversational formulas, 144
core vocabulary, 22
correctness of spelling and grammar, 133–4
costumes, local, 68
cross-linguistic research, 144
    conditioning factors, 147–9
    cultural considerations, 1, 99
customs, local, 68

Dalmatian, 84
Darwinism, 18, 29
data collection, 146–9
Denmark, 7
derivation, 115–17
derivational morphemes, included in
    etymological studies, 115–16
diachronic lexicology, 96, 99
    and etymology, blurring of boundary, 73–4
diachronic linguistics *see* historical
    linguistics
diachronic phonology, 45
diachronic semasiology *see* lexical
    semantics
diachrony, 135
dialect geography, x, 34, 58–9, 80, 84, 87,
    112–13
    impact on etymology, 72–7

213

Indexes